THE THERAPIST
IN THE
REAL WORLD

A NORTON PROFESSIONAL BOOK

THE THERAPIST IN THE REAL WORLD

*What You Never Learn
in Graduate School
(But Really Need to Know)*

JEFFREY A. KOTTLER

W.W. Norton & Company
New York • London

For information about permission to reproduce selections from this book, write to
Permissions, W. W. Norton & Company, Inc., 500 Fifth Avenue, New York, NY 10110

For information about special discounts for bulk purchases, please contact
W. W. Norton Special Sales at specialsales@wwnorton.com or 800-233-4830

Manufacturing by Edwards Brothers Malloy
Production manager: Christine Critelli

Library of Congress Cataloging-in-Publication Data

Kottler, Jeffrey A.
 [What you never learned in graduate school]
  The therapist in the real world : what you never learn in graduate school (but
really need to know) / Jeffrey A. Kottler.
       pages cm. — (A Norton professional book)
  Previous edition published in 1997 as: What you never learned in graduate
school : a survival guide for therapists / Jeffrey A. Kottler and Richard J. Hazler.
  Includes bibliographical references and index.
  ISBN 978-0-393-71098-4 (pbk. : alk. paper)
1. Psychotherapy—Vocational guidance. 2. Psychotherapy—Practice. 3. Psychotherapists. 4. Mental health counselors. 5. Mental health counseling. I. Title.
  RC480.5.K683 2015
  616.89'14023—dc23
                              2015017864

W. W. Norton & Company, Inc.
500 Fifth Avenue, New York, N.Y. 10110
www.wwnorton.com

W. W. Norton & Company Ltd.
Castle House, 75/76 Wells Street, London W1T 3QT

1 2 3 4 5 6 7 8 9 0

CONTENTS

Preface   7
Acknowledgments   11

PART I: MORE THAN YOU BARGAINED FOR

1	What You May Not Have Learned in Graduate School	15
2	Seismic Shifts in the Practice of Therapy	37
3	Walking on Water and Other Unrealistic Expectations	55
4	Organized Confusion: Making Sense of Change Processes in Clients, the Profession, and Ourselves	77
5	Returning to the Basics When It All Starts to Sound Familiar	101

PART II: SECRETS AND NEGLECTED CHALLENGES

6	Clients Are Your Best Teachers	123
7	Relationships Are (Almost) Everything!	147
8	Honoring and Telling Stories	159
9	Private Practice and/or Public Service?	185

PART III: ONGOING PERSONAL AND PROFESSIONAL DEVELOPMENT

10	Upgrading Your Presentations	205
11	Writing and Publishing for Pleasure, Purpose, or Profit	221
12	Navigating Organizational Politics	239
13	On Supervision, Mentoring, Mastery, and Creativity	257

References   291
Index   309

ways we do treatment planning; (2) the paradigm shifts from single-theory allegiance to broad schools of thought; (3) the introduction of new conceptual models that are more responsive to contemporary needs of diverse clients; (4) the call for greater moral responsibility on the part of clinicians, especially as it applies to promoting social justice issues; (5) the demands for greater cultural and gender sensitivity; (6) the widespread use of computers, mobile devices, and other technology; (7) the resurgence of qualitative research methodologies; (8) the increased preference for medications to cure maladies, even with sometimes limited evidence for their effectiveness; and (9) the increased popularity of short-term interventions rather than long-term relationships. It is this last change that has been among the most dramatic, considering that many experienced therapists who completed their training years ago had been prepared to do a kind of work that is now becoming increasingly obsolete, at least for now. The tides may very well change once again as the population ages, enjoys more leisure time, and feels a greater interest in exploring the underlying meaning of a life's journey.

Therapists and counselors are not only struggling to adapt to the changing landscape of the profession but also to a number of other demands that are directly related to professional and personal success. Graduate school couldn't possibly teach us all the skills and knowledge that we might need; the rest has been on our own, through trial and error, and via an underground network that provides both useful information and inaccurate advice. For example, we were not sufficiently warned that (1) there are negative side effects to being a therapist that can compromise our personal relationships, (2) life is not a multiple-choice exam where there is always one right answer, (3) even with advanced degrees we might still not be taken seriously by our families nor feel that we know enough to do our jobs, (4) our feelings of ineptitude may continue to persist, (5) there are personal reasons we chose to enter this field that we didn't fully confront, (6) we take ourselves far too seriously, (7) the answers to our most important questions are not always found in textbooks, (8) there is a lot of hypocrisy within our ranks and absurdity in what we do, and (9) we may never, ever feel good enough to do the job that we want to do. In addition, there are so many important things that we may not have been taught, such as how to get the most from supervision, recruit and "train" mentors to be most helpful, present talks in front of large audiences, and construct and implement a viable business plan for therapeutic practice, to mention just a few.

This book is written primarily for three groups of readers: (1) practitioners of social work, psychology, counseling, marital and family therapy, human services, psychiatry, psychiatric nursing, and other mental health disciplines; (2) advanced students in these professions; and (3) intelligent readers who are interested in learning about the inner world of therapy and the dramatic changes this field is undergoing. Never before in our history have so many new developments in research, theoretical constructions, technology, training methods, and diagnostic and treatment methods, not to mention changes in broader cultural trends and economic trends, occurred so quickly and require so many adaptations on the part of practitioners.

While this volume satisfies the demands of traditional scholarship, it is written in an accessible style that engages the reader on a personal level. Citations have been held to a minimum in favor of an author's voice that speaks directly to the reader about subjects that have often been ignored.

The focus throughout this book is on themes, issues, and critical areas that may not have been addressed in formal educational experiences. The first part is conceptual and provocative in nature, addressing seismic shifts in the field, the limits of professional training, and a review of the most critical areas for which practitioners are not prepared. The second part explores some interesting and neglected subjects that may not have been explicitly discussed during training years, including the ways our clients become our greatest teachers, the power of storytelling as the essence of our work, the factors that lead to creative breakthroughs during sessions, and the ways that deception plays a role in our helping relationships. The third part focuses on several practical areas where even experienced therapists need additional growth to maximize their potential: mastering new conceptual paradigms and cutting-edge technology, learning innovative forms of therapy responsive to the marketplace, preparing and delivering speeches and lectures, doing professional presentations, the process of mentoring and supervising therapists, publishing books and articles, dealing with organizational politics, sustaining a private practice, dealing with the media, transforming oneself through travel and risk taking, and planning for the future. Finally, we end by talking about the ways that the most satisfied and successful therapists are those who practice what they preach, applying to their own lives the most important lessons they teach to others.

ACKNOWLEDGMENTS

It's been almost 20 years since a friend and colleague, Richard Hazler, and I first wrote a book about some of the practical, brutally honest, and provocative realities of practice as a therapist or counselor, highlighting many of the most critical lessons and knowledge that would rarely be included in formal education. Since that time the field has been transformed in many ways and training programs have been considerably expanded. Yet even with all these developments the one thing that has not changed very much is the complaints by beginning and veteran clinicians that they were not fully prepared for the daily challenges they face in the real world. I'm grateful to Richard for helping to conceptualize this project during its earliest stages and for his many excellent ideas.

Benjamin Yarling, my editor at Norton, was the driving force behind this project. His vision and persistence, as well as clearheaded and focused thinking, helped to create this volume in such a way to maximally reflect the realities of therapeutic practice that are rarely discussed. I'm also grateful for the input of several therapists who contributed valuable ideas: Anjelika Gordon, Audrey Grider, Jamie Alger, Amanda Thoreson, Jerry Corey, Matt Englar-Carlson, Jon Carlson, and Jamie Bludworth.

PART I

More Than You Bargained For

Chapter 1

WHAT YOU MAY NOT HAVE LEARNED IN GRADUATE SCHOOL

A beginning therapist had been working with a young woman over the course of a few months, making substantial progress, so much so that the client wanted to return with her husband for some marital counseling in addition to her individual sessions. The therapist asked her supervisor a relatively simple question about the case: "Would it be all right to see them together if I've already established a relationship with the wife during our individual sessions?"

This seems to be a rather straightforward question that deserves a direct response. I suspect that you've already formulated an opinion on this matter, based on your own experience. Asking a similar question in a staff meeting, the beginning therapist would expect consideration of her opinion, specific guidance on the policies that her colleagues follow, an example of similar cases they had worked with in the past, and there would likely be general agreement reached about how to proceed. All of this, of course, would need to take place in a matter of minutes since staff meeting time is so precious, the therapist is not the only one in the group with specific needs, and clients are waiting to be served.

Efficiency, accuracy, practicality, and immediacy are the driving forces behind such a gathering, but they are not necessarily the most important factors in graduate school. A new therapist is likely to hear quite different feedback than an experienced practitioner in the field.

The question of whether it is alright for the therapist to see the couple after having seen one spouse remains so basic that surely experts would agree on how the case should be handled. Shock, however, sets in when she realizes how many different options are presented from a variety of supervisors, all of whom are experts in their fields. The different opinions expressed left her more confused than ever.

"Clearly, you already have a close alliance with the woman," one of the elder therapists in the room casually observes. "There's no way that you could ever be objective with the husband as well. You must refer them both to someone else who can treat their relationship."

Hmmm, the intern agrees. That makes perfect sense.

But then another of the senior staff chimes in. "Since you already know so much about her background, it gives you a head start on the case. The woman already trusts you. The husband is the one who wishes to join her, so he obviously doesn't see a problem. I would say that it would be possible for you to work with both of them if you guard against taking sides."

That makes sense, too, but before the idea is fully processed, another voice is heard in the room. "I just don't think that you can switch back so easily from intrapsychic to systemic dynamics. Once you have negotiated one sort of relationship, engaged in treatment planning that addresses her individual issues, you can't just change gears to start treating the couple. You will have to pass them along to someone else who hasn't yet been distracted by these other issues."

Before the therapist can pose a question about making a referral, still another staff member jumps into the fray. "Look, I respectfully disagree," he interjects, not very respectfully. "I think you *can* see them together—eventually. But there is a danger that you may be perceived as too closely aligned with the wife. So, if I were you, I'd first see the husband for a few sessions alone to get his take on things, then you can see the couple together."

"Are you kidding me?" the previous supervisor responded. "Absolutely not! You should know that in marital counseling the relationship is *always* the client, not the individuals. There is no way that she could help them together right now without doing some damage."

The therapist's head is now spinning. She is turning back and forth between the combatants as if it's a fierce battle, which it seems to be. There is now dead silence in the room. Finally, the clinical director, whose job it is to help staff come to a consensus regarding treatment planning, offers the following summary of the case. "First thing is to refer the husband to another therapist in the clinic. Let them get acquainted and do some initial work together. Meanwhile you keep seeing the wife, preparing her for how to get the most from couples counseling. After both you and the other therapist agree that the time is right, schedule conjoint sessions with both of you present. Each of you will be able to bring a different perspective to the sessions, and each spouse will feel there is an advocate in the room."

Whew! Crisis averted.

This situation might seem ridiculous to someone outside our profession who views therapists as experts working with agreed-upon treatment policies and techniques. Most therapists, on the other hand, would hardly be surprised by this lack of consensus, even about such an apparently simple dilemma. Conflicting feedback is not the exception but rather the rule, and this was particularly so in graduate school. Ask any group of faculty how they would handle a specific situation and you will see a certain pride in their different outlooks. Even more amazing is how certain instructors and supervisors believe themselves to be absolutely right and everyone else clearly wrong. This same scenario is played out at every professional conference or gathering in which there are such divergent views expressed about the supposedly correct way to conceptualize or treat a case.

Is there any wonder that professionals recall how, as students, they felt confused, disillusioned, and overwhelmed with anxiety and frustration? The changeover from student to professional requires far more than learning to work with more clients more often. Each therapist has had to come to grips with the tenuous nature of truth, the mythology surrounding what it means to be an expert, and the vast differences between what we learned in school versus what is required of a practicing professional.

Different Needs at Different Levels of Development

Why does the discussion in the opening example lead to a satisfactory practical solution for the senior staff while the beginning therapist only feels more confused? The answer lies in the differing developmental needs of emerging professionals and the purposeful structure of most university training programs.

Professional preparation is neither designed nor able to equip individuals with everything they will need in the real world. There is simply too much to learn and the field of knowledge expands and changes too quickly. Instead, professional training provides a foundation of knowledge, attitudes, and skills that permit beginners to learn the rest of what they will need on their own. School cannot teach specific correct answers about what is the best solution to every possible case. However, it can teach professionals how to think for themselves and to formulate a defensible rationale for behavior that is supported by theory, research, and practice. At its best, professional training provides a solid foundation for the beginner, but it is never intended to create an expert.

Law schools are a good example of professional training programs that demonstrate pride in how impractical their education is when compared to what attorneys really do on the job. Medical schools require prospective applicants to spend years studying subjects that have no direct relevance to actually helping people. These programs seek to convey general conceptual knowledge rather than the specific minute-to-minute bits of information and tasks that a vocational school might promote. Preparation of therapists, attorneys, doctors, or architects exists primarily to build the consistent ways of thinking and problem solving needed by active professionals in ever-changing situations.

"That's all very well," one new graduate reluctantly acknowledges, "but there was precious little in my classes that prepared me for the real world with all the billing practices, office politics, and daily stressors of dealing with clients who don't want help. And there was absolutely nothing about the most rudimentary aspects of running a private practice as a business."

While that certainly may be true, this raises an important question related to the limits of what professional training can actually do, perhaps even what it *should* do to prepare therapists for the realities of what they will be expected to do in order to survive, much less flourish.

A therapist fresh out of school is most concerned with finding and keeping a job, paying off debt, and learning the basic policies and procedures of the agency or organization. After those first few years there is time and interest to move far beyond survival mode, and it is then when additional, focused training is usually better suited to cover what was missed. But full disclosure: I'm a professor, as well as a clinician, so I'm more than a little defensive about what is covered, and what is neglected, during these years in school.

It is even clear that distinct differences exist between the ways novice and expert clinicians function, especially with regard to their cognitive activity. Whether in the practice of medicine, physics, chess, or therapy, experts are better able to encode information, organize memory, retrieve relevant knowledge, observe inconsistencies, connect disparate areas, discriminate judgments, track multiple tasks, explain rationales for action, correct mistakes, and develop novel responses (Chi, 2006; Orlinsky & Ronnestad, 2005; Skovholt, 2012). These qualitative changes require a base level of training, plus additional time, quality experiences, reflective practice, and varied data that cannot be provided within the limitations of training programs.

The practice of group therapy provides an example of how experienced leaders process what is going on much more quickly, reach deeper levels of exploration, and exhibit greater flexibility in their interventions (Kottler & Englar-Carlson, 2015). By contrast, beginners rely more on conventional theory, tend to be more cautious in their approach, and more regimented in their reasoning. Obviously, the readiness and ability of a novice to learn are quite different from what is available to professionals at a later stage of their development. Cognitive structures and processes continue to evolve as we gain experience, requiring us not only to learn new skills and strategies to match our developed capacities but also to unlearn old ones that no longer fit.

Many appropriate styles and practices that may have been appropriate at earlier stages of training lose their viability as things progress to greater levels of expertise. You may find that skills that were once relied on change from benign, active listening early in one's career to more forceful, confrontive, strategic interventions as you gain ability, knowledge, understanding, and confidence. The complexity of how you conceptualize cases may also increase in direct proportion to your level of experience and expertise. Cases that at one time seemed hopelessly complicated will often appear relatively straightforward, while at the same time you may come to appreciate intricacies that you would have missed earlier. The breadth of your knowledge base expands well beyond the parochial boundaries of your own discipline as defined by graduate school courses. Finally, the fluency and flexibility with which you can change direction depending on what you observe and sense become quite remarkable compared to the therapeutic ruts you found yourself in so consistently early on.

No matter how well conceived a training program might be, it is impossible to meet all of a beginning therapist's needs. It is inevitable that mistakes are made and weaknesses revealed once a beginner operates in the real world. Graduate school is designed to provide a start because of its inherent limitations, time parameters, and the myriad and evolving demands of the profession.

Doing the Best They Can

Although it is easy to be critical of the limits, if not the shortcomings, of graduate school, especially with regard to preparing therapists for real-world practice, there are practical considerations regarding what can actually be covered within the time parameters, resources available, and mandated requirements by licensing boards, university curricula, and accreditation agencies. As mentioned earlier, professional preparation for any field is primarily designed to teach basic skills and foundational knowledge; it is the mentoring and supervisory system afterward that is supposed to provide ancillary and advanced skills.

It's Impossible to Learn Everything

Once upon a time therapists were once trained in a single year or less. Modeled after apprentice programs in many of the skilled trades, practitioners were supposed to learn much of what they needed on the job. Over the years, professional training has continued expanding to the point that even a 3-year master's degree is sometimes not considered sufficient to cover all the territory. In some cases, newly minted doctoral graduates have spent more than a decade in school only to discover they must continue postdoctoral programs in order to make themselves more marketable.

Most experienced practitioners recognize that no amount of time will *ever* be enough to fully prepare someone for the future challenges of therapy practice; there is simply not enough time in a single lifetime. In addition, there are so many incremental, if not dramatic changes, in technology, research, conceptual models, and standards of care that knowledge redoubles itself every decade or so. Meanwhile, the myth continues that if only additional courses were added onto programs, somehow this would provide beginning practitioners with everything they might need.

One new graduate, for example, complained that she was unprepared for professional practice because she had been offered only limited exposure to new developments in eye movement and desensitization reprocessing, equine-assisted therapy, somatic experiencing, and other alternative modalities. "They hardly taught me anything beyond cognitive therapy, narrative therapy, and some basic psychodynamic stuff. But I've always been interested in stuff that's more cutting edge." The surprising thing about this representative comment is that she really believed that some of these more advanced, "cutting-edge" approaches should have been offered in lieu of models that have far more supportive evidence tested over time.

There is an inherent conflict between stated need for more and better training versus cost-effectiveness and time commitments. Every few years licensing boards and professional organizations seem to mandate additional requirements, extending the length of time needed to complete a program. The number of credit hours for a master's degree in many states has actually *doubled* since the time I graduated many years ago. More recently state licensing boards have required new courses added onto an increasingly burgeoning curriculum to include psychopharmacology, trauma, addictions, child and spousal abuse, aging, sexuality, gender issues, advocacy, plus all the continuing education units that are required to maintain a credential. It isn't that these classes are not useful and important but rather that they are always heaped on already overloaded schedules. Programs must therefore be selective in what they choose to provide for students. Most often schools choose basic information over specialization and thinking over action.

Learning Is Divided Into Arbitrary Pieces

Graduate training tends, by its very nature, to break concepts and behaviors down into their smallest, most recognizable parts. The idea is that while you may see the whole, you must study and practice the individual parts to understand and implement ideas effectively. The concept is accepted practice in most learning situations, but it clearly has its drawbacks.

Students consistently report their confusion trying to make sense of everything that is thrown at them in disparate and often conflicting fragments. During any given week, a student might be introduced to some novel conceptual model for diagnosing mood disorders at the same time another instructor goes on a rant about how diagnostic entities themselves are fictional creations that only exist in our imagination. Perhaps in one sense this prepares us for what happens in the real world where there can be so much debate and disagreement over some ideas, but it also leads to problems because of a lack of coherence and synchronization of curriculum from one segment to another. You may be asked to take courses in Assessment I and Assessment II, but that doesn't mean they necessarily fit well together.

What is lost during this process is the bigger picture in which beginners are helped to integrate, synthesize, and personalize what they've learned into some type of reasonably coherent framework. One therapist remarked that she wished there had been a little less emphasis on content and "stuff" in her program and more focus on the underlying process of helping others. When she first began seeing clients, she found herself "lost trying to hold onto everything the client was saying." She was thinking and analyzing so much, trying to include everything that had been stuffed into her head, that she missed a lot of what was really going on in the session. "Finally I figured out on my own how to follow the energy in each session, which is much more revealing to me than the client's words alone. This helps me to recognize where the client stands and where things are shifting, allowing us to go deeper than could be possible by attending to content alone."

Faculty and supervisors may talk a good game about the importance of process in therapeutic encounters, and the significance of direct experience in sessions, but this stands in direct contrast to the content-driven approaches that are dominant in school. The emphasis in most programs is overridingly slanted toward mastering specific domains of knowledge rather than understanding the underlying processes of change related to individualized personal experience. Ironically, with all the required coursework in multicultural issues and sensitivity to diversity, there is a marked absence of recognizing how these differences translate into distinct learning styles, especially if the goal is to help students to customize and adapt the concepts to their own needs and interests, as well as their diverse clients.

This applies equally to the emphasis in graduate school on testing and evaluation of performance. Certainly it is critical to assess learning outcomes to determine the effectiveness of instruction, as well as identifying weak areas to bolster, but sometimes that is *all* that students think about. Some of the most frequent questions asked in classes are not driven by passionate interest in the subject or curiosity regarding a deeper understanding of concepts but rather reflect obsessions with grades: "Will this be on the weekly quiz?" "When you say the paper must be 12 pages, what size font can we use?" "If I miss class next week because I have to attend a wedding, will that count as an unexcused absence?" "When you said earlier that CBT is not the same as REBT, will you be distinguishing between the two on the final exam?"

Students often spend more time figuring out how to work the system, attain the best possible grades, and satisfy instructor expectations than they do trying to learn the concepts and skills in such a way that they become most personally relevant.

Academic Qualifications Versus Personal Characteristics

Based on research studies of therapy outcomes, we know that a significant factor is related to the therapist's own personal characteristics, especially those qualities that lead to more trusting, engaged relationships with clients (Baldwin & Imel, 2013; Bowen, Brown, & Howat, 2014; Duncan, 2010; Wampold & Imel, 2015). In many ways, it isn't only what we know, or what we can do, but how we fold this knowledge and skills into a way of being that allows us to connect with clients in a meaningful way. It isn't only what we do in sessions but who we are and the ways we present ourselves.

Given the virtually universal acceptance that personal characteristics do potentially empower (or limit) therapeutic interventions, it is surprising how little such qualities are taken into consideration when admitting new professionals into the guild. Graduate schools often rely on test scores like the Graduate Record Exam that are culturally biased and privilege academic knowledge over life experience. Likewise grade point average may be a record of past academic performance, but it doesn't necessarily predict much related to therapist effectiveness. Other information collected from reference letters or personal interviews may highlight limited personal qualities, but they are unlikely to be sufficient to assess integrity, trustworthiness, compassion, and caring. This means that we may attract some really smart people to the field but not necessarily those who would do the best therapeutic work. It is no wonder, then, that most of us graduate as unfinished products with still plenty of work to do.

Even if particular programs wanted to de-emphasize academic criteria and increase the importance of other factors and personal characteristics of their candidates, they are not positioned to assess and develop the relational or emotional aspects in the thorough way they handle intellectual abilities and academic performance. Such a process may be necessarily imprecise, subjective, and overly personal.

Our legal and educational systems have developed the means by which to evaluate applicants and make decisions on their suitability based primarily on cognitive aptitude and achievement. Written and observational assessments of personality or moral characteristics, on the other hand, are given much less credibility. We will remain in this intellectually driven selection model until there is greater acceptance of our ability to identify and evaluate nonacademic characteristics as critical to learning and therapy. In the meantime, there are still many positive things each of us did take away from graduate school.

Lessons That Were Learned

The reality is that graduate training programs, and even continuing education in the form of seminars, workshops, and additional courses, provide a great deal of lasting impact. Those influences are sometimes tied to specific course titles, content, lectures, exams, or papers, as might be expected. More often, though, lasting effects are tied to a variety of experiential learning opportunities that surround formal training where students personalize their exploration of ideas, behaviors, and techniques. Relationships with faculty, students, supervisors, clients, and the demands of being continually evaluated on performance in a wide variety of pressure-packed situations each offers its own set of valuable experiences that create our professional selves.

The Scientist-Practitioner Model

There has already been enough debate about whether therapists are essentially scientists or artists, logicians and problem solvers, or intuitive relationship specialists. Obviously we are all of the above, both scientifically grounded in what has been learned from empirical studies as well as pragmatic practitioners who operate from the gut when the situation calls for it. We rely on what normative data have informed us about human behavior, developmental stages, and interpersonal patterns, just as we trust our felt experience about what we sense is going on in any given moment.

The scientist-practitioner model for therapists has become the norm in our profession. We are urged to consult research and best practices related to a given presenting problem. We are taught to develop hypotheses and test their viability. We are prepared to think objectively and dispassionately about phenomena that arise, reasoning through decision-making processes to arrive at optimal treatment choices. The model has been effective in solidifying and standardizing the therapeutic practice to a certain extent, a necessary component of any profession that seeks public credibility.

The scientist-practitioner model makes a lot of sense when you consider the potential pressures involved in clinical practice. A judge in a civil case will be favorably impressed with the ability to demonstrate that work with a client was based on validated, reputable research. Not only is the legal system pleased with the scientist-practitioner model, but therapists themselves feel greater confidence knowing that their strategies are based on consensual standards of care.

One therapist felt like everything she had to do in graduate school was focused on evaluating outcomes and measuring progress, all of which seemed to create distance from her clients. "Now that I've been in practice for a few years," she admitted, "I get to relate to my clients the way I want to, and I love it. Sometimes it's hard to admit what they did for me, but one of the best things I learned in grad school is this habit of evaluating everyone and everything as clearly as I can. I don't make nearly as many stupid mistakes mostly because I never take for granted the words, actions, and information that people, including myself, convey."

Validity and reliability are the critical issues in judging therapist knowledge accuracy, observations, appraisal activities, and outcome measures just as they are in basic psychological research. The scientist-practitioner model emphasizes a well-reasoned approach to collecting information, applying it in an objective manner, and evaluating outcomes before going on to the next set of actions. This information collection, implementation, and evaluation process is what most follows students into their professional practice, more so than the specifics that were memorized and recalled for tests, papers, and projects.

The scientist-practitioner model can also be far more inclusive than the rigid parameters that might be associated with an emphasis on empirically supported knowledge. Rhodes (2012), for example, describes four different research methodologies that can help us to explore process features of the therapeutic experience, examining more deeply the interactions between clients and therapists, as well as those aspects of the conversation that are most meaningful and enduring.

One of the legacies of our early training, even if there might have been some resistance along the way, is learning to evaluate progress systematically and hold oneself accountable for results. This helps us to address a number of critical questions: Does what's going on between us in session match what is to be expected? What kinds of observable behavioral changes are evident, and how do they compare to what the client reports? How should I revise my diagnostic assessment in light of certain criteria that are not being met? What are some of the problem areas that are getting in the way? What does the client appreciate most and least about our work together?

It is this last question that brings the client into the assessment process as an equal partner. After all, clients are experts on their own experience even if their self-reports might be flawed. One of the strongest movements in the field these days is becoming far more proactive in asking clients for their input about what is most and least helpful to them and making adjustments accordingly (Duncan, Miller, Wampold, & Hubble, 2010; Miller, Duncan, Brown, Sorrell, & Chalk, 2006; Miller & Hubble, 2011).

Regardless of the extent to which therapists conceive of themselves as "scientific practitioners" or "practical scientists," there is little doubt that the emphasis on empirically supported and evidence-based treatments is an integral part of transitioning our profession into a viable member of the health care system, entitled to all the privileges, reimbursements—and scrutiny—afforded to other medical specialties.

A Common Professional Heritage

Regardless of one's professional identity, whether a social worker, psychologist, family therapist, counselor, psychiatrist, nurse practitioner, or pastoral worker, whether a specialist in substance abuse, group work, couples counseling, mood disorders, posttraumatic stress, eating disorders, career decision making, acculturation, pain management, or a dozen others, we all share a common lineage.

Historical figures in our field have become something like shared family members that we gossip about at social or professional events. Freud is like a quirky great uncle of sorts, just as Carl Rogers or Virginia Satir might feel like legacy grandparent figures. Jung's collective unconscious, Erikson's developmental stages, the other Erickson's induction procedures, Adler's inferiority feelings, Bowen's systemic model, Rogers's core conditions, Horney's basic anxiety, Maslow's needs hierarchy, Skinner's reinforcement, and Bandura's modeling are some of the building blocks that have added bits and pieces to modern-day therapy. What were once all-or-nothing theories for their originators have now become pieces of a larger whole. Professionals of all orientations and persuasions blend these and other ideas into a set of beliefs, techniques, and styles that promote their own personal therapeutic model. Part of that choice is made based on understandings created by the study of the people and stories at the heart of those theories.

The study of historical figures in our field also provides a framework by which to understand the evolution of ideas, as well as our own individual contributions to the advancement of these concepts. It is, after all, a myth that any of us are actually applying any theoretical paradigm in its pure and unadulterated form; the reality is that each of us is unique in the ways we interpret and apply concepts, no matter what we might call ourselves. Behind closed doors with our clients we are all more pragmatic and flexible than we might pretend to be.

Sure there are ongoing power struggles, turf battles, and conflicts among various practitioners. And yes, there are also a number of petty disputes about who is most deserving of recognition and who is best qualified to deliver services, but this seems to reflect the nature of human competition in any domain. Where we can possibly come together is by collaborating on a far more unified front that transcends discipline and specialty, that focuses on points of agreement, and that works to improve the quality of our services. This could include a far more integrative approach to our work that recognizes contributions from a variety of disciplines, conceptual models, and traditions, and allows for greater flexibility in adapting what we do depending on the particular cultural context, presenting complaints, and needs of any particular client.

Preparation for Complex Choices

Most contemporary training programs have moved away from introducing students to only one theoretical orientation, one diagnostic model, or one assessment package. Programs are still pressured to include whatever current "hot model" captures attention for a period of time, in addition to the old standbys like psychodynamic, cognitive-behavioral, existential, behavioral, and so on. The fact that programs continue to promote the study of a variety of models, even if part of a historical survey, ultimately prepares beginners to make ongoing choices throughout their careers. Most of us continue to evolve and alter the ways we work as we grow, develop, and integrate new experiences into the fold.

If most programs do one thing exceedingly well, it is helping students to learn to make informed decisions at any clinical choice point, including which model(s) may be best indicated in a particular situation or with a particular client. We would hardly stick with the exact same therapeutic plan helping someone in imminent crisis who is self-medicating with drugs as we would another client who is struggling with acculturation issues adapting to her new home, or a third client who is attending sessions for self-awareness and growth.

A new therapist who works with culturally diverse clientele remembers being incredibly frustrated with an instructor who refused to provide definitive answers to his questions regarding the ideal theoretical model, or the optimal assessment tool, or the best strategies for dealing with particular complaints. "He just kept challenging us to keep searching for different perspectives, new ideas. Somewhere along the line it convinced me that I should never be satisfied with just what I currently believe about people." In other words, he was pushed to always consider adapting his thinking, and interventions, to fit every unique situation and person.

Ideally, graduate programs help students to clarify their beliefs, support them with evidence, alter those that don't fit with compelling evidence, and express their ideas persuasively. This is often a challenging adjustment for those who've spent 15 or more years learning to repeat what others have told them or else supporting opinions without much convincing data. This is where almost all professional training programs intersect in that they are geared toward helping students to think critically, reason logically, and work through problems systematically.

The Struggle for Approval and Professional Recognition

Let's face it: any academic experience, graduate school most of all, is a competitive environment in which students troll for attention and struggle for recognition. Even when attempts are made to reduce comparisons to others and focus is directed toward individualized development, it is virtually impossible to avoid evaluating one's own performance compared to others. This, in fact, represents a parallel process that instructors experience in their own academic environment in which there are limited resources. Tenure, promotion, and access to external funds, even to travel money, are all based on a merit-based system in which only the mighty succeed. This filters downward to students: They are also continually evaluated, judged, and assigned grades as symbols of their ongoing ability.

Given that most of us represent successful products of the competitive academic environment, we are used to external evaluations and judgments regarding our behavior. Most of us thrived in such a system that depended on doing our best work to please others in positions of power and authority who would affirm that we were good enough. It has been difficult for many of us to shed this search for approval ever since then.

Instructors and supervisors had a responsibility to make sure that therapist candidates were of sufficient moral character and met the professional standards for competence, if not excellence. The public expects that we would police our own ranks and make certain that only the best and brightest qualify for appropriate credentials. This may have created additional pressure and stress during training, but it also helped us to internalize self-evaluation standards and taught us how to attain a degree of recognition.

Upon graduation, therapists still find themselves competing with one another for employment opportunities, promotions and raises, and access to resources. Supervisors and mentors still hold power over us, making judgments about our worthiness. Those who do research or wish to publish their ideas are in the most competitive arena of all, submitting their work to editors and referees who will likely reject 90% of the submissions. Those in private practice compete for clients in a limited marketplace. And at one time or another, we look at our own skills and abilities compared to others and find ourselves falling short.

If graduate school taught us one skill set, it was how to secure the approval and recognition of others, even if we have tried to avoid this whenever possible. First we become attuned to what others like and don't like regarding our actions. In some ways this serves us well as we sensitize ourselves to what clients prefer and what they need, even if it also leads to approval seeking in other areas of life.

After becoming aware of things that are not appreciated, the next thing we learned is not to do those things anymore. When a professor told us to convert papers to one-inch margins, or to stop using gendered pronouns, or restrain from interrupting a lecture with comments, or avoid close-ended questions during interviews, we made instant adjustments rather than face continued ire and disapproval. Likewise, we learned to read what others expected from us and how to meet those demands. Given that we have been specifically trained to become interpersonally sensitive and responsive, we have been ideally prepared to continue to excel in these areas. This has become a gift as well as a burden.

Functioning as Part of a Team (for Better or Worse)

There were times in graduate school when we had to function well as part of a team (think group activities and presentations), as well as others when we had to show initiative and take charge of situations. We still juggle these roles, especially those therapists who find themselves caught in the middle between reconciling their clients' perceived needs, their supervisors advice (or mandates), and their own preferences.

We were actually well prepared in graduate school for navigating these complex dynamics and seemingly conflicting pressures. It may not have been very enjoyable at the time, but we have actually logged many hours figuring out how to function well despite the challenges of working as part of teams that may not have been as high functioning as we would have liked.

One therapist looks back at what he hated most about his school experience, and yet what has since served him well in his professional life afterward. He avoided group projects like the plague whenever he had the option. "Other students in those groups never seemed to agree on how to do things and you never got appropriate credit for your contributions. Some jerk would talk big and do absolutely no work whatsoever, which always meant a lower grade and put more responsibility on everyone else's shoulders." He also recalls that, to make matters still more frustrating, the person who would step up and who just had to be in control might be doing that for self-serving reasons rather than because he or she had much useful to offer. This only led to more dysfunction and inefficiency.

"As much as I hated those projects," the therapist says, "I can say now that they taught me more about dealing with other professionals, and even clients, than anything I read in books. I learned that the blowhard would need to say his stuff no matter what, but if I waited him out, I could still do what I needed to do to get the work done and keep my sanity intact. I learned how to invite the quieter people to become more involved so that I didn't wind up doing their work later on. I learned that sometimes I had to push and other times I had to sit back and wait (the part I hated most). I learned that if I have to work with someone who *must* be the leader, then it's best to just surrender—and then work around him or her in the background."

As I'll discuss in a later chapter, one of the most surprising and disturbing aspects of working as a therapist is that we discover that that we have more than our fair share of narcissistic, toxic individuals in our organizations who seem to have been attracted to the field not because they want to help people but because they want to inflate their own egos and meet their own needs for power, dominance, and control. As annoying as this might have been in classes, things can become significantly more challenging in our workplaces.

In some ways, many of us were casualties from conflicts we suffered in graduate school or the workplace. There are times we've felt misunderstood or even abused because of some perceived injustice. We also learned under such circumstances to thicken our skins so we could accept feedback, or criticisms, directed our way. We strengthened our resolve to both improve our behavior and to immunize ourselves against those who may have bullied us in some way. Although we may have preferred learning certain lessons in other ways, graduate school taught us how to deal with interpersonal difficulties, as well as prepared us to serve in both leadership roles and as effective team members.

Skills for Maintaining Self-Discipline and Self-Confidence

Every experienced therapist I have ever met can relate to a time when, if only for a moment, he or she wanted nothing more than to escape the pressures of a particular client or a difficult situation with a colleague, supervisor, or supervisee. Just the fact that many therapists become "experienced" means that they have found ways to overcome these urges, since such pressures are a normal part of the therapist's work. Becoming successful requires self-discipline under pressure, which is often a developed characteristic encouraged both directly and indirectly in graduate school experiences.

It comes as a big shock to many students when they find that the excellent achievement they experienced as undergraduates will not be sufficient to get them through graduate school. The quietest students will be pushed to become more engaged in class, expand on ideas in discussions, and challenge themselves to be more direct and assertive in their relationships. Extroverts are asked to test themselves by becoming better at listening, reflecting, thinking, and speaking less often. Students are commonly challenged to confront personal conflicts in ideas, thoughts, and behaviors rather than avoid pressured situations in which conflicts arise.

Developing the self-discipline needed to face difficult situations in productive ways is no easy task. We have been tested under fire during exams, debates, and interviews we've conducted with instructors or supervisors critically observing the sessions. This prepared us for the inevitable challenges we would face on the job when a client or parent says, "Are you sure you know what you're doing?" or a supervisor asks, "What exactly *are* you doing with that client?" It's not like we can just pull out the *Book of Solutions*, find the right answer, and then calmly report back what we found.

Whether it was pulling an all-nighter to study for an exam, writing a paper or thesis that seemed beyond what you were capable, or conducting a session with others watching when you felt *way* over your head, such training experiences did prepare you for what lay ahead.

Moments of Wonder

Graduate school prepares students for the many troubling realities of professional practice, but it also highlights the most inspiring parts of our work. Looking back on a career that began many years ago, one practitioner talks about the joy he feels even after all these years. "There's still nothing that gets to me as much as the light in my clients' eyes when they see the way out of what seemed like a dark hopeless corner. I float home after those sessions."

The experience of therapy provides moments of wonder not only for our clients but also for us. Even during those times when it feels like a session will drag on forever, something remarkable, almost magical, seems to make all the difference. A burst of insight occurs that radically changes the way clients see themselves and the world. This flash of sudden illumination turns the session from mundane conversation to a bold search for new and exciting possibilities.

Consider a recent time in session when you felt giddy with excitement, relief, or moved to tears of joy and exaltation. Despite the aggravation and frustration you might sometimes feel, it is precisely these moments of wonder that sustain us, that make us feel so grateful that we were fortunate enough to have chosen this profession.

Were we prepared for professional practice as well as we might prefer, perhaps as much as we deserve? Of course not. But even in our disappointments and unmet expectations there are holes that we learn to fill in ourselves, hopefully with the assistance of other mentors, supervisors, colleagues, and especially our clients, who are our greatest teachers.

Chapter 2

Seismic Shifts in the Practice of Therapy

To say that the fields of psychotherapy and counseling are undergoing rapid changes hardly does justice to the magnitude and scope of what has been taking place during the past decade. There once was a time when preparing to be a professional therapist held promise of a stable and prosperous future, one in which you could expect to earn a decent salary and enjoy the benefits of being part of a very exclusive club. All the sacrifices you have made to join this profession—the money you have spent, the time you have invested, the challenges you faced, the anxiety and pressures you have survived, the hard work you spent reading scholarly material, wading through textbooks, writing papers, taking exams, gritting your teeth through certain classes, competing with the best and the brightest—all seemed worthwhile as long as you would have your prize at the end. Throughout all the hoops you were made to jump through, the rites of passage you earned every step of the way, there was always that dream waiting for you at the end.

You may have imagined yourself sitting in a perfectly appointed office. While dozing in boring classes you distracted yourself with fantasies about exactly what your space would finally look like. You selected your furniture carefully, pondered exactly how you would arrange things in the absolutely perfect configuration guaranteed to make the most reluctant clients open their hearts to your compassionate scrutiny. During particularly tense or slow times in class, you might have lapsed even further into the most minute details of what this new stage in your life would be like. You thought about how you would arrange your books, where to put your diplomas, which colleagues you would associate with, what kinds of clients you would see, and how you would market yourself and your wonderful new skills. And yet by the time you graduated it may have seemed like quite a shock to discover that the job options and therapy world were quite a bit different than you had hoped.

Things Ain't What They Used to Be

There once was a time, not too long ago, when all therapists needed to begin practicing their craft was a quiet room, a few good referral sources, an appointment book, a phone, and an answering machine. This was during that era when many people had insurance policies that subsidized psychotherapy in such a way that most people paid a nominal fee and could easily afford to come a few times per week as long as they liked. The only justification that was required was certification that a person was indeed undergoing some sort of adjustment reaction, marked by anxiety or depression, or perhaps a combination of both. We were not asked how long our treatment would take, and it was perfectly reasonable to assume that our clients could attend sessions as long as they liked and were profiting from the experience.

It must seem awfully strange for newcomers in the field to hear these stories about the good old days, kind of like the claims by our parents or grandparents that they had to trudge three miles to school every day, braving snowstorms and any number of obstacles along the way. Indeed, it does seem like there is a different world for therapists today, a seismic shift in professional practice that now requires a whole new set of skills and knowledge, many of which were not introduced—and could not possibly all be covered—in graduate school.

End of the Golden Era

One of the most significant changes in the role of a therapist during the past few decades has been a shift away from the tradition of serving as a dependable confidante over a lengthy period of time to that of a very temporary advisor. Some practitioners have even rebranded themselves as a "personal coach" or "personal consultant" in order to increase their "market share" and expand new opportunities. This might work fine for those described as the "worried well," or who require only assistance in their growth or development, but leaves quite a number of people with more severe disorders or intractable problems without sufficient support. These are often individuals suffering from deep-rooted intrapsychic struggles, certain personality disorders, or chronic conditions that are not necessarily amenable to a "quick cure."

It was during the Golden Era of our profession when insurance companies would subsidize treatments to the tune of 90% of whatever fees were reasonably charged, no questions asked. It was perfectly normal that therapy might last a year or longer with a focus not only on the presenting complaints but also on underlying issues that might be brought into the conversation. While there were certainly abuses of this system, not to mention unnecessary client dependence, there were also far more opportunities not only to fix current problems but also to provide an ongoing forum for future growth.

What a luxury it would be these days to work with clients according to what we believe is actually in their best interests, not only to address what brought them into treatment but also to help them develop the self-awareness, personal skills, and resilience to deal with other problems in the future. And while we are reimagining bygone years, how lovely it would be to design therapeutic plans based on what is actually best indicated, no matter how long that would take. Perhaps it is better in some respects that we are now held more accountable for our efficiency and outcomes, but there's also a lot that has been lost in this new climate.

Doc in the Box

Sprinkled liberally around most communities today are little clinics that offer the public medical services in the same spirit as department stores or chain restaurants. You can even find such operations squeezed into the corners of drug store chains that advertise "health screening," "medical consultations," and "minute clinics." Gone are the times when you had a personal physician, one who knew your family and history intimately. Some of us are old enough to actually remember doctors making house calls! Now you show up at one of these mini-medical centers (no appointment needed), take a number, and then take your chances that the doctor on duty is someone who knows something about what is ailing you. Forget about anything resembling personal service: Their job is to administer medicine cheaply and efficiently, not necessarily to deal with you as a human being.

I recently had the misfortune to visit one of these convenient clinics after sustaining multiple injuries in a bike accident. I could barely move and was experiencing excruciating pain in my back, shoulder, and side. "I wouldn't worry," the doctor told me as she was typing into the computer screen, rarely even bothering to make eye contact. Even more remarkable, during the whole "examination" she never once touched me.

"It's probably just a severe muscle strain," she said, glancing up from her typing for a moment. She sat on the other side of the examining room, entering data into my file, looking up only when I inadvertently screamed from a muscle spasm. She gave me prescriptions for a muscle relaxant and a painkiller, neither of which I could tolerate.

It turned out I had two broken ribs and a fractured scapula, neither of which was diagnosed because she was so rushed to attend to other patients who had been waiting in other rooms. I could forgive the doctor because she was operating as part of system that valued efficiency and cost-effectiveness rather than quality care—or even reasonably competent care. And I know I'm not alone in this acceptance of mediocrity.

The public is growing so used to this doc-in-the-box mentality that when it comes time to see a professional for some personal concern or emotional difficulty, people don't even flinch at the prospect of choosing a random name from a published list of "approved providers." One therapist is as good as another, they reason. The important thing to consider is: Can I see this professional who is covered on my plan?

These are indeed the days of managed care, health maintenance organizations, employee assistance programs, and preferred provider networks. If the concept of private practice is not being systematically eroded, then it is at least being altered to the point where therapists are working more hours, for less money, doing homogenized treatment for prescribed intervals. It is not just the solo practitioner who is losing autonomy; any community agency, organization, or mental health service has had to streamline the ways it operates.

During the past few decades, more and more articles have been appearing in professional journals that urge practitioners to consider economic risks, cost-effectiveness, market research, sales strategies, program marketing, and branding. Such aggressive self-promotion goes against the grain of all we were ever taught in school about the importance of professional integrity. Yet this has become the new reality in order to survive in the therapeutic marketplace.

If the trends continue, it appears that we may have even less autonomy in what we choose to do with our clients and how we prefer to do it. The emphasis continues to focus on doing therapy as briefly and efficiently as possible, dealing only with the original presenting complaint, and measuring outcomes as quantitatively as possible. In one instance, a friend of mine who worked on a psychiatric unit was appalled that benefits were cut off for one patient who was determined to have made "substantial progress" because now he reported there were only four poisonous snakes that he imagined were crawling around inside his belly instead of the twenty when he first entered treatment.

Although this situation may at times seem discouraging, there have also been some significant advances in making therapy more responsive and efficient, as well as more cost-effective. Some clients appreciate the greater convenience of being able to schedule sessions via alternative delivery systems (video, phone, etc.) and report that they can be even more honest and forthcoming than during face-to-face sessions. It remains to be seen whether research will support some of these testimonies.

One major problem seems to be the degree of competition rather than cooperation that now exists between members of the therapeutic community. The truth of the matter is that between social workers, psychologists, family therapists, counselors, pastoral care workers, psychiatric nurses, and psychiatrists, not to mention all the paraprofessional mental health workers operating without licenses and primary care physicians functioning outside of their specialties, there are too many of us in the marketplace. Whereas the prospects look most promising for masters-level counselors and therapists, there is a far bleaker picture for more "expensive" doctoral-level practitioners (Norcross, Pfund, & Prochaska, 2013). It is now a matter of survival of the fittest—and those who adapt most smoothly to the changing landscape of professional practice.

Economic and political realities have turned one profession against the other, and even within specialties practitioners undercut one another, outbid one another for contracts, and act as if we are all fighting for a limited number of customers, which in a sense we are. This is especially ironic when we consider that the waiting lists at community mental health centers, veterans' hospitals, and charitably funded agencies (NGOs) are staggering. Although there may be competition for affluent clients described as the "worried well," there remain substantial numbers of economically disadvantaged and marginalized clients who desperately need help that is not available. Unfortunately, they can't pay for services and the government continues to reduce funding for their mental health needs, leaving the poor and homeless without much support.

This situation has indeed caused considerable resentment and frustration, but it has also had some constructive impact. The call for increased accountability has motivated us to improve our effectiveness. Clients are profiting from more efficient methods of symptom alleviation even if they are sometimes being left out of opportunities to explore deeper issues of meaning in their lives. It is also true that more and more middle-class working people are able to afford to seek our services than ever before.

Finally, it is only reasonable that our profession is expected to ante up in the effort to control spiraling health costs that have resulted from decades of abuse by some irresponsible individuals and organizations. In one such case, a social worker who worked within a private practice group would bring in large extended families, see them together, but then bill their insurance company for individual sessions, sometimes even 90 or 100 billing hours per week! In another case within the same agency, a psychologist would simultaneously schedule two or even three clients at the same time, just like doctors do. He would then run back and forth between each interview room, giving clients assignments or tasks to complete while he would alternate every few minutes between each of the sessions. Naturally, he would then charge different insurance companies for the same hour, knowing that they would not compare their records to discover what he had been doing. I am certain that most of you can think of a few similar examples of your own in which unscrupulous colleagues have tried (and succeeded) in ripping off the system. It is no wonder that strict controls have had to be implemented as a way to prevent such abuses and document more stringently the impact of our efforts.

Yet even with the pressure to become more accountable and work within a system that emphasizes efficiency over quality care, there are still practitioners who manage to provide excellent service within these parameters. When I returned to the same "doc in the box" for a follow-up visit to change my medication because the pain from my fall was intolerable, the new doctor shocked me when she pulled up a chair to face me. "So," she said, "before we get into what brought you in to see me, tell me a little about yourself."

I was so surprised at the attention I stammered for a minute, not sure where to begin. We spent the next few minutes chatting before she actually gave me a complete physical exam and accurately diagnosed the fractures, adjusting my treatment accordingly. When I left the appointment, I felt so much better, not only because of the way I'd been treated but also because I'd actually been heard.

The Prozac Generation

First there was cod liver oil and Carter's pills, then Valium and Xanex, followed by Prozac and its successors, heralded as the new miracle cure for everything from depression, shyness, anxiety, chronic gambling, sociopathy, lower back pain, obesity, premenstrual syndrome, fear of public speaking, lack of confidence, or even a lackluster personality.

Guess what is the most commonly prescribed medication among adults under 45 years of age? That's right: antidepressants. More than 40 million prescriptions for Prozac alone have been prescribed (Mukherjee, 2012). Most of these prescriptions are written by general practice physicians who spend less than a few minutes talking to their patients about their problems. The doctors are happy because they feel like they did something useful, and their patients leave satisfied because they believe all they have to do is take a pill to not only feel better but also to fix all their problems.

After the publication of such books as *Listening to Prozac* and *Prozac Nation*, the public became even more convinced that relief was just a swallow away. Designer drugs (so-called because they are intended to work on a single neurotransmitter) are becoming so popular that in a small town in rural Washington one practitioner coerced over 700 of his patients to take Prozac! His defense: "There is a huge amount of unrecognized depression out there. I was just a little bit early in making the diagnosis" (Roberts, 1995, p. 16).

Prozac and its derivatives don't represent so much a medical breakthrough as they do an interesting cultural phenomenon. Prozac became a metaphor for quick relief and it turns out that its effectiveness is not much better than previous generations of antidepressant medications, and in many cases not much better than sugar pills (Healy, 2004). As such, there is a rising backlash from researchers and practitioners (especially those not in the pocket of the pharmaceutical industry) challenging many of the reported claims that it would not only "cure" depression but also migraines, PMS, and everything else under the sun (Breggin & Breggin, 2014). It turns out that not only do we not really understand how this class of serotonin-enhancing drugs operates in the system, but we also can't really be certain that they work at all (Kirsch, 2011).

Nonmedical therapists, who have only their powers of persuasion as their primary tools, are facing stiff competition from psychiatrists (and primary care physicians who prescribe the vast majority of antidepressant and antianxiety medications) who are offering the public chemical alternatives to alleviate what bothers them emotionally. What is a therapist to do when a client presenting symptoms of panic attacks or depression believes that symptom relief is only a few weeks away by taking a few pills each day? Sure there are a few annoying side effects, but what is a little insomnia, nausea, jitters, or lack of sex drive compared to immediate changes in one's demeanor, or even a perceived personality transformation?

The initial promise that all psychological ills could be cured by the new generation of psychotropic medications has now been reevaluated—and it's mostly good news for those of us who rely on the "talking cure." After extensive outcome studies related to the administration of antidepressant drugs, it isn't altogether clear whether results are generated by the chemicals themselves rather than placebo effects related to the doctor's belief that the pills would be helpful. It's pretty obvious that even if these medications could deliver what they promise, their impact is heightened, if not dependent, on the interpersonal context in which they are administered. In other words, it seems to take a skilled increasingly feeling alienated, disenfranchised, and marginalized, there is a desperate need to feel understood.

I remember some time ago devoting a year of professional development to upgrading my skills in the latest breakthroughs in brief therapy models. I couldn't wait for opportunities to move my clients along a faster route toward deliverance. After all, I have long been far more attracted to dramatic confrontations than I have to more low-key interpretations—not because I believe they work better but because they satisfy my own impatient need for progress.

I had been working with one woman for some time, making modest progress, but certainly not by the standards of my more solution-focused colleagues. I felt like a dinosaur still resorting to the "primitive" ways of working I had been practicing for years—listening carefully and compassionately, slowly building a solid alliance, exploring deep issues of freedom, personal responsibility, love, and breaking free of the past.

Clearly it was time to get to the "bottom line." My work with this client had been "dragging on" for months now, and I was feeling a little guilty that I was not meeting the current standards of what is expected. I interrupted my client on several occasions, especially proud of the deftness with which I introduced reframing, externalization, miracle questions, exception-seeking questions, deconstructions, paradoxical directives, and even an old-fashioned direct confrontation when I told her that I thought she might be needlessly stalling the pace of things in order to avoid facing the world on her own.

The tears that had been streaming down her face abruptly stopped. I could see anger in her eyes and in cords of muscle in her neck. "Kottler, what is your problem?" she asked none too politely. "In case you haven't noticed, I have not felt that many men have ever listened to me in my life, not my boss, my father, my brothers, my ex-husband, or certainly my current husband, and not even my own son. I am used to being interrupted. I have never been taken as seriously as I deserve. I had sincerely hoped that with you I might feel a little understanding. After all, I am paying you to listen to me. Is that clear?"

I nodded my head contritely, feeling ashamed.

"I wish you would stop trying to fix me," she continued the deserved scolding, "and just listen to me. I want you to understand what I'm experiencing. I want *someone* to finally understand who I am and what I want."

She actually said all that. I, of course, immediately protected myself from this censure by telling myself that this "intervention" clearly worked: Look at how assertive she had become, and all because of my technique of challenging her. While patting myself on the back, I also felt confusion settle over me. I realized that in my urgency to move more quickly, I had focused more on technique than on the person in the room with me.

Prove It

There is not only an imperative to move more quickly in our work, regardless of what the client wants or needs, much less what we believe is appropriate, but also a mandate that we must better assess the results of our efforts. And we damn well better be able to demonstrate that what we are doing is consistent with what is expected and considered normative by whoever is paying for it. It makes little difference whether solution-oriented therapy is appropriate for a given case or whether you even practice that sort of intervention; that is what you are ordered to do because its results can be easily measured.

Medical personnel and corporate executives who make up utilization review boards sometimes struggle to understand the work that we do because we can't show them the offending tumors or body parts that we have excised from the patient's body. They are not even certain that things like depression and posttraumatic stress even exist in the real world, nor are they convinced that there is anything we can really do to help these people.

On one level, it *is* absurd that we make people better by simply talking to them. This stands in contrast to the healing traditions in most of the world throughout history, traditions that are still practiced today among indigenous groups, in which those who are troubled almost never talk about what's bothering them but instead are invited to participate in community-based rituals that involve dancing, movement, prayer, and assigned tasks.

I once tried to explain to the head shaman of a village in the Kalahari Desert what I do for a living to help people and he just laughed at me. He wondered if talking about problems ever helps anyone.

If you think about it, that's a really good question. It does sound rather ridiculous to a shaman describing what psychotherapy is all about. The healing traditions among many indigenous peoples have been refined over thousands of years. They almost never involve talk but rather various rituals, movements, spiritual incantations, and community involvement. Compared to all the rather dramatic and potent activities that are part of traditional healing, including the use of difficult trials, public confession, vision quests, fire walking, dance marathons, shaking movements, communication with the spirit world, our therapeutic conversations appear rather feeble. It is no wonder I had such difficulty making a case that I was truly a competent healer. And it's also not surprising that many within the medical establishment question our legitimacy.

Others are constantly looking over our shoulders, and they are not the sort of benevolent supervisors who seem to care much about client welfare, our continued professional development, or such matters as autonomy, confidentiality, and quality of service. Quite often, the person who approves our treatment and decides whether we are allowed to continue seeing a client is not even trained in our profession. Such a case manager or utilization review worker may be a practical nurse, a general doctor, or even a company overseer who is consulting computer data and graphs but has never, ever even spoken to a person like our client.

Nevertheless, if we expect to continue doing business with the handful of organizations that will one day control all health care in this country, we must be able to document exactly what we did, what effects it had, and what results are likely if they should be kind enough to grant us another few sessions. This is not an unreasonable request if you are talking about engineering or even traditional medicine. The problem for us, however, is that if we are really honest, we would have to admit that most of the time we don't really know what it is that we said or did that had the greatest impact. Oh, we can make stuff up, and we *do* have our theories that we are quite fond of. Nevertheless, when a client improves or gets worse, we delude ourselves that we think we know why. It is always a humbling experience to follow up years later and invite clients to tell us what they found to be most helpful, often things that we don't remember saying or doing, or even things completely unrelated to our treatment.

The Call for Greater Moral Responsibility

The subject of morality has rarely been dealt with in our profession except for a few notable contributions (Doherty, 1995; Holmes & Lindley, 1989; London, 1986; Rieff, 1961; Wallach & Wallach, 1983). Family therapists such as Cloé Madanes have been introducing the morality of shame into their sessions, even urging perpetrators of violence to beg their victims for forgiveness. We have long been told that morality is something that belongs in a seminary, or at least in a philosophy department, but not in the secular study of therapy. And spiritual dimensions of being a healer? That is completely out of the question! In a scientifically based discipline such as the practice of therapy, which is advocating greater precision, measurement of outcomes, and reliability of interventions, what place is there for something as soft and ethereal as spirituality?

Doherty (2008) claims the therapy profession is suffering a crisis of confidence not because of our inability to help people but due to our failure to take a stand for what is obviously right. Therapists often promote personal self-fulfillment over interpersonal responsibility and accountability. A client may be lying to others. Another abandons his family in order to pursue some dream. Granted, what is "right" is often open to debate, but in some cases therapists have gone to such absurd lengths to avoid dealing with the moral implications of behavior, they have lost all credibility.

We learned in graduate school about the importance of neutrality, being nonjudgmental, detached, unpolluted, a condition that, while often desirable, is impossible to attain. There are times when we must take a moral stand—and can't help doing so because of some injustice we have heard about or witnessed. We were told that this loss of objectivity represented countertransference or, at the very least, evidence of personal overinvolvement or a lack of professionalism imposing our notions of right and wrong.

Despite these dangers, moral issues are unavoidable in our work. Neutrality is a myth. We have even been mandated by our ethical codes that we have a responsibility to stand up against racism and oppression, and advocate on behalf of those who feel powerless. Instead of apologizing for our abandonment of moral neutrality, we are actually in the business of character development and promoting virtue (Hamilton, 2013).

Therapy is inherently a value-laden enterprise in all kinds of ways. We make choices about what we consider is important and worthy to discuss and what is inconsequential. We talk a lot about issues of truth and responsibility. We help people to find or create greater meaning in their lives, itself a conversation about morality. Even our preferred model that guides our clinical decisions is infused with moral choices regarding life priorities, desired goals, and what best leads to a satisfying life. And we are frequently confronted with thorny moral issues that provide no simplistic resolutions.

There is nowhere for us to hide when clients bring us their conflicts that are fraught with moral implications. They want to know whether we think it is best to stay in a loveless marriage or to get out. We do our best to make some benign interpretation or reflection regarding the struggle with obligations to oneself versus others, but the reality is that we will subtly, if not unconsciously, push a little to consider moral nuances of one choice over another.

To add to the challenges, the public is asking us to be morally responsible in our actions and to help our clients to do the same, especially when they have acted inappropriately or antisocially. This applies not only to those clients referred to us by the courts, or those mandated to attend sessions because of drunk driving, drug addictions, or anger problems, but more recently therapists have been called upon by some sectors of the public to engage in "conversion therapy" to supposedly change a gay client's sexual orientation. Obviously, the therapist's own moral position—not to mention familiarity with scientific evidence—will influence such a choice.

On the other hand, legislative and legal actions are limiting more and more of our freedom to make choices. We are cautioned by our professional associations and state licensing boards to be more conservative and cautious than ever before, more compliant to the strictest norms for professional conduct. Both the frequency of malpractice suits and complaints to ethics boards are skyrocketing due to a change in public sentiment, more assertive consumers, and more aggressive lawyers who work on commission. The issue has no longer become whether a therapist has done anything wrong, but rather whether malpractice insurance will settle a nuisance suit for the price of a threatening letter.

Riding the Seismic Waves

It boggles the mind to consider how rapidly much of what we once learned is quickly becoming obsolete. The types of presenting complaints that we were used to working with seem to have transformed themselves into new maladies. During Freud's day there appeared to be a rash of hysteria, followed afterward by syphilis, "alien syndrome," dissociative disorders, and more recently, an increased prevalence of eating disorders, posttraumatic stress, and newer or revised forms of mental illness added to the latest *Diagnostic and Statistical Manual of Mental Disorders*. Just as diagnostic entities have evolved, so have our treatment options.

Even among practitioners who identify strongly with a particular theoretical orientation, it is difficult to ignore the innovations in technique and research that have been developed in the past decade. In fact, conceptual purity is now quite difficult to maintain in the face of new research and clinical improvements that are being made across a wide range of disciplines and schools of thought. We are all becoming more alike, converging toward the center, as would be predicted in a profession that is maturing into its second century of evolution.

For the past decade I've been interviewing many of the notable theorists in the field for several other book projects. I've been struck by how even these notable figures have abandoned their own exclusive systems to borrow ideas from colleagues. They sit on panels with one another sharing their thoughts, debating points of conflict and agreement, but mostly listening to one another and altering some of their conceptions in light of what they hear from others. In the cases Jon Carlson and I have collected over the years profiling successful outcomes (Kottler & Carlson, 2003, 2006, 2008, 2009, 2015), many of the stories feature creative interventions that were highly integrative and pragmatic. I remember asking William Glasser about a case he shared that seemed to have no direct connection to his signature "choice theory." He just shrugged and confessed that he does whatever is needed for a client, regardless of where the idea originated. In other words, we have all become far more integrative and that trend is going to continue in spite of the ways we may have been indoctrinated into a particular system.

To return to the metaphor associated with this chapter's title, there have been some huge seismic waves that have shaken our profession to its core, many of which present new challenges and a changing landscape that bears little resemblance to what may have once been expected. If we are to survive professionally, much less flourish, we have to roll with these swells, making adjustments to augment our knowledge and skills. If there is one thing about which we can be certain, it is that the tsunami of change is relentless and ongoing.

Chapter 3

WALKING ON WATER AND OTHER UNREALISTIC EXPECTATIONS

Therapists are godlings. We walk on water. We can read minds and predict the future. We know all the answers. We even know a few of the questions. Whatever we don't already know, we can search out online, in books, or by *consulting the literature*. This mythical body of wisdom contains all the knowledge we could ever want to unlock the mysteries of the soul and cure human suffering. This is one of the things that we learned in graduate school—there is truth, it resides in a single form, and it can be unearthed quite easily if only you know the right combination of search modifiers for the databases.

Are You Really Helping Anyone? How Do You Know?

You may have graduated as a professional therapist hopeful that you were prepared to deal with almost anyone or anything that might stroll into your office. You subscribed to journals, accumulated cherished books, attended workshops and required continuing education credits, and recruited supervisors who could guide your further development.

Some very wise and knowledgeable experts have been telling you for a long time that you *must* know what you're doing. After all, your clients get better, don't they? You must be doing something right.

You nod your head in agreement.

Indeed, the vast majority of therapists, estimated well over 90%, consider themselves more accomplished and competent than their colleagues (Sapyta, Reimer, & Bickman, 2005). Lest you feel defensive about this "illusionary superiority effect" in which we tend to grossly overestimate our effectiveness compared to others, this trend holds true in almost every aspect of life. The vast majority of people believe that they are better drivers, more popular, smarter, and more competent at their jobs than everyone else (Dunning, Johnson, Ehrlinger, & Kruger, 2003).

I don't think that I'm the only one who hears a little voice in my head, one that sometimes whispers quite loudly, "You don't believe that you really know what you're doing, do you? Do you really think that you are helping anyone with that primitive-level stuff you try to do? Do you think people actually get better by just talking to them? And even when they do improve, do you actually believe that *you* had something to do with that? Heck, they got better in *spite* of you, not because of anything you said or did."

I remind myself that's ridiculous, attempting to pacify the doubts. I learned in graduate school a long time ago that if I build a solid relationship, diagnose client concerns accurately, and match interventions to the specific requirements of the case, good things will happen. I think of all my satisfied customers. I can recite case after case in which crippled people walked out of my office throwing their emotional crutches away forever, or at least until the last time I checked on them. . . .

We are therapists, professionals. We learned in graduate school that as long as we follow the time-honored recipe, all will work out for the best: (1) listen carefully, (2) respond back with what we hear and see, (3) structure opportunities for learning and growth, (4) help create alternative realities that are more beneficial, and (5) allow clients to proceed at their own pace. The ingredients may change a bit from case to case, but the process remains basically the same.

Armed with such confidence, reinforced again and again in The Literature and by our professors' and mentors' voices that still talk to us during times of doubt or need, we often feel like we can conquer the world. We know stuff that most people don't seem to realize. We can get to the heart of things in a matter of minutes sometimes. We can talk in silky and soothing voices, utterly convincing the client, if not ourselves, that a particular course of action is righteous. We learned this from our professors and supervisors, who learned it from their mentors. Thus armed, most of the time we help to make a tremendous difference in people's lives even if there are occasions when we overstep. We have gotten ourselves in trouble a few times when we forget that what we learned in graduate school isn't necessarily what happens in the realities of daily practice.

Feeling Like an Imposter

We present an aura of almost perfect serenity. We embody the best in human beings, all-knowing and all-loving creatures. Clients always see us in a good mood, endlessly patient and wise; we've got the perfect response for every situation, an answer for every question.

I learned in graduate school that I was expected to be strong, to be a model of composure for others. I also learned how important it was to distance myself from other people's pain; to do otherwise would be to condemn myself to a life of vicarious misery. Nobody ever told me, however, the consequences of this therapeutic stance—that I would cut myself off from my own feelings, that I would begin to see my clients as cases rather than as people, that I would become addicted to relationships in which I was always the one in charge, that I would become a know-it-all. There was a time, early in my career, when I had begun to believe in my own omnipotence, so much so that I had the misguided belief that I really could do anything, maybe even walk on water.

I felt singularly unprepared to confront my doubts, to face my imperfections, to own up to my mistakes, to acknowledge my limitations. And yet how freeing such honest revelations are, helping us to face our failures, and in so doing, teaching us humility, prompting greater flexibility, improving our frustration tolerance, promoting reflection, increasing resolve, providing useful feedback on what works and what doesn't. It turns out that we actually learn far more from our mistakes and failures than we do our successes and when things go perfectly smoothly.

It has been challenging to forgive the inevitable lapses and misjudgments that occur. I'm harder on myself than anyone and have made a career talking about all the things I don't know, don't understand, and can't do as well as I'd like. It took years and years after graduate school to learn how to metabolize these disappointments, to accept that I'll never be as good as I want to be, and yet to realize that it is precisely this striving that leads to greater excellence.

One reason this task is so difficult is that certain perfectionistic myths were perpetuated in our training. We observed many of our instructors presenting themselves with confidence and authority, seemingly never at a loss for words. We watched films of master therapists demonstrating their magical skills, without ever appearing stumped. We felt surrounded by other professionals who, even if they didn't always know what they were doing, were certainly good at pretending they were. It is no wonder we have felt so much pressure to be perfect, and why often we may feel like impostors.

It was only later, *much* later, that I was able to pull back the curtain and see that the great wizards I most admired were masters of illusion. It turned out that they were often as clueless as I sometimes feel but were better at hiding their doubts and faking their confidence. I learned that some of the most famous theoreticians were actually not that skilled in the application of their own ideas. When demonstrating their models in action, it was sometimes challenging for the producer to record a decent interview; sometimes the theorist would be invited to return several times until a satisfactory session could be created. They were human after all with their own foibles and weaknesses.

It is no wonder that therapists are sometimes prone to an imposter syndrome, believing that deep down inside we aren't really doing much of anything and don't understand nearly as much as we sometimes pretend. Every time we manage to help someone, there is that seed of uncertainty in which we wonder whether we can do it again. There is always the risk that we've lost our magic.

When Education Is Limited, If Not Obsolete

We learned in graduate school that hard work would pay off for us, that excellent grades in life come to those who study carefully and prepare meticulously in order to perform at the highest level. What we don't learn until *after* graduation is that certain beliefs that we inherit from our instructors may not actually reflect the realities of our jobs.

Even though there have been such dramatic changes in the ways therapists operate today, there sometimes have been considerably slower adaptations in training programs. Many institutions are still preparing clinicians to do primarily relationship-focused, insight-oriented work with middle-class clients in a private practice setting. Beginning therapists are still being told decade-old clichés to "try to be yourself" or "take your time to get to know the client before you attempt any interventions." While this is still legitimate guidance, it hardly fits within the parameters in which most of us must now operate. When you've got a handful of sessions with a client, utilization review members breathing down your back wanting to know your outcomes and how you will measure them, and a desk full of paperwork waiting to be processed, it is sometimes challenging "to be yourself."

These omissions, misinterpretations, and maladaptive lessons were hardly the fault of our professors who did the best they could. Coursework and curricula were also structured as best they could be at the time to provide as much useful training as possible within the time constraints. Regardless of where fault is placed, in the system, in our mentors, or in ourselves, there are several glaring holes in our preparation that must be filled in through experience in the field. This is not only unusual in any professional training but, to a certain extent, is to be expected.

Looking back on aspects of their education that was less than complete, several newly graduated therapists I interviewed mentioned what stood out to them most. Although practica, internships, and other opportunities had been provided to get a taste of clinical practice, one such therapist had not been alerted to the sheer stamina that is involved in seeing multiple clients every day. "I was just so surprised and overwhelmed when I started seeing clients full time. I would come home utterly exhausted. I didn't want to do anything but sit on my couch in silence. The thought of another conversation, or any outside noise, just felt like more than I could handle. I didn't understand that I was taking in the energy of my clients, and most of the time that energy was deep and heavy. I felt weighed down. Yet, I mistook this feeling for the typical exhaustion that comes with making life changes. I didn't grasp that I was not only dealing with my own energy and fatigue but also the fatigue of others."

Along a similar vein, another therapist was not sufficiently prepared to handle all the ways her own unresolved issues would impact her therapeutic work. "When I started working with clients, I eventually realized that in order for me to avoid critically judging them, first I needed to learn how to accept and not judge myself. In order for me to be present with my clients who experienced trauma, I first needed to work through my own childhood trauma. To see my clients' strengths, I had to learn to recognize my own. In order for me to attend to my clients' needs, I needed to take care of my own emotional and physical needs."

Another therapist isn't quite sure what she doesn't know or didn't learn yet, because she has just begun practice. If there's one critical takeaway that we should all have at the end of our training it should include a rather clear and specific plan for what should follow in terms of additional preparation and training, as well as template of weaknesses that require ongoing work. That is one function of this book: to help assess areas in need of further development and upgrading.

Obviously a few years of graduate school can't cover everything, nor can such an immersive experience highlight every facet that might someday be encountered. Nevertheless, there are probably some glaring holes that each of us can point to. Following are a few of such important lessons that may have been neglected.

Practicing Therapy Is More Than a Job

Somewhere along the line, we may have gotten the distinct impression that being a therapist is like any other profession— accountant, lawyer, or doctor. We would learn our lessons well, become duly licensed, and then enjoy the fruits of our labor in a well-paying job that would give us the security, respect, and satisfaction that we have longed for.

Little did we realize that after all the sacrifices we made in order to become a therapist, we might very well end up feeling the same way about our work as we did in previous careers or even part-time jobs. Although we may be trained professionals, there is no guarantee that we can find employment that feels as satisfying as we had hoped.

A therapist looking back on her training laments how expensive graduate school was, compounded by financial losses while she was out of employment circulation. "This lost income was in addition to the costs associated with tuition, transportation, fuel, parking, books, and electronic equipment. I didn't realize how few students enter into well-paying positions straight out of graduate school and, on the contrary, many graduates work for free at their internship sites. And for those who hope to go into private practice, I didn't realize it would be up to five years before I'd be earning a decent income."

Boundaries Are Sometimes Permeable

It isn't that finding meaningful work is necessarily difficult, but that the boundaries between our work and personal lives are not quite as clear as we were told they would be in our texts, lectures, and supervision sessions. Perhaps for therapists practicing in large cities, it is certainly possible to arrange your life so you never run into a client when off-duty. Furthermore, in large cities, you also have career options that would not be available if you are committed to staying in other geographical regions.

Representative of therapists who work in rural areas, or smaller towns, Edgar marvels at how uninformed the authors of ethical codes must be when they don't take into consideration the realities of working in places other than huge metropolitan areas. "They talk a lot about maintaining boundaries, and separating work from family, and maybe some therapists can do that easily. What am I supposed to do, though, living in a place where I am one of the only therapists around for miles? I see my clients in my kids' school. I see their parents in the store or post office. I serve on a commission with one ex-client; another is the mechanic who works on my car; still another has been my son's teacher."

Edgar describes his role as a therapist as involving far more than what he does during sessions; in a sense, he is a public figure. "People watch the way I handle myself in public, the ways I parent my children. Nobody would ever seek my services unless they thought I was a person of honor and integrity."

We need not live in a small town to face similar pressures surrounding our image in the community. Maybe a doctor can get away with smoking cigars or a lawyer can be an eccentric crank, but it is not altogether paranoid to insist that people are watching us carefully for signs of instability and immorality. Most of us were never prepared for this responsibility or even warned that practicing as a therapist is not simply a job but a calling.

You Still Don't Feel Good Enough

Becoming credentialed as a therapist was supposed to bolster our sense of competence and earn us respect. Certainly this is the case to some extent, but probably not nearly as much as we had hoped. Most of our personal doubts, our insecurities, our core issues are still in residence even if they are relegated to the outermost suburbs of our souls. Although I'm owning these feelings, I'm also well aware that many readers vehemently disagree and feel little of such insecurity.

I remember seeing my professors and supervisors as the embodiments of all that I wished to be. They seemed to know everything, to know just what to do in any situation. They were so articulate and poetic in the ways they would explain themselves. They appeared calm and unconcerned during situations in which we would feel utterly panicked. There was an implicit promise in our contract together: If I would study hard, read the books they recommended, practice the skills they introduced, adopt the values and attitudes that they modeled, I would eventually be like them.

They lied. They lied not in their promise that I could someday be like them, but in the ways they presented themselves to me in the first place. I realize now, after hanging out with faculty for the past 40 years, that deep down inside most of them were not anymore secure and confident than I feel now. They interpreted their jobs to act like they knew what they were doing all the time even though they were just faking it, just like most of us do now. They lied by telling us all about their wonderful successes and neglecting to tell us about their failures. They lied by revealing their strengths in all their glory while covering up their weaknesses.

Because failure was a topic that was so rarely discussed in textbooks and class sessions, even in the workshops we attend upon graduation to fill in the missing gaps, it is no wonder the secret of our own imperfections has to stay underground. In many job settings, and among most groups of colleagues, it is simply not safe to admit that we don't always know what we are doing or that we don't have a clear idea of where to do go next. Instead, we imitate our mentors, pretending a degree of confidence and expertise that we may not feel.

In many settings there is an underground conspiracy to talk only about what is working quite well and to sweep the failures under the rug or, at the very least, to explain some clients away as resistant, noncompliant, difficult, poor risks, borderlines, or similar labels that imply it is their fault for not cooperating with our best intentions. It may not be safe for us to admit to ourselves, much less to anyone else, that much of the time we are flying by the seat of our pants, improvising, ducking incoming shrapnel, trying to keep things under control when we may feel lost. Those clinicians who do seem to exhibit such total confidence that they always know exactly what they are doing and where they are headed are downright frightening: That either means that we are really incompetent or that they are deluding themselves in a certainty of truth that doesn't really exist.

Practicing Therapy Has Negative Side Effects

One of the therapists mentioned earlier talked about the ways she had been unable to metabolize all the clients' burdens and energy she encountered during sessions. She also found herself transformed personally in ways that were both disturbing as well as gratifying. "My days of watching TV vanished. I found myself sitting among friends feeling like I no longer knew how to relate to the more surface-level topics they were discussing."

She didn't quite understand what was happening at the time, and that was just as upsetting as the disorientation itself. "I was taking on my clients' problems and confusing them with my own. I didn't quite know how to separate from them."

Ideally, supervision would help sort out these kinds of issues related to overpersonalizing what happens in sessions, but sometimes there just isn't the time or opportunity to get as much help as might be needed. Indeed, once Jamie did have the chance to talk to colleagues about what was going on for her, she was able to regain some sense of balance. "I learned to gravitate toward a new way of being that allowed me to unwind and restore my energy after sessions. I have shed superficial relationships and discovered new ones that are more sustaining. I have come to truly appreciate solitude as it allows me to get in touch with my true self. I think one reason this process was so difficult for me is because I didn't understand what was happening. I thought I was alone until I talked to others. I sure wish I had been warned ahead of time."

In fact, there have been all kinds of warnings about the hazards of practicing therapy, at least in published sources (Guy, 1987; Kottler, 2010a, 2012; Norcross & Guy, 2007; Skovholt & Trotter-Mathison, 2011; Sussman, 1992). Some of the dangers that are most often mentioned in these sources include the following:

- A sense of isolation: a feeling that we are alone in the world bearing the burdens of other people's secrets
- Narcissism: an inflated sense of self in which we begin to believe that we really do know what truth is, that we really are special people
- Emotional depletion: resulting from coming too close to others' suffering
- One-way intimacy: becoming used to the kind of relationship in which we are always the one in control
- Boredom: the inevitable result of doing basically the same thing, in the same place, the same way
- Cynicism: seeing clients no longer as people but as "cases" or "borderlines" or problems to be fixed
- Countertransference: personal issues are triggered or aggravated as a result of getting so close to others who are struggling with themes we have yet to fully resolve
- Burnout: general malaise, disinterest, or disengagement that often occurs as a result of not maintaining spirited enthusiasm for the work

Would we have become therapists if we had known that the consequences would be that we would have to get even closer to the demons that lurk within us? Certainly we had been warned that we might have to examine personal issues a bit, perhaps muck about in a countertransference or two, even do a few rounds as a client (for educational purposes, of course), but did we honestly believe that we would have to deal with our worst nightmares on a regular basis? We could either learn to hide from our own raw vulnerabilities, at the expense of cutting ourselves off from our deepest feelings, or even more painful, to stay intimately connected to our clients, keeping our hearts open to their stories and, in so doing, setting ourselves up for many sleepless nights.

Mindy has been practicing for a number of years and so has a wider perspective from which to assess both the hazards and benefits she has experienced. "I like parts of what I've become," she admits. "I've become more sensitive to nuances in behavior, being more analytic in the ways I approach problems, feeling more in control of myself." Yet there are changes she has observed that are less desirable. "Ignorance is a kind of bliss, and I don't like knowing some of the things I know about what people do with their lives. I don't like that I can't seem to turn my brain off anymore—it is always racing, whirling about, thinking of strange ideas, going over cases, plotting future actions, making up new theories to explain things that I don't understand. Sometimes I wish I could just turn my mind off."

We do see things and hear things in sessions that sometimes we wish we could erase from our memories. It is not unlike what law enforcement professionals report after being on the street for a while. One practitioner asks how it is possible to treat sexual perpetrators and serial abusers, as well as their victims, and expect to be the same afterward. "I'm not nearly as trusting as I once was," she admits. "Now I'm beginning to question whether really any relationship can ever work out."

Despite these cautionary tales, it turns out that there are far more positive consequences to becoming a therapist than there are unexpected hazards. We learn so much about the inner worlds of human beings when they demonstrate the greatest courage and resilience. We have access to a wealth of experience and wisdom from clients that would take a dozen lifetimes for anyone else to accumulate. Over time our interpersonal skills and relational sensitivity become honed and refined, allowing us to enjoy greater intimacy and satisfaction in all our relationships.

Most of us are well aware of how honored and privileged we are to be part of a profession that contains so much incredible satisfaction and joy. The problem is not that there is a price to pay for the privilege of helping others, but that most of us were unprepared, through neglect or denial, to address these issues in constructive ways.

The Real Reasons You Became a Therapist

Fess up: What drew you to this field in the first place? Skip the altruistic part about trying to save the world and get to the part where you are trying to save yourself.

Certainly at the top of the list could be the desire to work through one's own emotional conflicts. There was the initial hope that perhaps going to graduate school would equip me with knowledge and skills I could use to address my own issues so I wouldn't have to resort to the time-consuming and expensive alternative of actually going to see a therapist as a client.

Once it became clear that I could make some inroads in my own self-treatment but not cover nearly as much territory as I had hoped, the next plan involved using my sessions with clients to continue explorations into the land of the forbidden. This strategy actually worked quite well—for a little while anyway—as almost every day someone walks in the office who is struggling with an issue that I haven't yet fully resolved. Sometimes it is difficult to tell whether I am talking to my clients or myself during particularly passionate speeches. I caught myself recently telling someone in a therapy group I was leading that she really needed to break loose from the bonds of predictability that were holding her back. When she looked at me curiously, wondering where *that* came from, I realized I was mostly talking to myself.

Obviously, getting into our own personal therapy, as well as supervision, helps sort out these points of confusion that may have been neglected in graduate school. We were probably never pressed that hard to talk about why we were studying therapy in the first place, and even if we had been, I question how honest we would have been to reveal the hidden motives. When asked to talk about their secret intentions, a few of the most frequent and revealing responses I've heard resonate with themes related to (1) redeeming themselves in some way for a life that has yet to feel productive, (2) feeling powerful and in control, (3) increasing feelings of self-worth by earning gratitude and respect of others, (4) feeling validated that they have something useful and significant to offer to others, (5) enjoying hearing about the secrets and forbidden thoughts revealed in sessions, and (6) appreciating the knowledge and skills they learned that make them more effective in every other aspect of life.

Your Family Still Will Not Take You Seriously

My true confession is that I became a therapist, in part, because I desperately wanted my parents to respect me. I struggled academically during the early years and was a very marginal student. I was a disappointment to my father in the sports arena. I felt socially inept and also had some speech and vision problems—which also contributed to my other difficulties. Not surprisingly, I didn't feel very useful or successful in any domain of my life.

I had hoped that being the first in my family to attend college, much less graduate, might earn me some accolades, but it wasn't nearly enough. I thought that maybe graduate school would do the job, but I still felt like I was treated like a wayward child who had gone astray, particularly since my family members didn't seem to think much of my new profession. To the best of my knowledge, I don't think my parents ever read one of the books I wrote or attended one of my lectures.

It always seemed utterly amazing to me how within the domain of our office or lecture hall, people will pay exorbitant fees for anything that comes out of our mouths, even take detailed notes on our pearls of wisdom, but a few hours later, our parents, siblings, or children won't pay any more attention to our opinions than they do anyone else's. Some misguided colleague, who knows far less than you do about a subject, may be quoted in the newspaper, online, or on television and his or her words will be treated as gospel. You could try to set the record straight, but you would only see their eyes roll up into their heads.

One expert in the area of child discipline complained about his frustration related to this exact predicament. "My daughter calls me to tell me about the latest problems she is having with her son, my darling grandson who never gives me an ounce of difficulty." He then calmly and succinctly tells his daughter exactly what she needs to do to understand what this behavior is likely about and suggests several possible courses of action, advice that his clients or readers would clamor to follow. "People come from all over the country to solicit my expertise on identical problems," he says, shaking his head. "But does my daughter listen to me? Of course not! I'm just her father."

It is not that there is anything all that wrong if our families don't take us any more seriously than before we were therapists—it is just that this is so surprising. Nobody ever told us that after we went to all the trouble to become experts on human functioning that the people we are closest to wouldn't defer to or revere us the way others do on the job.

Life Isn't a Multiple-Choice Exam

If only our decisions were limited to four choices and we could be certain that one of them was correct. Imagine a new client coming in, and he was considerate enough to present us with four possible diagnoses (first item), four conceivable treatment plans (second item), and then four different ways of getting through to him so that he would be amenable to following our plan (third item). Even better, imagine that there was a way to determine that we had chosen the single correct path.

In graduate school, even when professors didn't use multiple-choice examinations, there was still a pervasive expectation that there were right answers and wrong ones, and that it was possible to identify which were which. What a wonderful world it would be if things actually worked that way in reality!

A client comes in complaining of frequent and recurrent headaches. He is depressed about his predicament and feeling frustrated because he has yet to find out the causes of his problem. A physician has already ruled out any organic causes, so it appears the headaches are psychogenic in origin. Immediately, a few diagnoses come to mind: (a) chronic anxiety, (b) acute situational tension, (c) depressive syndrome, or (d) hypochondriasis.

After further investigation, it seems as if the symptoms are most typical of chronic anxiety. Indeed, the man does lead an extremely busy and challenged life, and although he appears calm on the outside, he is obviously metabolizing the pressure in unhealthy ways. Pleased with your assessment, you continue with your treatment plan.

You are quickly able to develop a solid working alliance and begin exploring some of his early associations with performing under pressure, his unresolved issues related to pleasing his parents as well as contemporary authority figures such as yourself. He is quite responsive and insightful, grateful as well for the new understanding of himself he has developed. Of course, his headaches are still a problem, maybe even a little worse, but you explain that it is probably the result of the deep-level work that you are undertaking together. He seems patient enough to stay with the program.

Next you try a stress reduction program, exploring ways that he can make changes in his lifestyle, learning relaxation methods and cognitive self-talk. He is a highly motivated and able student, excited about his new life skills, even though they don't seem to be having the desired effect on his painful symptoms.

You decide to switch gears, moving again to the level of narrative, but this time concentrating on his internal constructions of his life story, as well as his own perceptions of what his symptoms might mean within that context. Although his headaches persist, he seems much better able to cope with them and tolerate the discomfort. He has learned many things about himself. He has mastered several new skills that are useful to him both at home and at work. He may not have reached his primary goal of reducing the headaches, but he leaves reasonably satisfied that he got his money's worth.

At times, your thoughts come back to him. You wonder what the symptoms were really all about. Did you handle the case correctly?

What would others have done differently? Like most of your work, you sometimes never really know for sure what is going on with your clients nor do you have any definitive notion of what you did that made the greatest difference.

Months go by and one day the client calls for another visit. You are curious and also a bit apprehensive. You didn't know what to do with his headaches last time; what makes you sure you will have any more success this time?

He very quickly lets you know that he has not returned for more therapy, merely to give you the courtesy of a follow-up report. Quite by accident it seems, he learned the origins of his problem and was able to banish the symptoms from his life forever. What did you miss, you wonder.

The client decided to sell his house and as part of the preparation to get things in order, he had a mandatory house inspection. Rather quickly it was discovered he had a leak in his furnace that had been sending toxic gas through his house for months. The headaches had been the result of being poisoned. So much for selecting the correct diagnosis and treatment.

This case is somewhat rare in that we do not often have the luxury of finding out the definitive answers to the questions we must regularly confront. Most of the time we are dealing with ambiguous situations, with clients who can't easily articulate what is wrong, and what they do say is not necessarily what is really bothering them. Furthermore, a half dozen different practitioners may very well come up with just as many preferred therapeutic options.

The Answers Aren't in the Books—or Online

During those times when we are most confused, at a loss for how to proceed with a given case, or with our careers, the answers needed are rarely found in books or on the Web. There is a point in our development when reading, even attending lectures and workshops, does not produce the kinds of transformative experiences that are really needed in order to work through personal and professional impasses. As students, we learned to look in books or other resources for answers; as veterans, more and more we look both within and in the wider world.

Each time I've felt stuck, I do two things as a first line of attack. First, I try to Google an answer, which is often just a tease. Then I go buy a book. It doesn't seem to be enough for me to borrow one from a friend or the library, nor is it quite the same to check a website or an article online. I have to own the book in order to feel like the knowledge will be mine. That way I can underline things, write in the margins, savor its wisdom between my hands. I feel immediate comfort just looking at the books around me. They are symbols of what I must know and understand.

After that doesn't work (and it usually doesn't do the job), the next thing I try is to consult with trusted colleagues. There is no shortage of advice. Because my friends are just as frustrated as I am, having restrained themselves all these years from telling clients what to do with their lives, they can't wait to unleash their advice on me. Most of these opinions are actually quite brilliant. I feel humbled by their creativity, also more than a little chagrined that I wasn't smart enough to think of these things myself. Unfortunately, the relief that I feel is short-lived and by the time I'm ready to put their advice into action, whether in my sessions, my classes, or my life, it just doesn't seem to fit anymore.

It is at this point that I remember to look within myself. I assume for a little while that I have the answers inside me if only I could locate them. I search my past experiences for clues. I reflect on what I know for sure and what has worked for me in the past. I ask myself what I am hiding from, as well as what I am afraid of. I revisit old themes that have gnawed at me from the beginning of my awareness—issues of approval seeking, of not being good enough, of being afraid of failure, of wanting to feel loved and accepted by everyone all of the time. I may recruit some help at this time from a friend or colleague to help me look deeper, but the emphasis throughout is to unearth what I already know even if I don't know that I know it.

Although looking inward has its draw, looking outward beyond the world of self, of books, of our own parochial discipline, also has its benefits. I remind myself to stop reading about something and start living it. If I read anything at all now, it is fiction or anthropology. Better yet, I start traveling. I travel literally by exploring other cultures, but I also travel by engaging people outside my work to find other layers of what I am capable of knowing. Mostly I travel with my clients and students to places in our minds that we have never gone before. If you have been practicing for a while, this is quite a challenge because it often seems that we have seen and heard it all before. It takes a heck of a lot of energy to force ourselves to give up what has already worked for a long time in order to try something that we are not altogether familiar and comfortable with. When I balk at this prospect, I usually remind myself that I am asking no less of my clients.

Differences Between Ethical Theory and Reality

Ethical dilemmas seemed so clearly demarcated in graduate school. Certain standards of behavior are expected; you meet them or pay the price. There are just some things that you must do, some things you don't do, ever, and things you don't tolerate in others. Period.

Yet there are certain unethical behaviors that we all engage in and pretend we don't. There are the little white lies we tell clients—for example, that we know we can help them when we are not even sure what is really going on, that of course we like them (when we really are appalled by their behavior), or that therapy is a safe place even though there are definite risks involved. There are the times we are experimenting with new methods that we have not adequately tested. There are the periods of self-indulgence when we pursue avenues of exploration that are less for the client's growth than they are for our own entertainment.

In graduate school we learned about legal statutes and precedents that dictate what is considered appropriate within various jurisdictions. We learned about consensual standards of care, supposedly what we all agree is supposedly the best way to act in various circumstances. We learned about appropriate professional conduct, that is, what will be expected of us in certain situations.

We learned about what we are supposed to do when faced with predictable critical incidents. Mostly, we learned less about what many professionals actually do and more about what they *say* they do.

In all arenas of ethical conduct, there is often a great difference between what people claim they believe in and how they actually act when faced with difficult conflicts. For example, among faculty and students in the profession, we could get almost universal agreement that bartering practices are clearly unethical; it even says so in the ethical codes. After all, such an arrangement could easily compromise the clear boundaries of the therapy as well as perpetuate conflicts of interest in a dual relationship. Indeed, there has been shameless exploitation of clients in which, in exchange for their sessions, they have paid their therapists with goods and services that far exceed the debt that is owed, or that involve them in activities that actually sabotage any therapeutic work that had been accomplished.

Clearly we need to be able to distinguish between subtle shades of unethical conduct in order to make choices based not only on what we were told by others but also by what we have reasoned through on our own. The world is simply not as black and white as we were led to believe, nor are ethical decisions a simple matter of blindly following the rules that were authored by others.

How to Be

Mostly what we learned in graduate school is what to *do*, not how to *be*. We learned behaviors, techniques, plans, strategies, procedures, programs, interventions, and actions. We collected alternatives that could be employed in various situations. We learned what to do when we were confronted with a particular case or dilemma. We learned where to go if we were stuck.

Raise your hand if you were prepared to be loving and caring. Au contraire, the culture of training is conducive to competition not cooperation, to achievement not serenity, to developing knowledge and power, not compassion.

Maybe it is not so much what we do with clients as who we are when we are with them that matters most. We are in love with our techniques. We can't wait to try out some new intervention that is supposedly guaranteed to cure people of their suffering. It is not that this new technology of helping works; it is that most everything seems to be helpful at some time or another.

We didn't learn much about being loving during our training years. We didn't spend much time identifying which of our personal strengths might be harnessed to promote healing. We weren't given much opportunity to explore in depth the nature of our "dark side" that might sabotage our efforts to be helpful, nor did we spend a whole lot of time developing our personal characteristics of integrity, honor, courage, kindness, sincerity, and yes, love. The assumption was either that we already had these traits, or that we would somehow grow them on our own.

It turns out our greatest challenge is not what to *do* with our clients but to *be* with them. One of the ways that we can erase the myth that we are able to walk on water is to accept our personal limitations and the contradictions they produce in our work. Consider just a few of them that have been highlighted in this chapter: that we may seek perfection but will never attain it, or that we must somehow give our full attention and energy to our clients all the while we take care of ourselves.

It is obvious that we are entrusted with more power than our ability to reach perfection would dictate. Clients want to give us the power to cure them whether we truly have such an ability or not. Allowing clients to set the agenda for sessions does not make the power differential disappear. Our responsibility is to recognize and accept our potential influence in order to use it at only the most judicious times and places.

We must also face the reality that the better we do therapy, the more clients will see us as potential saviors and the more we may feel the accompanying pressure to meet their unrealistic expectations. One starting point is to share our personal feelings and reactions with other professionals we trust, especially about those aspects of our work—and our lives—that most confuse us.

Chapter 4

ORGANIZED CONFUSION: MAKING SENSE OF CHANGE PROCESSES IN CLIENTS, THE PROFESSION, AND OURSELVES

A Quiz!

What is the relationship that determines the progression of the following set of numbers?

8 5 1 7 2 0

(To be continued. . .)

When Confusion Reigns

A few of you may have quickly figured out the answer to the opening question. Regardless of whether you arrived at a satisfactory solution to the problem, the process you followed was one of pattern recognition, which comprises much of what we do to help our clients make sense of their experience. Despite what we claim, much of the time—perhaps even most of the time—we don't really understand the complex and multifaceted nature of what leads to change in our work. Even those instances when we can point to some specific event that transpired in session, some breakthrough that appeared to make all the difference, there are still a multitude of other factors in the client's life, in our interactions together, past and present, that exerted some influence. We have mostly come to terms with a default position of confusion and uncertainty.

A therapist welcomes a new client for the first time. "Hello," she says, "my name is Dokwan." It immediately becomes apparent that these are the only words of English that she knows. The therapist doesn't understand a single word of Japanese other than "sushi" and she isn't sure if that is even a Japanese word. Dokwan immediately begins crying, speaking urgently and rapidly in her native language at a pace that the therapist can't follow even if she did have some grasp of the dialect.

"I couldn't leave her in obvious distress," the therapist later recalled, "but I also couldn't understand a single word she was saying. Nothing I ever learned prepared me for this, but we were there together and I had to do something. So I tried to remain attentive to the nuances of what she was communicating. I offered her tissues and tea. I used gestures and a kind of sign language to let her know that although I couldn't understand her words I could feel her distress. I held her hand when she reached out to me in gratitude."

This may be an extreme example of how confusion is so much a part of our work, but it also illustrates the ways that we seek the most basic structures to make sense of what we observe and hear, as well as to engage our clients. In this particular case, the therapist relied on the most essential thing of all, remaining fully present in the moment. She also relied on the most fundamental framework that she'd ever learned, which is to focus on the relational connection with her client that transcended mere words.

Mostly Understanding How Change Occurs

After all the centuries of philosophers, epistemologists, social scientists, and other experts studying the mechanisms regarding how change takes place, whether within an individual life or a social movement, we are still in a period of relative infancy. Oh, we have plenty of theories and ideas about the subject, and we even espouse them with misguided overconfidence, but the reality is that a lot of the time we really have no idea what is going on. This, of course, is quite a contrast with what we were exposed to in graduate school, where we often got the distinct idea from instructors that there were particular "truths" that were unassailable. In many cases, this represented their own strong opinions rather than any verifiable certainty.

Graduate school was the place that most of us were first introduced to the notion that there were vastly different ways to conceptualize people's problems and the best ways to help. Faculty and books explained "theories" as the ways we systematically organize knowledge and make it applicable in a wide variety of circumstances. These systems provided assumptions, accepted principles, and rules of procedure to assist us in analyzing, predicting, and otherwise explaining what was happening with our clients and in therapeutic relationships. It was less clear to us why there were so many different theories and associated assumptions, principles, and rules.

The more I looked at all the different and conflicting theories, the more confused I felt. It reached the point where there seemed to be voices competing for attention in my head. The voices, which verged on being hallucinations at times, each spoke a different language:

"The unconscious and unexpressed desires of people will lead you to the root of their problems."

"People enjoy certain benefits from remaining stuck. Until you can address those underlying issues any change effort will be futile."

"We all suffer from feelings of inferiority that must be overcome in order to lead a productive and satisfying life."

"It is the things we tell ourselves about our experiences that largely determine how we subsequently feel and respond."

"It is really the ways that we are acculturated, indoctrinated, in some cases colonized by media and the larger culture, that most influences the ways we see ourselves and others."

This is but a mere sampling of the ways that change is understood and explained by members of our profession. We had been told by various experts that change doesn't reliably and permanently take place unless we focus on the past, while others told us authoritatively that the action is best guided toward the present or future. Likewise others told us unequivocally to help clients deal with feelings, while others told us to focus instead on thoughts or behavior. We were urged by some to concentrate on intrapsychic dynamics and then soon afterward instructed that we should instead be looking at family systemic factors or rather larger cultural scripts. We were lectured (or scolded) to consider gender as a major variable that shapes experience but then told by others that gender, in itself, is a social construction and we should be exploring more broadly at the level of societal influences. We were taught to rely primarily on relational engagement, then cognitive patterns, then interpersonal influences, then. . . Well, the list goes on and on. Suffice to say we've all heard way too much about the "truth" related to how change really occurs.

When all of these wonderful and conflicting ideas are filtered, processed, metabolized, integrated, personalized, there are some conclusions that can indeed be reached, some universal factors that we almost all agree are significant and useful regardless of preferred ideology and beliefs (Boston Process Change Study Group, 2010; Castonguay & Hill, 2012; Kottler, 2010a, 2014; Lambert, 2013; Miller, Hubble, Chow, & Seidel, 2014; Prochaska & Norcross, 2014). Let's review several of the features that we know, beyond any reasonable doubt, are significant in producing or facilitating lasting changes. It is presumed that almost everyone would agree that these variables play some important role, including studies of client reports on what they say was most helpful (Bowen, Brown, & Howat, 2014; Lambert & Shimokawa, 2011; Larsen & Stege, 2012; Manthei, 2007; Paulson, Turscott, & Stuart, 1999). I'll just mention a few that I'm reasonably sure will elicit the most agreement. A more comprehensive list of factors is shown in Table 4-1.

Table 4.1. What Makes a Difference in Promoting Change in Therapy?	
Positive expectations and hope	Relationship factors (trust, caring)
Disclosure and processing of content	Permission to explore new areas
Telling personal story	Feeling understood and heard
Emotional arousal	Emotional regulation
Facing fears	Constructive risk taking
Reduction of stress	Honesty and directness
Rehearsal of new skills	Task facilitation
New insights and understandings	Sensitive confrontation
Challenge of dysfunctional beliefs	Suggestions for resolving problems
Focus on present, past, and future	Modeling of new behaviors
Modeling new behavior	Creation of meaning
Public commitment of intentions	Social support
Reframed narrative	New options and alternatives
Secondary gains eliminated	Responsibility for consequences
New resources accessed	New solutions generated
Understanding past behavior	Planning for future
Interpretations of behavior	Tolerance for ambiguity/complexity
Inviting and responding to feedback	Flexible adjustments over time
Integrity and mutual respect	Follow up and accountability

Relational Connection

Regardless of the ways the therapeutic alliance is conceived, in all its manifestations, it remains the glue that holds everything we do together. Whether it remains the focus of work, or an ancillary part of the treatment, the trust, respect, and intimacy that evolve make it possible for honest disclosures. Almost half of all positive outcomes can be attributed to some facet of the relationship and healing atmosphere that is created in sessions, in spite of how much we might be in love with our own favorite techniques and strategies. Without a strong connection, accompanied by high degrees of trust and caring, not much else is going to be accomplished.

Hope

We may have different ways that we encourage and support our clients, yet the one thing that we do for them, sometimes above all else, is provide them with a far more optimistic perspective on their capabilities and future possibilities. This encompasses placebo effects, planting favorable expectations for the treatment. We instill hope in an assortment of ways whenever we challenge dysfunctional thinking, counter negative attitudes, or ask a "miracle question" regarding how things could be different. Our mostly sunny disposition and optimistic nature also can inspire clients to climb out of their doldrums and have faith in their own ability, as well as the therapy, to transform them in constructive ways.

Talking About Stuff

The "stuff" that is introduced may depend on particular client needs and therapist preferences, but there is somewhat universal agreement that sharing one's story is essential, whether as part of catharsis, narrative elaboration, or heated discussion. We invite clients to tell their stories, after which we help them to elaborate on details, flesh out the context and effect, and then help them to reauthor alternative versions of their experience that are more empowering. We encourage them to talk about difficult subjects, perhaps things that they have never spoken about previously. We offer them safety and privacy to further encourage them to speak deeply about anything that might trouble them. Then we collaborate together to talk things through in order to promote new insights and understandings, which hopefully lead to action.

Emotional Arousal and Processing

Like everything else I'm discussing as examples of almost universal acceptance, all therapists work with strong feelings in sessions. They may be reflected, deepened, elaborated, challenged, processed, or logically analyzed, but they still remain a focus of much of our work. This is true as much for the most passionate humanist who believes it is important to access and express strong emotions as it is for the nitive therapist who may seek to uncover the underlying through patterns. We do far more than ask clients to talk about how they feel; we also teach them to work through these feelings in more helpful ways.

New Insights and Understandings

Every system of therapy makes use of some kind of insight, whether this remains the primary task of the treatment or more of a transitional step to help motivate changes in behavior. Although Jay Haley and a few other brief therapists have described promoting insight as distracting, if not dangerous, most clients find some value in gaining a deeper understanding of their motives, beliefs, and actions. They really do want to know how they got in their current predicament so they can avoid such situations in the future. They are curious about the ways that past patterns have so profoundly influenced their current choices. They often feel a hunger to make sense of their life experience, especially some of the key existential questions that relate to meaning making.

Rehearsal of New Behaviors

It is precisely because sessions are conducted in a safe and supportive place that clients are willing to take risks and experiment with new behaviors that they would otherwise avoid. They are provided with opportunities to try alternative ways of thinking—and especially of doing things differently. They practice responding in new ways. They role-play or rehearse actions they intend to take once the session is over. On the most basic level they are afforded the chance to enjoy a far more open, honest, and intimate relationship that, hopefully, makes them eager to recreate similar relationships with others.

Task Facilitation

Talk is clearly not enough if it doesn't lead to changes in behavior. Once sessions end clients are asked to take what they've learned and apply the lessons or new skills to the outside world where it may be given (or better yet, give themselves) ents. They may be assigned particular tasks to o enact. They may commit to following through e been neglecting or avoiding. Most critically, insights and understandings into actions they lowed by bringing those trails and experiments back to therapy to process what happened and refine future strategies that are likely to be even more successful.

Paradigm Shifts Within the Profession—and a Solution to the Quiz

Although I've been discussing change phenomena that occur within the therapeutic process, there are parallel processes that are taking place within our field at large. As mentioned earlier, there has been a noticeable shift away from single-theory allegiance to a more global adoption of particular paradigms that are more encompassing and flexible to address the individual and cultural differences of our clients. This has become a more constructive way to organize our knowledge base as well as a celebration of the so-called common factors that are part of all systems.

Paradigms, for all the significance heaped on them, serve much the same organizing purpose as theories and frameworks. Thomas Kuhn, in his classic *Structure of Scientific Revolutions* (1970/2012), popularized the idea that progress does not usually proceed in a gradual and incremental pace, in spite of how attractive that idea might seem. Rather, there are series of groundbreaking paradigm shifts or "quantum changes" that forever alter the ways we think about the world and our place in it. When Einstein proposed his theory of relativity, Newtonian physics became obsolete. When Galileo, Darwin, Copernicus, Marx, Pasteur, or Freud proposed revolutionary ideas about the nature of the world (or human experiences of the world), our views were not the same. This has been true with respect to political shifts (Tea

Party, Arab Spring), social movements (gay marriage), the environment (climate change), and technology (movable type, compass, Internet, iPhone), as well as within our profession. One example of this might be the paradigm shift we are currently experiencing in which therapy is being increasingly conceived as a member of the larger health professions instead of only the *mental* health specialty (Cummings & Cummings, 2013; Johnson, 2012). We are now, more than ever, called upon to consult on cases related to lifestyle choices, stress management, persistent pain, chronic disease, and related health issues. Similarly, the contributions of cybernetic epistemology, systemic thinking, constructivist and social constructionist models, feminist ideas, and especially multicultural issues represent other major paradigm shifts that have transformed the ways that we work.

Any such models or frameworks help to conceptualize our thinking and actions. They represent internal belief systems that add necessary efficiency to our lives by eliminating the need to think through, evaluate, judge, and only then, to act on aspects of our world in every moment of our existence. They help us to make sense of what we witness, as well as experience, and then provide guidance for selecting suitable responses.

As one example, you were presented at the beginning of the chapter with a quiz that requires you to make a paradigm shift in order to arrive at the correct answer. Relying on the usual ways of making sense of numbers would not be useful in this case because the problem demands that you construct an alternative way of viewing the data. This is not unlike what happens in therapy when our job is to help clients abandon previous conceptual models that are not serving them well and instead to discover or invent alternatives that are better suited to their situations and the problem at hand. In many cases they are thinking too rigidly or have been overinvested in a limited conception of what is possible. They can't resolve the difficulties because they feel stuck following familiar patterns that are clearly not working, thereby unable or unwilling to abandon them in favor of others, perhaps those that represent radical departures from what they might have considered previously. The same thing happens when therapists, as well, persist in sticking with some rigid perspective that limits their ability and willingness to reconfigure a more useful alternative.

In the case of the little quiz that began the chapter, the standard way of thinking about numbers has been sufficient in almost any situation that you have encountered previously. Yet in this instance it turns out that in order to find the correct answer it is necessary to put aside what you think you already know and understand, to get beyond the obvious. The relationship that actually determines the order of the numbers in this problem is that they are listed in *alphabetical* order. The digits have no numerical relationship whatsoever. You would have to abandon a traditional paradigm of looking for relationships between numbers in order to arrive at a new way of seeing what might be present. This is actually a fairly representative picture of what we often ask of our clients, an often threatening and disorienting challenge that elicits a certain amount of resistance.

Clients have developed their own unique ways of looking at the world and the choices available to them. However limited and self-defeating these beliefs might be, they offer a certain amount of comfort, if not familiarity—even with their annoying side effects. "My world is over now that my husband died," a client says in session. "We did everything together. We were our only real friends. There is nothing that can be done about that. There is just nothing for me to live for anymore."

The phenomenological world in which this woman lived has disappeared with her husband's death, so it's not surprising that she has given up hope. Repairing her old world will not work. The therapist will need to help her conceptualize a new world for herself in order to make a paradigm shift away from the model she has successfully lived with for years. This is not unlike some of the obsolete paradigms that have been abandoned with our profession, such as positivism, parochialism, and the overreliance on personal opinions over scientific scrutiny. One other discarded paradigm envisioned therapists working with clients to help them change their lives through a process in which change was completely within the client's control, without taking into consideration both biological and cultural influences.

Shifting Responsibilities and Growing Specialization

After World War II, the medical profession and insurance companies began recognizing that the vast majority of patient visits (somewhere between 60% and 90%) were not related to physical problems but to stress issues and other psychological factors. It became clear then, as it is now, that one's physical health was heavily influenced by outside stressors and that there ought to be other means to address these needs besides through a medical doctor. In fact, it was this recognition that gave the early development of professional therapy a major boost. Since that time there have been a number of new specializations and alternative responsibilities that have been assigned to our jobs.

A thoughtful young man, pondering a career as a therapist, sought the advice of an experienced professional regarding his choice of a graduate program. "I'm pretty sure I know what I want to do," he explained. "I've always wanted to work in the area of posttraumatic stress, and especially that stuff I've been reading about posttraumatic growth." It turned out that he had experienced his own life challenges and felt best qualified to help others with similar complaints.

"I'd like to work in a veterans hospital. In fact, I know that's what I want to do eventually. So I don't want to waste my time learning a bunch of stuff that isn't going to help me with that job. What would you suggest?"

We can quickly recognize the folly of this naïve idea that one can arbitrarily dismiss the foundational knowledge and basic skills of general practice just to focus on one very specific area. Such specialization usually follows a solid grounding in basic core competencies.

Besides the fact that this man's misguided plan does not match the reality of how therapists are actually trained for an ever-changing professional climate and marketplace, there is a very strong likelihood that he could eventually end up in a very different job for which he would have been completely unprepared.

How could you ever predict that you'd end up where you are now, whatever it is that you are doing, much less have a clear idea what you will end up doing a few years from now?

I've had more than a dozen distinct jobs as a therapist in settings and specialty areas that didn't even yet exist when I was in school. I could never have imagined in my wildest dreams that I would end up working in so many different communities and cultural settings. I thought my first job as a substance abuse counselor would be my life's work. Next it was working as a counselor for a community college, a preschool, then a middle school. I worked as a research interviewer for a career development project. This was followed by a job in a community mental health center that eventually led me into private practice. And the list goes on. I am now running a foundation that rescues and supports lower caste girls in remote villages in Nepal. Never in my wildest fantasies did I ever consider, much less prepare myself, for therapeutic work traipsing up and down Himalayan peaks. The point of this chaotic narrative is that we can't possibly know where our careers and lives will end up or what opportunities will come our way.

There is nothing on your diploma or license that says that practice is limited to treating posttraumatic stress, or eating disorders, or depression, or any other specific problem. You are expected to be able to help a great variety of individuals regardless of what they bring to you; you would only refer those who are way outside your area of competence.

That's not to say that it isn't important to develop specialty areas, whether in trauma, aging issues, peak athletic performance, forensic and family court cases, executive coaching, pain management, bicultural adaptation, spiritual issues, multiple personality disorder, obesity, addictions, or attachment issues, to mention just a few possibilities. Almost every book or workshop for therapists on marketing strategies emphasizes how critical it is to define an area of expertise and brand oneself to the public in this domain.

For those of us who still want to retain some dignity, class, discretion, modesty, and professionalism, the very idea of trying to imitate mental health celebrities in the media, the very thought of branding ourselves, is absolutely abhorrent. Yet many, like Bavonese (2013), insist "that old attitude has become a crippling handicap. These days our brand needs to be highly visible and energizing, offering an authentic picture of who we are and what we can do for people who need our services" (p. 56). All very well, but as we'll talk about in a later chapter, this is another area that wasn't exactly taught in graduate school. Instead, we got the distinct idea that if we studied hard, practiced diligently, treated people with kindness and compassion, lived up to the highest moral standards, good things would come to us in the end. That may very well be true but certainly not without some very proactive effort on our part to let the world know we exist and that we have something useful to offer.

Regardless of the way you brand yourself and specialize, each of us brings a unique perspective and therapeutic style into the room. We may have felt pressured at times into adopting the favored ideas of professors and following the prescriptions of supervisors, but many of us have managed to filter out those things that don't fit and added others that feel more compatible. We've read widely, incorporating additional concepts that have been supplemented through workshops, consultations, and conference programs. Most of all, we've had a lot of discussions with colleagues and conversations with clients that have been instrumental in helping us to sort out all the confusion, formulate our own notions about how change best occurs (and lasts), and then developed a personalized style unlike any other.

Chaos as an Organizational Construct

Chaos theory sounds like an oxymoron. The definition of chaos, "a condition or place of great disorder or confusion," would seem to be the opposite of the definition of theory, "systematically organized knowledge." Perhaps it is this strange combination of terms that most directly identifies the significant nature of this paradigm shift and the difficulty people have in rearranging their thinking to fit it. The chaos paradigm asks us to consider a systematic organization of the knowledge surrounding those things that will continue to be disordered and confusing. This has not been Western society's normal pattern of thinking, learning, and living.

Virtually all the information and skills we began learning as early as primary school presumed that order in the world was based on a linear relationship between cause and effect. ("See how A causes B to occur, and then how they combine to produce C.") Before the influence of chaos theory, major scientific paradigms allowed us to reject the unexpected, the unwanted, and the incomprehensible as merely extraneous variables. We could run our lives and work with clients in ways that assumed the information available would lead us to logical, controllable outcomes. Chaos theory pushed us to accept the idea that although we can envision connections between ideas and behaviors based on a theory, we are, and always will be, ignorant of most of the connections within that theory.

Chaos theory began its attack on traditional theoretical views within the world of mathematics, but it quickly spread to physics, meteorology, ecology, and other science-related fields where it is now well established. The social sciences expanded use of the theory by quickly moving to evaluate its potential impact in many human circumstances. Counseling and psychotherapy have also embraced chaos theory as a means by which to explore relevant issues because of its potential to help articulate a more strength-based, adaptive view of human experience, especially during times of disequilibrium and transition—in other words, during chaos. Furthermore, such a model not only recognizes but embraces the inherent complexity and unpredictability of human behavior.

Brief therapies were among the first to recognize the ways that concepts from chaos theory might help explain the ways that tiny changes can have magnified effects, or what Gladwell (1996) called a "tipping point." This idea emerged from meteorologist Edward Lorenz's (1963) "butterfly effect" in which he demonstrated in weather forecasting how fractional alterations in the atmosphere, even a butterfly flapping its wings, can eventually lead to a hurricane elsewhere in the world. We might recognize the way this has been translated into therapeutic work by Jay Haley and other strategic therapists when they talked about how resistance can be avoided by encouraging the client to make little changes that eventually accrue to represent significant transformations. Such thinkers might not appear to care how and why these phenomena take place, but they are huge fans of the results that can be produced through bypassing obstructions to changes that appear too ambitious.

Chaos theory, with its respect for uncertainty and complexity, honors the wonder of the unknown and the inexplicable. "Both client and counselor can let go of the illusion of control and instead face the precariousness of life experiences with compassion and an attitude of positive uncertainty" (Bussolari & Goodell, 2009, p. 100). Well, that's certainly one way to reframe confusion. According to the authors, the model also provides ways to conceive of chaos and disorder as useful forces that help promote reorganization. It also introduces more robust and flexible language to describe and understand behavior, more consistent with what actually happens in sessions.

Various life transitions don't necessarily follow the orderly, sequential, incremental, predictable, invariant stages of development that we learned in graduate school. Jean Piaget's stages of cognitive development, Lawrence Kohlberg's stages of moral development, and all the other stage models made for interesting reading but life doesn't always follow such scripts. Bussolari and Goodell make the point that chaos theory creates more space for variability, the unexpected, and makes a clear connection between emotional discomfort and corresponding growth and adaptation; it is precisely the chaos of uncertainty that makes change possible. This is how systems of any kind are inclined to reorganize themselves.

We see examples of the chaos model on a regular basis in our clients where the unexpected can either make or break their progress. For instance, a middle-aged woman is suffering from an incapacitating depression brought on by her husband suddenly leaving her for a younger woman. The life she had accepted as being totally devoted to being a dutiful wife was now crumbling around her. Two months into therapy the woman had acquired a more positive perspective of herself, taken actions to explore new careers, and created situations where she was developing enjoyable new male and female relationships. It was an orderly progression from the depths of despair to logical actions and thinking that would produce an exciting new future. However, the best-laid plans of the therapist were unexpectedly reversed in an instant when the client called to cancel their next session.

"I know you'll think this is crazy," she began the conversation, "and maybe it does sound strange, but I've decided that I want to work on getting my husband back. I'm going to fix up the interior of the house, do some landscaping outside, and keep myself available for him to come back. I just know it's a matter of time."

The therapist is dumbfounded by this abrupt, apparently irrational turn in events that had been proceeding so well. He doesn't know what to say, so he keeps his mouth shut while she continues.

"I saw my husband with his new girlfriend in the store yesterday and, if you ask me, I don't think they were very happy at all. I think he'll be getting tired of that little apartment they're shacking up in and start thinking about home. Fixing up the house will show him what he is missing even more. I'm not coming to therapy anymore, but thanks, you've been very nice."

A chance encounter stirred the client's imagination to reverse course and run down a path that seemed to lead nowhere. Chaos theory calls attention to how small influences that are unknown to us ("sensitive dependence") can change physical as well as cognitive patterns. A small stick breaks off from a limb, frightening a fish to move closer to shore, where a bear jumps in after it and creates a major wake. Downstream, the small wake moves the last stone that had held a giant boulder in place for the last 40 years. A fisherman is astounded to see a 10-foot-high boulder begin moving in the middle of a placid stream for no apparent reason. Both the examples of the client and the boulder demonstrate one of several key chaos principles that tell us we can never trust the patterns we see to provide full understanding of what will occur next.

We may not be able to recognize what is causing many of the changes in our clients' lives, but we can study the patterns ("strange attractors"). The longer and more thoroughly we observe what's going on, the more consistencies in the details of patterns we see, even though the pattern's sources may remain unclear. Thus, a surprisingly positive or negative reaction by one client looks like an anomaly to a novice therapist, but it can be seen as the continuation of the general pattern ("iteration") by an experienced therapist. Neither novice nor expert may know what actually caused the reaction, but the experienced therapist can use recognition of the pattern for understanding and planning future actions, that is, if he or she also accepts the inevitability of ongoing chaos and uncertainty.

Recently I was leading a therapy group that appeared to be going extraordinarily well. We had been well into the working stage for some time, so all the most healing factors had been humming along at a high level. There was trust and caring among members that had led to some solid work. The group was winding down after a particularly fertile session in which one of the women in the group had been talking about the burdens she felt taking care of her sick, belligerent, ungrateful father. We enjoyed an excellent relationship so, in passing, and with a humorous edge, I moved the group toward closure by making a brief comment about the challenges of dealing with emotionally unstable family members. As I started to initiate the checkout, the woman abruptly turned away, put her head down, and started shaking her head back and forth. When she turned toward me again, I could see she was furious. "How dare you call my father unstable! That is one of the rudest, must disrespectful things anyone has ever said to me. Where do you get off saying something like that?"

Where the heck did *that* come from? There had been no sign, no warning, not the slightest indication that the outburst was coming. What had I missed, I wondered? There'd been nothing but the most pleasant interactions between us in the past. I could immediately tell that whatever happened, although triggered by me in some way, was not really about what I said but rather something else going on with her, something I might have missed. And that something might have been very, very small, a tiny pebble that got things rolling in a very surprising way. Alas, there was no time to process the explosion because the group was ending. That didn't strike me as a coincidence either, but there was never any resolution to the outburst because she never talked about it again.

If I resist the impulse to explain away what happened, to offer some theory that accounts for the unpredictable interaction, then I'm left to accept and hold onto the confusion. And it is important to make sense of the behavior so that I can prevent something similar from happening in the future, that is, if it is possible to do so (which I doubt).

The chaos paradigm tells us that with all the small, specific events in a therapist–client interaction, much less in a group setting where there are literally dozens of such micro-interactions going on at any moment in time, there is no way to accurately chart all the influences on the outcome. This is a far cry from the theoretical models that presume to understand and predict behavior within a quantifiable set of limited principles.

Chaos theory is one of several alternative paradigms, along with several postmodern approaches, that view the world, and our place in it, as an inherently ambiguous and complex phenomenon, one that transcends our ability to organize it, much less fully understand it. This stands quite in contrast to the lessons we learned in graduate school, where there was purported to be "truth" and "right answers."

The metaphor of chaos strikes me as actually a bit overwrought. I'd accept uncertainty, and even a modicum of confusion, but I also happen to believe that many processes do follow a somewhat familiar plan. It is possible to acknowledge that things are far more complex than we might often claim, but let's face it: We got into this business in the first place because we so enjoy making sense of and explaining things.

Modern to Postmodern Thinking

We have been privileged to witness (and participate) in one of Kuhn's "scientific revolutions" during the past years, a movement away from modern positivism to postmodern conceptions of reality in all its various forms, including religion, science, education, art, music, and psychotherapy. This has spawned all kinds of innovations in the ways we do research. For example, qualitative research methodologies such as phenomenology, narrative analysis, case studies, and ethnography have made a comeback since the days of Sigmund Freud and Margaret Mead. Newer developments in feminist and queer methodologies signal much greater appreciation for ways that power operate in research interactions. Even the language has changed from calling those who are studied "participants" or "co-researchers" instead of being objectified as mere "subjects."

Many of the most cutting-edge treatment models, such as narrative therapy, relational-cultural therapy, feminist therapy, solution-focused therapy, emotionally focused therapy, all recognize clients as active partners in the process that unfolds. Power issues are front and center. Issues related to marginalization and oppression become central to a lot of the work. Preconceptions are challenged and often let go.

Whether you identify with one of the postmodern approaches or not, some of the ideas have seeped into the ways that most practitioners now think and function. Yet this paradigm is not without its critics that take issue with the claim that reality is unknowable or that different versions of truth are equally valid. It may indeed be very flexible, caring, and respectful to honor a client's story that includes a report that he was captured by aliens who subjected him to horrific forms of torture. He says that he's depressed now because he fell in love with one of the bubble-head guards who showed him small kindnesses. I'm sure there's a metaphor, or at least a symbolic representation, related to the client's yearning for intimacy embedded in the story, which does have its own sort of truth, but that clearly isn't the same as what we consensually consider the experience of reality.

Therapist Paradigm Shifts to Help Organize the Confusion

We notice all the time the ways that our clients resist the prospect of change. It is not only disorienting but also uncomfortable, if not painful and exhausting. It requires abandoning what has been familiar, making all kinds of adaptations, learning new skills that will likely feel awkward and initially ineffective. It means, in some ways, not feeling like yourself because, after all, you are experimenting with the idea of being someone else. To add to the burdens, people around you may not be crazy about having to make their own adjustments to the new you.

If clients often resist change, even when it is obviously necessary, why should we be immune to the same prospect? Sure it's interesting, as well as exciting, to learn new things and add to our repertoire, but in some ways it can also be threatening. Just a few decades ago managed care was first beginning to exert influence over the profession, new paradigms like postmodernism were first taking off in popularity, and there were the first strident calls that our field must make the transition to a more empirically supported science. For those of us who have been around for a while, we may have felt some resistance to this new development.

I remember feeling annoyed, if not threatened, by some of these changes that meant I would have to abandon some of the ideas I most cherished. In some ways, my beliefs and values felt devalued. At the time, I was doing almost exclusively relationship-oriented, long-term therapy with clients who were primarily interested in their growth and development rather than presenting crises that required immediate intervention.

Wow, have things changed! When I go back and read things I've written in previous books, I hardly recognize myself. I can't remember the last time I had the chance to do insight-oriented, long-term therapy because so much of my focus now revolves around time-limited group therapy and social justice projects in neglected regions in which psychotherapy in any form is neither practical nor appropriate for the severity of the problems and their systemic nature. I mention this as just one example of the radical paradigm shifts that have occurred in the past and are likely to continue at an accelerated pace.

It amazes me how for a few hundred years about the only "technology" that people had to master was loading a firearm. Then there was a time early in my career in which the only technological skills required were changing a typewriter ribbon, operating a mimeograph machine, and perhaps programming a VCR television device. Now every few years almost everything we do, and the way we do it, becomes utterly transformed in ways that could never be imagined. Twenty years ago there was no such thing as an iPod much less a mobile device that holds as much computing power as the machines that were the size of buildings. When I was in graduate school, we still had to create huge stacks of IBM cards that would then be inserted into a window where attendants in white lab coats would "run" the program and produce results 24 hours later (which I could still never figure out). The advances in our profession are, in some ways, just as startling.

This is a renewed period of enlightenment in which each of us feels encouraged not only to stay current on the latest research and conceptual advancements but also to develop our own personalized notions consistent with standards of care. Here are two examples of how a few therapists have experienced this phenomenon.

Valuing Confusion

It had always seemed clear to Ann that the true causes of problems for clients, herself, and the world in general were confusion and uncertainty. Eliminate them and control, order, and reason would work everything out in the end. Of course, Ann was usually frustrated because whenever it seemed like control, order, and reason came together, the effects were never quite what she expected.

Ann had been working lately with several clients who were struggling with chronic illnesses so she sought additional training at a workshop that turned out to be extremely disappointing. The workshop seemed poorly organized, tedious, and lacking practical strategies that she hoped to gain from the experience. "I decided to write a letter to the presenter," she recalled. "I started putting down my thoughts and telling him what I had wanted from the experience and how far that was from what he delivered."

Recording these thoughts on paper helped Ann to clarify some significant insights. "Only later that day I realized that this was the best thinking I had done in weeks, maybe years. I had created my own new directions, ones that I guess were hidden somewhere in me all the time. It was all because of the confusion and frustration created in me by this dud of a presenter. His incompetence directed my thinking and allowed me to work my ideas out. I could hardly believe it; I was starting to feel grateful to this jerk."

It became increasingly clear over time that just as confusion is an important component of the therapy process, so too was it part of her own development. More than ever, that breakthrough insight helped her to let go of her previously determined need to put everything in a box that could be stored in its appropriate place on a shelf. She now felt more willing and able to help clients stay with their confusion and use it as an impetus for constructive changes.

Spiritual Awakenings

Duong had worked with a wide variety of clients during his 15 years as a therapist. He had helped severely emotionally disturbed clients to develop ways to get by from day to day, unemployed people to seek new career paths, and professionals to find new meaning in their lives. It was, however, some volunteer work in a hospice for the terminally ill that caused him to look at life and therapy from a very different angle.

"I had always operated from the belief that a therapist's work was helping people create the most viable physical existence possible," Duong explained. This had earned him plenty of accolades, but it wasn't quite enough for him to feel settled. "My patients at the hospice changed everything for me. They were all suffering, had virtually no time left to alter their lives, and many had no support system outside the hospice."

Always practical, Duong believed that medication was the key to alleviate their pain and discomfort so that their last days could be free of suffering. While this removed physical distress from the patients' lives, it did not add anything meaningful to the precious time they had left.

During one evening making the rounds, Duong observed a lay minister talking to one of the patients who was in the last stages of her illness. Duong recognized the patient and knew she had no particular background or interest in religion, so he was surprised that she seemed so engaged in the conversation with the pastoral care worker. "I came to realize that they were actually talking about hope and one's place in the larger universe. This was something that had always been missing in my work."

Duong admits that he didn't have this new paradigm all figured out yet and he doubts he ever will. "It's not about church, the Koran, the Torah, or the Bible, although I have found things in each of these books that bring me closer to a feeling of connectedness. It's the realization that the demands, agonies, and problems of everyday life are not the whole picture, and that somehow this realization gives my clients and myself more power to deal with each day as it comes. I now seek ways to clarify and maintain that perspective in my clients and myself, but it's not easy. The day-to-day pressures hit you in a physical way, but the spiritual ones need to be sought. I try to encourage that search."

Duong's inclusion of spiritual issues in this therapy is just one example of the ways that our models and paradigms are profoundly altered by our engagement with others. It is relatively rare after graduate school that we ever see other professionals in action, as occurred in this case, but most often such influences occur as a result of what our clients teach us—that is, if we are paying close attention to the lessons they offer.

We were warned about the fickle nature of knowledge in our field, ever-changing and evolving as quickly as we can grasp existing ideas. While this conceptual development is exciting, there is also something very faddish about the supposedly revolutionary trends we are faced with every few years. When many of the supposed new innovations and advances in the field appear to be cloaked in much that is already familiar, it makes us long for a return to the basic foundations that once operated so powerfully in our work.

Chapter 5

RETURNING TO THE BASICS WHEN IT ALL STARTS TO SOUND FAMILIAR

For anyone who has been a therapist for very long, it may very well appear as if we are reinventing the same ideas over and over again, just slapping different names on them. Every few years we are given notice that some new idea or theory renders everything we've already been doing obsolete and we better get onboard or we'll be left behind. There are usually initials or acronyms attached to the newest theories—EFT, DBT, RCT, MBT, ACT, EMDR, IFS—perhaps because we are so busy we don't have time to say the whole names.

Just when you think you have gotten a handle on the current state of practice, professional standards, conceptual models, and the most current interventions, you are alerted that the rules have changed again.

"I just wish they'd call a moratorium on new stuff for a year or two," one therapist complained. "Just until I can catch my breath. Maybe I'm out of the loop or something but by the time I figure out what is hot, manage to read the right articles and attend the right workshops, then practice it for a while, I'm told I'm already behind the times."

I can easily relate to this therapist because it so clearly reflects some of my experiences. I remember in the 1970s when neurolinguistic programming (NLP) was supposed to be the answer. I was skeptical. It seemed to me that the originators were more like marketing experts than they were genuine therapist trainers. I resisted as long as I could. After all, I was pretty pleased with what I was doing at the time. I had invested a heck of a lot of time and energy into learning what I was already doing. I got pretty good at it, too. Then I was told by a few colleagues that unless I learned NLP, I would always be living in the Stone Age. So I gave in, bought the required books, and signed up for a workshop.

I paid a lot of money to attend the sanctioned training sessions. Just a few weeks before I was to make my pilgrimage, I read somewhere that NLP was already old news. I wish I could say this was an infrequent experience, but it seems to reoccur over and over again. Currently on the new horizon is an assortment of new models that are purported to offer something innovative and "the thing" we've long been missing—integral spiritual therapy, functional analytic therapy, social action therapy, holotropic breathwork therapy, equine facilitated therapy, mindfulness-based therapy, metacognition therapy, schema therapy, Hakomi Buddhist therapy, harm reduction therapy, attachment-based therapy, sensorimotor therapy, shamanic therapy, nondual therapy, acceptance and commitment therapy—and this is only a *partial* list!

There's a point at which it seems as if almost everything is being recycled, altered in a new form and rebranded as revolutionary. And I can't think of another profession where this kind of faddish attachment to new ideas has so much legitimacy.

It is even more interesting how the originators of our various theories become rock stars. Can you imagine at a chemical engineering, landscape architecture, or neurology convention that participants stand in long lines to snag the autograph or take a photo with their favorite hero or heroine who developed a new way of processing a chemical compound or designing an urban park? Just as our clients put us on a pedestal, so too do we deify prominent figures within the profession. The irony of this is that many of the so-called master therapists who are most well-known are not necessarily the best clinicians; in some cases, they are barely competent as practitioners (which may be why they changed jobs to become public figures or workshop leaders). Many of the most accomplished therapists are content to work under relative obscurity, devoting their lives to doing the best they can to help their clients rather than promoting themselves on a bigger stage.

Back to Basics

There just doesn't seem to be enough time to get really good at anything new. Most of us promised ourselves in graduate school, before entering the "real" world, that we would finally get around to reading and studying and learning the things that interested us most instead of always having to satisfy our instructors and complete their assignments and reading lists. It didn't quite happen that way: Most of us are busier than we ever were during training years just trying to make ends meet, take care of personal business, stay current in the field, plus have some kind of social, romantic, and family life.

How can we possibly choose among the more than 250 theoretical options that might be best-suited to our clients, setting, and personal style? Many of us have been lazy, in a sense, taking on a particular approach—hook, line, and sinker—without investing the hard work of personalizing and adapting it to our own needs.

In the real world, the choice of framework is not based solely, or even primarily, on what a therapist believes is most useful but rather involves far more personal motives that reflect our values and preferences (Heinonen & Orlinsky, 2013). What kind of relationships do you enjoy with clients? What sort of presenting problems most interest and stimulate you? Which of your most significant values are prominently embedded in a particular model? A therapist's gender, culture, religion, sexual orientation, political stance, native language, geographical location, work setting, family history, not to mention outside interests, hobbies, and personal needs, would also come into play.

All the newest paradigms and innovative models provide alternative perspectives for looking at the work that we do, and in that sense they can open new and more creative possibilities. They don't so much change our lives as offer new language systems and conceptual maps to understand unexplained phenomena.

The earliest inhabitants of our planet explained events as the result of divine intervention. It really did appear as if the sun or moon disappeared and might not return again without some sort of appeal to the gods. These theories made perfect sense at the time, no less so than anything sacred we hold true today. Remember that it wasn't that long ago that "therapists" drilled holes in the skulls of the mentally afflicted, burned them at the stake, or subjected them to all manner of indignities like "trial by drowning" in order to "cure" their witchery. It leads me to wonder what beliefs and assumptions we hold true that are no more valid. Lest we defend that we are far more than mere faith healers, our practices empirically verified, it should be noted that many scientific methodologies are severely flawed and their results skewed, or sometimes even fabricated. I know that the question of falsified data is controversial and that reports of fraud and misconduct vary tremendously, but in a review of 18 meta-analyses of studies investigating this problem it was estimated that about 2% of published studies misrepresent their results, whereas in other studies as much as 35% of researchers admitted they used questionable practices: "cooking" their data, distorting or deliberately omitting relevant information, and in some cases, even making up the results (Fanelli, 2009). This doesn't exactly inspire confidence.

Considering that (perhaps) there's a remote possibility that our favorite ideas may not be as scientifically supported as we'd hope, how we can be so certain about our foundational knowledge? We can scoff at the primitive conceptions of reality that were espoused thousands or hundreds of years ago, but it wasn't that long ago that truth took on an entirely different shape than what we might believe today. For those of us who could be generously called "senior" therapists, we might remember some of the assumptions and supposed facts that ruled our childhoods. I can recall, with perfect clarity, being told by my parents, with utter certainty, that going into the water immediately after eating would condemn me to an excruciating death by stomach cramps. There was some precise, but unpublished, chart that moms of the world swore by as their guide.

Picture a hot summer day: 90% humidity, matching the temperature. The swimming pool is filled with raucous children soaking, playing, splashing, cooling off.

I'm dying to get in the water. But I just had lunch. I ask my mother when I can swim.

"Well," she asks, "what did you eat?"

"Uh, just a few fries and a coke."

"Okay," she answers, consulting some mysterious internal calculator that parents seem to be born with. "Fifteen minutes."

A sigh of relief as I try to make a fast getaway. "Thanks, Mom."

"Wait a minute! Did you have ketchup with those fries? And didn't you finish your brother's sandwich?"

Busted. "Kind of."

"Make that 35 minutes, and not a minute less!"

So I sit on the edge of the pool in the brutal heat, my feet dangling in the water but knowing that my mother is watching me like a hawk. But at least I never died of stomach cramps thanks to my mother's vigilance.

Years later, I will never forget, I first took SCUBA diving lessons and the instructor gave us last-minute advice before we showed up for our first open-water dive. "Remember," he said soberly, "eat a big breakfast before you go in the water. See you guys in the morning."

What the heck? My hand shot up in the air. "Uh, excuse me? I have a question."

The instructor turned toward me.

"Um, I don't mean to disagree or anything," I began by disagreeing, "but aren't we supposed to wait an hour or something after we eat before we go in the water. I mean, if we eat a big breakfast, won't we get stomach cramps?" I was now seriously mistrusting my safety under the care of a supposed expert who didn't even seem to know the most basic thing my mother taught me.

To add to my confusion, and frustration, he started laughing. "I bet your mother told you that."

"Soooo?" I responded a little defensively. I started thinking about all those summer days I spent sitting on the sides of swimming pools, dangling my feet in the water, impatiently waiting to be allowed in the water, asking my parents every few minutes: "Is it time yet? Can I go in *now*?"

The instructor casually responded, shaking his head. "That's all a myth. You don't get stomach cramps from going in the water after you eat. That was some crazy idea that people used to believe with absolutely no evidence. Tell me, have you ever actually heard of anyone dying of a stomach cramp after going in the water after eating? Have you even heard of anyone getting a stomachache under those circumstances?"

I wracked my brain. Surely there must have been someone who fit the bill. But all I could do was shake my head.

"In truth, your body needs nourishment to maintain its body temperature. Otherwise, you'll get hypothermia. And then you *will* die."

After I recovered, I started thinking in earnest about what other unassailable truths we accept as reality that are just as much myths as drowning from stomach cramps.

Common Denominators

One of the conclusions that we think we know—and I for one am a strong proponent of this conclusion—is that all effective systems of helping, whether traditional ideologies or contemporary innovations, subscribe to some fairly basic principles that are part of all effective therapy. We covered a bit of this in an earlier chapter and quite a number of authors have expressed similar opinions, identifying the essence that drives all successful therapies, some of them from a previous generation (Evans, 2013; Frank, 1973; Kazdin, 2009; Kottler, 1991; Mahrer, 1989; Norcross & Glencavage, 1989; Omer, 1987; Prochaska & DiClemente, 1984; Rosenzweig, 1936; Strupp, 1973; Truax & Carkhuff, 1967).

"Common factors" or "core ingredients" represent the essence of what we actually do in sessions regardless of what we say or think we do. These are the features that bind us together, that signify points of agreement, and that have the most consistent empirical support. Each of the factors such as instilling hope, promoting insight, developing an alliance, and others have different names and configurations in various systems but still retain essential characteristics that promote change.

The Human Connection

A common predicament of many clients is their disconnection from others, whether as isolation, lack of intimacy, persistent conflict, lost love, or unsatisfying relationships. Often there may have been some precipitating event that resulted in these feelings—a marriage breakup, children leaving home, relocation, job change or loss, argument, death of a loved one—but just as likely there may be some chronic, entrenched dysfunctional problem that sabotages deeper, more meaningful interpersonal engagement.

Often the heart of our therapeutic work involves helping clients build bridges to reconnect themselves with sources of support or create opportunities to build new and more robust support systems. In one sense, what therapy teaches people on *both* sides of the encounter is that it is indeed possible to enjoy a level of honesty, authenticity, respect, and caring that had never been imagined previously. Clients leave our care hopefully determined to recreate the kind of intimacy they felt with others in their lives.

Likewise, it is frequently reported by graduate students and new therapists how their own relationships have been "ruined" in one sense: They are no longer satisfied with the kind of superficiality they once ignored. One intern, Alyssa, talked about how she had been warned this might happen but still felt unprepared for the degree to which her own life would become transformed. "They told us the first day of orientation that all our friendships and family relationships would be impacted by our training. They scared us to death with predictions that if we didn't bring our loved with us on this ride, they would be left behind. I remember thinking that sounded crazy to me and it was never anything that I signed up for."

Although Alyssa was initially skeptical, she found almost immediately that her conversations with classmates, and experiences in class, required such deep sharing and disclosures that she was no longer satisfied with many of her relationships outside of school. "I used to be perfectly content to talk about gossip or movies or football, and I guess in some ways I kind of miss those mindless but fun interactions. But a lot of my personal relationships have changed in the past few years since I began my studies: I'm just not that patient and tolerant talking about inane stuff—I want to go deep and talk about real feelings." Alyssa shrugs as she says this, hesitates, then adds with a laugh that doesn't sound funny at all. "I guess I've lost some old friends who just couldn't adjust to where I'm at now."

This parallel process experienced by both clients and therapists as they deepen relationships is a direct result of what happens in sessions in which there is very little small talk and almost all discussion is about significant and meaningful issues. Indeed, this becomes addictive after a while.

The Person of the Therapist

The most obvious reason why clients come to therapy is to make their pain and suffering go away. They want their problems fixed as quickly as possible; if necessary, they'll return a second time but would much prefer if we could resolve things within that first session. Alas, we don't quite have a magic wand, and the process usually takes longer than hoped and expected.

Disappointed in their first priority, the consolation prize they hope for is that they've found a therapist who can truly understand them. Of course we don't really understand anyone, much less ourselves, but it turns out that that is less important than helping clients *feel* like they've been understood. We do this in a lot of different ways, reflecting their feelings, summarizing what we've heard them say, interpreting underlying meanings in their communications, acting as an advocate, validating their experience, reassuring and supporting them during times of trouble. But most of all we engage them most deeply through our own authentic way of being.

It isn't only our diagnostic acumen and therapeutic skills that we bring into the room or the therapeutic models we enact in sessions but also who we are as human beings. Even though there are certain therapist characteristics that are frequently mentioned as most important, qualities like being caring, respectful, patient, emotionally stable, and so on, we have each discovered ways to capitalize on our signature strengths, whatever those might be.

"I never thought I could be very good at this stuff," one therapist confided. She was a quiet, reserved Vietnamese American young woman, who had rarely spoken in class. "As you know, I'm not the most dynamic or charismatic sort of person." She is actually quite shy and soft-spoken and, knowing her for years, I was a little surprised myself how she managed to flourish as a practitioner. I'd since seen her work and it was pretty impressive. She had learned how to adapt her own style and personal characteristics to engage with her clients in ways that a more forceful or dramatic person could never do. She found that clients trusted her because they saw themselves in her. They didn't feel threatened by her. And in some ways, they worked harder for her than they would have otherwise because her modesty resonated with them.

We have all known colleagues who seemed barely able to function well in their own lives and yet they appeared to do extremely solid therapeutic work with their clients. Somehow they are able to compartmentalize their own troubles, or maybe their clients just find them extremely accessible because of perceived shared struggles. Nevertheless, if the relationship is the glue that holds everything else we do together, then it is our own unique personality and style that maintains the adhesion.

The Capacity to Influence

The laws of physics demand that stationary objects remain immobile and that objects moving in one direction will not move in an opposite direction of their own accord. A person's behaviors, feelings, and thinking patterns that have solidified over time are no less amenable to change. Whatever different methods we rely on, a common thread among effective therapists is our ability to influence clients toward change and persuade them to do things that they may wish to avoid or resist.

This power we hold is both exhilarating and frightening at times, as highlighted by one therapist who ran into an ex-client in a department store. "I saw her chatting with two other women and I flashed back to all the agonizing sessions we had together. She had been so unwilling to even leave the house or talk to anyone else except me." Now recognizing the woman in the store, appearing so casually at ease, it surprised him. "The idea that I was an integral part of that dramatic change still floors me every time I encounter it."

The therapist had never been comfortable with the power he wielded over others' lives. He was also uneasy because he didn't fully understand the extent of his influence and its lasting impact. "I don't exactly know what makes me successful. I just know that I've always had the ability to influence people's thinking and acting. As I've become better at it, I sometimes worry about how much it is like brainwashing because it could so easily be abused."

We do know and understand things that are useful to others, even if they initially resist some of the ideas. We can often explain complex or inscrutable concepts in the language that our clients can most easily grasp. And although they may not always want what we are selling, we have within our repertoire both subtle and dramatic means by which to convince them to at least consider what we offer as a possible path to deliverance.

Sometimes it can be the simplest piece of information or explanation that makes all the difference. I remember one of my very first couples cases when I first began practicing. They were so young, maybe still in their late teens, and they had this deer-in-the-headlights look about them. They had no idea what they'd gotten into. They had just gotten married and things were not going well at all.

After a lot of back and forth, beating around the bush, stalling and talking around things that were clearly not what brought them in to see me, they finally got to the point in the last few minutes of the session. "We're having some, you know, some marital problems."

"Yes, that's what you've been saying."

"You know, *marital* problems."

I still didn't know what they meant. The whole time we'd been talking about the problems in their relationship. Then it hit me: "You mean problems in the bedroom?"

Slow head nods. They both looked down and would not make eye contact.

"So, what seems to be the difficulty you are having in the bedroom?"

The husband looked at the wife who avoided looking anywhere else except at her lap. After a long pause, I could barely hear her whisper, "It hurts."

"Sex, you mean? You are saying that when you have sexual intercourse it is painful for you?"

Both heads nod again.

A whole array of thoughts was going on inside my head. Should I refer her first to a gynecologist to determine whether this is psychogenic, perhaps vaginismus, or if there is some physical or medical issue? Maybe their sexual problems are simply an extension of the other family issues they brought up earlier. I noted that they seemed very uncomfortable talking about this subject. They couldn't even say the word "sex" without blushing. I realized I was feeling uncomfortable as well because they seemed so distressed. Finally, I couldn't think of anything else to say except to ask a few more questions to find out what was really going on.

The responses I received were shocking and I did my best to appear calm, as if I heard this sort of thing all the time. It seems that when the husband wanted to have sex (and he was the only one who would initiate it), he would gesture toward the bedroom, kind of nod his head upstairs. "Okay," I pressed, "*then* what happens?"

"Oh," the husband answered, "you know, we just do it."

"Wait a minute. Slow down. What you mean you just do it? Could you describe in more detail how this happens for you?"

At this point the wife looked like she was going to die of embarrassment. She was twisting her hands, her neck was turning red, and I watched as the blush moved up her throat to her face. She still would not look anywhere other than her lap.

Finally, the husband answered me. "Well, we go in the bedroom and she lies down"—at this point he pointed toward his wife as if I might mistakenly think he was talking about someone else—and then I pull down her pants, and mine too, and then we do it." He stopped for a moment, then continued, "Well, we *try* to do it, but she says it hurts too much, so then we have to stop."

The wife nodded, almost involuntarily, confirming what her husband said was true.

"Okay," I pressed, "but I still need some more detail from you, as uncomfortable as this conversation might be for you both."

It turned out that this *was* all the detail. He was describing exactly how they had sex and it became immediately apparent why it was so painful. Considering this was so early in my career, it was seminal in helping me to understand how sometimes the things we can explain make all the difference. In this case it took about 5 minutes to tell them about the concept of "foreplay," that a woman needs some time to warm up, so to speak, that they might take a few minutes, even a half hour or longer, to undress one another, touch and kiss one another, and so on. Don't ask me how they never managed to hear about this, or how people could be so clueless about their bodies, but this brief explanation was all they needed. One session was all it took—my greatest cure!

What appear to be brilliant informational tidbits to clients are often taken for granted by therapists. After years of study with intelligent peers, more knowledgeable faculty, and then continuing contact with other professionals, we can begin to assume that our knowledge is not all that special. Like all knowledge, it serves little purpose when remembered or offered in isolation, but it becomes memorable and essential when we can provide it at the right time in the development of a client's life story.

Telling Stories

A case could be made that we are, above all else, in the business of telling and listening to stories (Kottler, 2015). We will talk a lot more about this in a later chapter, but suffice to say that so much of what we actually do is invite clients to tell their stories, after which we honor them, in some cases validate them, but in other instances coauthor alternative narratives that are a lot more functional and empowering. The shame of the matter is that although this is what we do most of the time in the real world, we had almost no training in how to become accomplished storytellers, even though it is such a critical part of our work.

We use stories as metaphors, self-disclosures, case examples, object lessons, or as part of prescribing books and films for clients to watch and process. We share stories from successes and failures of the past, from literature and real-life events, previous sessions, seminal moments in our own lives, and from all the things we've learned over the years. We use stories to impact clients in ways that nothing else could touch in quite the same way.

Apart from the stories we include and discuss and process in sessions, we are storytellers every time we write up a case report or even write a progress note. We use stories in talks we present, just as we do in supervision or case conferences.

One purpose of telling stories is to give clarity to the structure of one's life. We use the patterns of those stories to organize thoughts, learn from the past, operate in the present, and plan for the future. When people begin confusing that story or forgetting key parts while magnifying the importance of others, the process of learning, acting, and planning begins to break down. Therapists know how to help clients reconstruct their stories to include the parts that have been altered or eliminated.

We listen, reflect, envision the progress of a client's story and express the specifics of our confusion when the storyline is breaking down. Clients are regularly surprised to find out that they left out critical aspects of the story. In fact, one definition of trauma is that it involves some fragmented, chaotic memory that has yet to become fully integrated (Cummings, 2011; Hoyt & Yeater, 2011; Neimeyer, 2012).

Assigning Therapeutic Tasks

It is not just the behaviorists among us who believe clients need practice once they leave our office. All therapists recognize that we provide a safe environment to devise new ways of thinking and behaving, but that the real test comes with their implementation in the real world. Each of us has devised favorite methods to get people to apply new ideas to their lives.

Depending on theoretical style and clinical preferences, all therapists suggest or prescribe tasks that they think might be good for their clients. This can be simple and general, such as asking them to think about something that was discussed with the understanding that we will return to it later, or it can involve some more specific homework such as maintaining a journal.

"Clients often forget what they have done that is productive or nonproductive over the week," one therapist explains, "so they don't get a clear picture of their progress. I ask them to write briefly each night in a journal about the one or two things that they did that day related to what we are working on. We start the next session by recalling what happened and then go from there."

Some therapists, especially those with a more strategic, action-oriented bent, are inclined to be far more directive and provocative in their assignments, following in the footsteps of Milton Erickson, Carl Whitaker, Jay Haley, Albert Ellis, Cloe Madanes, and other brief therapists. Within time-limited parameters it is even more crucial to use opportunities outside of sessions to do most of the important work, whether practicing new skills, taking risks, or taking some constructive action.

One of my favorite examples of how therapeutic tasks can be

reconceptualized in a *very* different way is offered by Bradford Keeney, a former systemic theorist, who now identifies as a shamanic healer (Keeney, 2007, 2009; Keeney & Keeney, 2012; Kottler, Carlson, & Keeney, 2004). In a previous project (Kottler & Carlson, 2003) we interviewed him about one of his most seminal cases and he described working within the cultural context of a Native American medicine man who had been unable to have a vision (signifying he is a fraud). This would obviously not be a case in which the usual ways we conceptualize therapy would be appropriate, so the treatment took the form of prescribing a series of rituals that were consistent with the shaman's belief system. Among many indigenous healers this is the norm rather than the exception because of the ways that talk can be misleading but actions speak the truth.

Immunizations Against Stress and Burnout

It is because of the implicit ambiguity, confusion, and complexity of our work, coupled with hanging out all day with people in misery, that we are prone to burnout after a period of time, at least unless steps are taken to prevent such a condition taking hold. Whereas stress, or even distress, are relatively mild responses to the challenges we face on a daily basis, burnout represents a chronic, far more severe state of impairment characterized by reduced personal and professional effectiveness, depression, insomnia, and other negative side effects (Smith & Moss, 2009). Then there is also the vicarious or secondary trauma that penetrates our soul as a result of overexposure to so much tragedy, despair, and life struggles.

We try to balance our concern, perhaps overconcern, for those in our care, with the need to set boundaries that keep us sane. It is thus a paradox that we derive so much satisfaction from our (over) involvement with clients but also experience emotional exhaustion, depersonalization, and depletion as a result. Most of these negative feelings may result as much from a lack of social support as they do from caring too much or working too hard (Lee, Lim, Yang, & Lee, 2011; Puig, Yoon, Callueng, An, & Lee, 2014).

It is the lack of support, as well as increased conflict and feuds in the workplace, that only exacerbate the uncertainty, confusion, and complexity that we must juggle every day. We may try to remain grounded in the basics of what we do, drilling down to the essence of being most helpful to others, but this is a very grim business that often occupies us. That's why it is so important to keep things in perspective and try not to take ourselves too seriously. Keeping a sense of humor helps a lot, especially when it is the kind that is "self-enhancing" rather than "self-defeating," meaning that we try to make others laugh and lighten the mood rather than tease and ridicule or make self-disparaging comments (Malinowski, 2013).

What the Future May Bring

Anyone who has been out of graduate school for more than a few years would find the realities of daily practice distinctly different from what was initially prepared for. There are not only many new models and therapeutic options on the scene but completely new demands on our professional and personal lives. These changes are only going to continue at an accelerated pace as technological innovations, research advancements, and conceptual developments bring new options and opportunities for us.

So, what can we predict for the future?

Well, for one thing we need to be very humble and tentative in anything we might anticipate or imagine lies ahead. After all, how could we have ever predicted the ways that mobile devices would completely transform the way that people interact with one another in just a few years? Nevertheless, some wise and experienced experts (Norcross et al., 2013; Norcross & Rogan, 2013; Silverman, 2013; Tracey, Wampold, Lichtenberg, & Goodyear, 2014) have given some thought to the matter and concluded the following:

1. There will be increased pressure on accountability and assessment of outcomes, requiring us to learn and apply

more reliable and valid measures of progress in sessions. This will not only be based solely on client reports, or therapist perceptions, but more multidimensional sources of data.

2. Competition in the marketplace will increase as paraprofessionals and bachelor's-level mental health providers will be considered more cost-effective. This is not unlike what has happened in the medical field with physician assistants and nurse practitioners doing a lot of the work that was once exclusively within the province of physicians.

3. Economic pressures, reorganization of our health care system, and the pressure toward greater efficiency will put even more stress on therapists to employ brief therapies and manualized treatments. It is predicted that traditional psychodynamic and insight-oriented models will continue to become increasingly rare, except for those who are willing and able to pay for that service.

4. Therapy will become delivered in more flexible formats other than face-to-face individual appointments. Already we can witness the ways that sessions once conducted via telephone are now taking place through video-conferencing, online web programs, e-mail, and even text messaging. In the future we may see sessions conducted through virtual reality.

5. Mind-body integration will become much more important, not only in the ways that we understand client complaints and presenting problems but also in the ways that we treat them. The whole mindfulness movement, health and exercise movement, yoga and meditation practices, plus traditional psychopharmacology and the biopsychosocial model will exert increased influence.

6. We will be increasingly asked to translate our ideas and adjust our treatment modalities to serve a more diverse population of clients, not only in their cultural and ethnic backgrounds but across a variety of distinguishing characteristics, including their religious and value preferences, gender and sexual orientation, and especially socioeconomic background. The latter is particularly significant

given that so few of our services have traditionally reached deep into the communities that most need our help.

7. Psychopathological and problem-based systems will be replaced by more strength-based systems that emphasize personal resources, spiritual integration, and positive aspects of experience.

8. Therapy will increasingly become integrated into the larger health care system and develop further expertise and recognition in behavioral health issues, prevention of disease, and stress management. Therapists in the future will be reimbursed more often for primary preventative care and "well visit" checkups in which individuals have the opportunity for "tune-ups" even when there is no major complaint.

9. As psychiatry becomes less in demand as a specialty, psychologists and other mental health professionals will take over some of the medication management and also create new opportunities for nonmedical and paraprofessional therapists to expand their reach.

10. Relapse prevention, group formats, and social support programs will become increasingly popular to ensure changes remain stabilized and to help therapists reach out to a larger client population that is currently being met by self-help groups.

11. As the population ages, therapists will be increasingly called upon to address the problems and challenges of elderly clients who are struggling with corresponding developmental issues related to failing health, compromised mobility, existential themes facing the prospect of disability and death, grief and loss, and other topics brought into session for which we may not have been prepared.

12. Finally, the integrative movement will continue to exert influence, not only encouraging us to blend ideas from multiple theories and paradigms within our own field but also to include ideas and research from many other disciplines.

If you are currently in training, or graduated recently, hopefully some of these areas mentioned are being addressed before you hit the real world. It's interesting that although 80% of therapists were mostly satisfied with their graduate training preparing them for the real world (Norcross & Rogan, 2013), it's been estimated that roughly half of everything that was learned will become outdated and relatively useless 10 years later. This means that, in a sense, we are also "clients" throughout our professional lives, always upgrading our skills, adding to our knowledge base, and working to improve ourselves in a multitude of ways that go far beyond mandated continuing education credits.

The remainder of this book, beginning with Part II, is designed to provide the practical direction and tools you may need to navigate this journey. In the next part of the book, we will look at some of the secrets and challenges that we face in the real world, beginning with an exploration of the ways that our clients become our greatest teachers.

PART II

Secrets and Neglected Challenges

Chapter 6

CLIENTS ARE YOUR BEST TEACHERS

"I was thinking that maybe I should take the job after all. I mean, it would involve a promotion. And I'd have some new responsibilities. Plus it would cut my commute to work in half. The more I think about it, the more . . ."

"But," the therapist interrupted, "you said last week that you hated the very idea of working in that place. You said that although your job title would change that basically you'd be doing the same things you are doing now for less money." The therapist was visibly surprised by this change in attitude, considering that the client talked nonstop for a half hour during the last session about why this job offer would be the *worst* thing he could ever consider doing.

"No, I don't think that's what I said at all," the client disagreed vehemently. If the therapist had noticed, he would have seen the client's hands clinch, a reliable signal that anger was brewing.

"You may not remember," the therapist persisted, "but I distinctly recall you saying that going there would be—I think the expression you used is that it would be 'like trading jail for prison.'"

The client was shaking his head all the while the therapist was speaking. "That's not at all what I meant. You just misunderstood me. Besides, I pretty much decided I'm going to accept the offer. I think it's a good deal."

It was at this point that the therapist realized he was fighting a losing cause, only aggravating the client who was becoming more and more entrenched in his position. "I totally understand," the therapist replied, not really understanding at all. "If that's what you want to do, then you should go for it."

"What? Now I think you are just indulging me because you don't want to fight with me. You just can't admit that sometimes you're wrong, can you? Just because you sit in that bigger chair of yours, and have those diplomas on the wall, doesn't mean you always know what you're talking about. Like now for instance." As it to emphasize his point, the client crossed his arms and sat back smiling.

This client was indeed teaching his therapist an important lesson, but one that was being ignored because the therapist just couldn't let the interaction go. He knew his recollection of the previous session was accurate; he had the notes to prove it. But more than that, he felt that this was a perfect opportunity to confront the client with an observation about their interaction that was typical of the encounters that occurred in the outside world. This client had few friends, and almost no intimate relationships, and this sort of argument was partially the reason why. What the therapist was missing, however, was that being right was beside the point: The client was trying to tell him that he was threatened by this conversation, that he was off balance and trapped and was trying to extricate himself with his dignity intact. He was trying to tell the therapist, in his own indirect way, to back the hell off. But the therapist was too attached to an agenda to listen, much less take the feedback in stride and move things in an altogether different direction. The client will leave the encounter feeling misunderstood and annoyed, perhaps enough so that he won't return. The therapist, in turn, also feels confused and frustrated, but he reassures himself that his client just couldn't handle the truth and clearly wasn't ready to make the needed changes he claimed he wanted most.

If we are talking about truth, then the more significant point is that the client wasn't ready to take in what the therapist was offering, however accurate the comments might have been. He tried to tell the therapist several times, "No thank you. I don't want what you are trying to give me right now. Maybe later but not now. Can't you see that?"

Do We Really Know What's Going On?

We may have gotten the impression from graduate school that most of what we would ever learn would result from the books we read, the research we consulted, our own personal therapy as a client, and especially from our supervisors who would not only control our salaries and advancement but also guide our development as clinicians. In the real world, we do learn a lot from all of these sources, but not nearly as much as we do from our clients, who are the best experts on their own experience.

Relying on our own subjective evaluations of sessions is seriously flawed and presents a biased and distorted picture of what really may be happening. Therapists aren't actually the most reliable and accurate judges of their own work, as I noted in an earlier chapter in which almost all of us consider ourselves more accomplished and effective than any of our peers. In one study, it was determined that not a single therapist surveyed considered himself or herself below average in ability, and half of them couldn't think of a single case in which a client even deteriorated (Lambert, 2010). It would appear that either the sample in this study represented a remarkably improbable group of super-therapists or else their perceptions were significantly skewed. One conclusion, based on a review of studies that examined therapist assessments of their own performance, summarized that like any other mortal beings "our human nature confers a vulnerability to biases, blind spots, and self-enhancing illusions, which frequently distort our capacity to make rational sense of ourselves and our environment" (Macdonald & Mellor-Clark, 2014). And why should we be exempt from the same errors in judgment that befall everyone else?

It is obvious that therapists tend to overestimate how effectively therapy is proceeding, sometimes failing to recognize problems in the relationship. We sometimes hold entrenched, rigid beliefs that compromise our ability to read what is actually going on in sessions and how satisfied clients are with the results. Our ability to predict outcome accurately is negligible and just better than chance due to a number of cognitive distortions that have been described (Herbert, 2014; Lilienfeld, Ritschel, Lynn, Cautin, & Latzman, 2013; Macdonald & Mellor-Clark, 2014).

Novelty Effects

Expectations for treatment and placebo effects often produce immediate improvement (estimated to be as high as 15%) even before clients show up for a first session. They feel better just as a result of making an appointment and taking the first constructive steps. They rehearse the things they want to say and imagine what the experience will be like. They tell others about their intention, which starts some other things in motion. Even before the first interview they have already imagined conversations and clarified what they hope to gain from the sessions.

Therapy is not quite like anything else, and it is precisely that differentness that makes it stand out and be remembered. In some ways it doesn't matter that much what we do to make a lasting impression: The encounter is virtually guaranteed to become memorable; we even design it for that purpose. Where else in the world can you sit face to face, quietly and privately in a sanctified space, with no interruptions or intrusions, and talk about the most intimate aspects of your life? Where else would you encounter a professional whose very training and being have prepared him or her to respond with almost perfect clarity and caring?

Regardless of what we do, and how we do it, the uniqueness and foreignness of the experience is partially what contributes to its impact. Clients may point to the most insignificant (to us) comments, things we don't even remember saying. They recall conversations that we aren't sure ever took place. Most of all, they are likely to remember anything that struck them as really unusual and outside their previous experience.

"It was that role play," one ex-client kept telling me over and over again. "Remember when we did that role play and you asked me to confront my mother-in-law?"

I nodded. I did remember she had issues with her in-laws, but I also recalled that she would frequently bring that up as a way to hide from other stuff that was far more pressing. Apparently during one session we must have spent a few minutes having her imagine saying some things to her husband's mother, but my recollection was that was just a brief interlude before we moved on to something else. It seemed like no big deal (to me), but she talked about it like it was the ultimate breakthrough for her. Maybe it was, but it reminds me how we just don't really know what we do that matters most, even when we do ask for feedback immediately after sessions. This particular client revealed that she didn't realize how powerful that experience had been for her until many months later, long after our work together had ended.

Naïve Realism

Our optimism and hopefulness lead us to see the world through distorted lenses in which we are convinced—and try to convince others—that everything is just fine and will work out in the end. Through such perceptual filters we may ignore conflicting data that signal something is badly out of sorts. This occurs largely through the arrogant and misguided belief that what you see and hear, and what you interpret based on that perceptual data, actually represents some kind of objective reality. This leads to erroneous conclusions, invalid assumptions, and poor decision making.

"I am a sensitive observer," proclaimed one prominent expert, "and my conclusion is that a vast majority of my patients get better as opposed to worse after my treatment" (quoted in Dawes, 1994, p. 48). The treatment to which he is referring was a prefrontal lobotomy, and although this was a very popular treatment for schizophrenia and depression a half century ago, it was later found to be essentially worthless and harmful. This is but one example of the ways that we delude ourselves into thinking that it is solely our own actions that are responsible for client changes. There are many other factors operating behind the scenes, such as (1) placebo effects and client hopeful expectations, (2) spontaneous remission in which symptoms improve on their own over time, (3) regression to the mean in which many extreme behaviors eventually dissipate upon checking at a later time, (4) effort justification when clients feel the need to report successes because of the time and effort they invested into the process, and (5) multiple treatment interference in which clients have simultaneously sought out other forms of assistance (consulting with clergy, meditation practice, yoga, exercise, change in diet, attending a support group) (Lilienfeld et al., 2013).

Related to this last point of how we may erroneously attribute therapeutic success to our own efforts when there may be other influences operating outside of sessions, I was once doing a workshop on "working with difficult clients" in a relatively small community. I had assigned participants the task to share in small groups about the challenges they faced with their identified most difficult clients. I walked around the room listening in on their conversations when I overheard one therapist in the triad talk about a client who was driving him absolutely crazy with frustration. As he described the details of the case, a second therapist in the group revealed that sounded awfully familiar to her because she was seeing someone very similar. The third therapist jumped in: "That's really weird because I'm seeing someone who is also like that. It's almost like we are all seeing the same client."

Guess what? Each of the three therapists *was* seeing the same client! She had been secretly consulting three (or more?) different therapists, all at the same time, and all without mentioning it to the others. A situation such as this certainly causes us to consider all the things that might be really going on in a client's life about which we really have no idea.

Illusion of Control

Ever the optimists, therapists strongly believe that with sufficient motivation, control, and commitment, almost anything can be accomplished. That may be just dandy for the privileged who have access to all kinds of resources and support, but it does not quite match the experiences of others who have felt powerless their whole lives, who live in poverty and deprivation, who have been subjected to oppression and prejudices. There are, in fact, many things that are not in our control, including inborn abilities, environmental factors, financial resources, economic and political events, not to mention other people's behavior.

One of the most consistent messages we like to pass on to clients, whether they are ready for it or not, is that you have far more control than you imagine to determine the course of your life and the choices you make. I've seen the look in some clients' eyes when I tell them that, and I can sense immediately that they want to smack me and tell me I have no clue about what it's like to be them. "You sit in that comfortable chair, Kottler, surrounded by all your trappings and books and you live in your own world. You just have no idea what it's really like when I leave this office. Do you know that it sometimes takes me two hours to get home by bus because of the transfers? Between paying for these sessions, getting my kids to child care, taking time off from work, how the hell am I going to take control of my life? When am I going to have time for that? Maybe *you* can do that, but I don't have control over hardly anything in my life. I'm just trying to survive."

No client has actually said that to me, but I imagine that sometimes that's what they are thinking when I spout that rah-rah cheerleader stuff of eternal optimism. That illusion of control also relates to our belief that we can completely control what happens in therapy, for better or worse.

Confirmation Bias

Unfortunately this is perhaps the most common bias among therapists. We all have our favorite theories, and we just love it when events follow the formula that we come to expect. We hold certain hypotheses that we look to confirm and support, regardless of what is actually unfolding. And we don't like it at all when our precious assumptions are challenged and our theories don't fit; it's a lot easier to "massage" the data and select only supportive evidence rather than to alter or change theories.

Each of us holds onto certain myths and misconceptions about ourselves, about our clients, about how therapy works, and about human nature in general. We may have adopted some of these ideas in graduate school, in our own reading and conversations, based on our limited experience, from media and popular psychology outlets, or by subscribing to certain supposed universal "truths" that really have little support in reality (Lilienfeld, Lynn, Ruscio, & Beyerstein, 2010).

One example of this phenomenon was the notion of "symptom substitution" in which it was fervently believed by early psycho-analysts that without deep-level explorations of underlying causes to problems, people would just develop new problems if only the surface issues were addressed. It turned out there wasn't much actual evidence to support this belief, even if it appeared to make intuitive sense.

Other examples of entrenched beliefs adopted by therapists that have not been supported by much evidence include current debates about recovered memories, traumatic stress debriefing, symbolic representations in dream interpretation, complete abstinence required for recovery from alcohol dependence, hypnotic induction procedures for past-life regression, and the primacy of early experiences that would necessarily rule our lives unless they were completely resolved. In all of these cases, and many others, we may be inclined to confirm what we already think is true rather than examining more carefully what might be really going on.

Misinterpretation of Cause-Effect

Attributing progress to therapist actions or interventions when, in fact, incidental events had the most impact would obviously lead to misunderstandings. As therapists, we have a strong propensity to find (or create) cause-effect relationships when none may actually exist. We see clear connections between certain events and their corresponding results. We pretend that similar-appearing behavior results from a single cause, one that can actually be identified and named. Even when we acknowledge a kind of circular causality in which behaviors become both interactive causes and effects, we still insist that we have accurately tracked their influences.

Sometimes therapists confuse the meaning and application of research results, trying to generalize results from a large study to the unique and individualized experience of a given client or therapeutic relationship. Everything that we do is, in some sense, a totally unique interactive phenomenon even if we see some similarities and make connections to other cases. We get in trouble when we impose patterns and templates, based on a massive scale, that don't take into consideration many of the other forces and influences that might be happening in a particular situation. This can lead us to find relationships between variables where none actually exist and to ascribe meaning to events or behaviors that represent more fantasy than actual reality.

There are indeed certain probabilities and patterns that function for most people much of the time. But there are also a lot of exceptions to these rules, many of which we may fail to recognize if we are also looking for ways to identify clear connections between certain outcomes and their particular causes.

It has always bothered me the ways that certain figures of authority in our field have spoken with such (over)confidence about what they believe is happening with a particular client or situation: "This is clearly a case of . . ." or "What is certainly going on in this scenario . . ." or "You are obviously missing a key factor. . ." I appreciate the input and alternative perspectives, but I wonder how it is possible to truly *know* that this is what is going on, that a particular person, event, or interaction was actually the trigger or cause for what followed. There is no doubt that there are times when all of us are tempted to make gross or inaccurate generalizations that are not supported by much specific evidence in an individual case.

Misperception of Progress

Just because clients are talking doesn't mean they are getting better. We have seen that it is not uncommon that our most cooperative clients, those who talk nonstop, report all kinds of things they are doing, thank us profusely and enthusiastically for our help, and tell us we are the best therapists ever, still don't necessarily change much at all. Likewise, there are times we think we are failing miserably, when the client is actually doing quite well. Most of the time, they just tell us what they think we want to hear. Also, as we will discuss in a later chapter, clients also lie a lot, shade the truth, exaggerate and minimize what is really going on, and sometimes present themselves in ways that bear little resemblance to the ways they function in the world. As such, we sometimes don't have the foggiest idea of what progress is actually being made.

If We Don't Ask, We'll Never Know

It is clear that clients and therapists sometimes have very different takes on what is happening in the room. When one party might very well be quite satisfied with the proceedings, the other could have considerable doubts. Sometimes clients leave a session and we feel utterly bewildered by what transpired, not to mention uncertain about what ultimately resulted from the interaction. This is but one instance in which the respective needs and interests of the participants might not necessarily match.

Even factors like the way you design and furnish your office can elicit very different preferences between therapists and clients. Whereas practically everyone would agree that comfort and quietude are important, clients consistently prefer spaces that convey a sense of orderliness, as well as show personal touches that reveal the therapist's humanness. This doesn't necessarily fall in line with what therapists think is most important, considering they usually underestimate these features (Devlin & Nasar, 2012). Like so many other facets of the encounter, therapists rarely ask clients what they think about the space.

Recently there has been a call in our profession that we attend more carefully and systematically to client feedback, soliciting specific input after sessions so that we might better adjust our efforts and better address client needs. Quite a number of researchers have been engaged in assessing the most effective ways to gather this input and data from clients, relying on an assortment of qualitative and quantitative measures (Frankel & Levitt, 2009; Haber, Carlson, & Braga, 2014; Hodgetts & Wright, 2007; Lambert & Shimokawa, 2011; Manthei, 2007; Miller et al., 2014; Reese, Toland, & Sloane, 2010; Shaw & Murray, 2014). Regardless of the method employed, ranging from simple questionnaires, brief forms, in-depth qualitative interviews, follow-up phone calls, texts, letters, or e-mails, the idea is that we all need to be more proactive in finding how we are doing.

Personally, I find it rather intrusive and awkward to ask clients to fill out forms at the end of a session. I once attended a workshop for department chairs that was related to assessing outcomes in the classroom. By the time instructor evaluations are distributed at the end of the semester, it is too late for faculty to make any adjustments that might improve the quality of the experience. So it was suggested that we encourage professors to distribute a brief assessment after a few weeks with only three questions, which I have since adapted to therapy sessions. I not only like how brief and simple the device is but also the use of plural pronouns that imply *shared* responsibility for the results. The way the questions are phrased implies that all the participants have a role in shaping the sessions to be more responsive. Whether asked verbally, or presented as a brief form, these are the questions that could be asked:

1. What is it that we are doing together that you would like us to do more of?
2. What is it that we are doing together that you wish we would do less often or not at all?
3. What other changes could we make in the ways we work together that would make the experience more suitable and valuable for you?

Any attempt to solicit feedback from clients helps them to be more responsible for their sessions and also helps us to become more responsive to what they say they want most. However, it's also important to acknowledge that clients don't often know what is in their best interests, nor do they necessarily want us to know their plans and preferences. As we are aware, clients often have their own hidden agendas, one of which may very well include sidestepping or avoiding any real attempt to address the presenting problems for which they were referred.

Mechanisms of Mutual Influence

When therapists speak about the ways that clients affect us, it is often couched in critical or complaining language: "This borderline is driving me crazy." "I'm haunted by what happened in the last session." "I can't believe how resistant and defensive this client is being." "She really pushed my buttons." "I can't get him out of my head." "I dread seeing my 4 o'clock." We often spend a considerable amount of time complaining to colleagues, loved ones, and ourselves about how unappreciated and sometimes abused we feel. We compete with one another as to who has the most challenging and obnoxious clients. We speak about them sometimes in the most hateful language, as though they were sent from hell to make our lives miserable. And it does sometimes feel that way.

If you consult the literature on the subject of difficult clients, you will find all kinds of nasty labels for clients who get under our skin. We call them names and relegate them to diagnostic categories that make us feel better. And it is true that sometimes we do have to work with people who were referred to us in the first place because they are so ornery and abusive that nobody else will deal with them. We see people referred by the courts or law enforcement personnel. We are stuck with people who would just as soon strangle us as listen to whatever we are telling them. And, yes, this does get under our skin over time.

And yet . . . and yet . . . we receive incredible gifts from our clients, even the ones who we complain about the most.

When we talk about the ways we are changed and influenced by our clients, the ways they become our best teachers and supervisors, there are several different ways this can occur. First, we review some of the more traditional conceptions of mutual influence in sessions like countertransference, projective identification, and secondary trauma, and then we move on to far more constructive processes for which we feel fortunate and grateful. What is obvious in each of these examples of mutual influence is that we are potentially the recipients of incredible growth and learning as a result of what we learn in this work. Even though we are (hopefully) not meeting our own needs, there are still incredible lessons we learn every day.

Don't take my word for it: Just review your own experiences. Think back on all the people you have helped or tried to help in some capacity. Who stands out as the one client who had the most impact on you, personally and professionally?

Before reading any further, let your mind wander to the first person you think of. This is someone whose influence and impact on you could have been construed as either positive or negative but still continues to this day.

Try to remember what this person looked like, perhaps including some particular mannerism, quirk, or article of clothing that sticks in your memory. Recall the sound of this person's voice, including something he or she would often say that was unique. Picture where this client used to sit in the room, how he or she would express himself or herself, and especially something that he or she characteristically did or said that you will never, ever forget.

Now that you have this person so vividly in mind, what do you now best understand about why your interactions together were so powerful and memorable? There are a number of conceivable reasons you might nominate, including a case that was a tragic failure, a relationship with brutal conflict, or perhaps one with high levels of emotional arousal. Just as likely, this could have been an instance of a spectacular success that affirmed your competence or validated your favorite ideas. It could also have been a time when someone penetrated *way* underneath your skin, stabbing your soul.

Countertransference and Projective Identification

Of course, I'd begin with the historical legacy from psychodynamic theory. It was first postulated by Freud and others that it is not only inappropriate but potentially dangerous for us to collapse boundaries and allow ourselves to be personally affected by our clients. That is why we adopt a position of perfect neutrality, assuming that is indeed possible—and if that can't be done, then at the very least we need to set up safeguards so we can keep our distance.

This illusion was first shattered for me decades ago when doing research with *curanderos* or shamans in the Amazon basin. They found it improbable, if not hilarious, that I believed it was actually possible to avoid becoming "infected" by my clients' toxic energy. One shaman gave me a magic vial as a parting gift, one he said would protect me against such evil spells. (It has been sitting on my desk ever since and appears to still be working.)

Even if the original conception was a bit extreme, the idea that any feelings or reactions we hold toward clients, or those they have for us, represent fantasy distortions, the transference legacy is an excellent reminder about the complex nature of therapeutic relationships. We are authority figures and, as such, are bound to stir up feelings in clients in which they make connections to people from their past. Likewise, clients do sometimes remind us of others we have known and that can very well spark us to react in unexpected ways. But more to the point, our own unresolved issues do crop up as a result of what happens in the room. That possibility must be considered—and respected. And we must be able to distinguish between genuine reactions in the moment versus those that may be triggered by some illusion. Regardless of their origin, there's no doubt that we are strongly impacted by our clients in a variety of ways, no matter how much we might deny this effect to ourselves—and to them.

Haunted by Secondary Trauma

"I've never told anyone what happened before, not even my wife, not my brothers, and the guys in my unit—we never talked about what we did either. Never." That last word is spoken with such finality that it leaves no question that the secret about to be revealed is a doozy.

Brian had served in a unit in Afghanistan whose main function was the interrogation of prisoners. He hadn't asked for this assignment and was surprised he had been transferred there because he had no special language skills.

"I did things over there. I saw things over there." It was at this point that he collapsed in on himself, sobbing uncontrollably.

I reached out a comforting hand to Brian, but it felt awkward to touch him while he was so vulnerable. Finally, my hand rested on his shoulder and he leaned into it. Still, I didn't know what to say so I just waited, literally holding my breath.

Brian's story was so vividly told that I could picture myself there with him. I could smell the fear. I could hear and feel the suffering. Maybe I've seen too many movies and read too many books about similar kinds of brutality, but nothing had ever come close to being as real as this was for me. I was in the room with this gentle, kind, compassionate man who was now telling me about difficult things he witnessed. I was both disturbed and confused. But I couldn't help myself when I pressed for more detail. I wasn't sure, then or now, whether I thought this would be helpful to him or I was just fulfilling my own morbid curiosity.

Brian talked at length about some of the things he had seen, but mostly he spoke about wanting some kind of redemption and forgiveness. I'm pleased to say that I think that eventually happened for him, and I'm truly happy for him. But here's the thing: His lingering trauma was contagious and I caught a piece of his suffering. I just can't get certain images out of my head. I picture what I might have done in similar circumstances and question whether I could have resisted. My dreams sometimes include remnants of this powerful and disturbing story, somehow linked to other war narratives I've read and seen.

As a function of our role, we hear some of the most horrific and distressing stories imaginable. Clients tell us about the molestation or abuse they have suffered. We hear about traumas that were so intolerable that they drove people into madness. We listen to stories of hopelessness and despair. We sit with people who are suffering such intense depression they can barely get out of bed, or such intense anxiety they are visibly vibrating in the chair across from us. People share with us their deepest, most terrifying insecurities and their darkest secrets, the things that were never safe to tell anyone before. And we hold all of this. We become receptacles for others' unrelenting and extreme pain.

Of course, we have been taught ways to counteract these effects and to process the experiences. We use supervision and personal therapy to let go of what still haunts us. We use self-talk and all the things we teach to clients to challenge our thinking. Over time, some of the feelings dissipate and we may enforce stricter self-protective boundaries in the future. But therapists who say that they aren't haunted by some of the stories they've heard over time weren't paying very close attention.

Witness to Profound Change

Although almost everything that is written about how clients impact us frames the discussion in negative terms, I've made a career talking about the gifts that they offer us and the privilege we hold having access to their struggles and resilience. While it is certainly true that therapists are exposed to more than our fair share of disturbing material and upsetting stories, we also are offered so many opportunities to accompany people on their journeys toward growth and spectacular changes in their lives. Even more incredible, we are allowed to help guide this path to enlightenment, basking in the glory of such seminal experiences.

I've long found it interesting the ways that each session we conduct is very much like any other form of vicarious entertainment, whether on television, films, plays, or novels. Each day we see soap operas unfold before our very eyes, sometimes situation comedies, but often tragedies and dramas. Yet unlike these passive forms of viewership, therapists are actually fully involved in the plot developments. We are directors of the script that plays out, as well as key characters in the drama. Rather than simply watching events play themselves out, waiting with bated breath for the next installment, we become active participants in the process.

We are moved profoundly by the courage and resilience of those we help. Sometimes we sit in awe of the ways clients surprise us with their determination or ability to recover from circumstances that, at first, seemed so hopeless. Over time we witness the most incredible transformations, so much so that we (and others) hardly recognize the clients anymore.

I became a therapist in the first place because, in some ways, I'm addicted to change. I love (and hate) the excitement that comes with major shifts in my life. Because I get bored easily, I thrive on new challenges while I might complain about the difficult transitions. I've changed jobs and locations so often because, in some ways, it is an easier, lazier way to seek out new stimulation rather than investing the much harder work in recommitting and reinvigorating a current situation. I've also found that being a therapist allows me to live through my clients, experience their joys and disappointments, and at least vicariously, to feel the changes they are undergoing. Of course, this isn't nearly as much fun as taking risks and trying new things myself, but it sure is easier.

Vicarious Learning

Not only do we enjoy (if "enjoy" is the right word) the benefits of watching our clients make dramatic changes in their lives, but we also learn so much from them along the way. We live a hundred—or a thousand—lives by having access to the most intimate details of so many life experiences. We learn from our clients' mistakes and misjudgments. We hear about some of their most misguided choices and ridiculously poor decisions and vow to ourselves not to do the same. We are privy to their hard-won victories, internalizing the lessons. We help them to come to terms with their failures and disappointments and, in doing so, unconsciously work through some of our own. We talk to clients about their dysfunctional thinking, self-defeating attitudes, self-limiting beliefs, entrenched defenses, and unrelenting resistance to change, and simultaneously talk to ourselves about our own unresolved issues.

I've heard so many therapists confess that as exhausted and

depleted as they might feel after a hard day's work, they feel the most psychologically healthy and mentally stable when they've spent so many hours challenging their clients' self-sabotaging behavior. I remember Albert Ellis saying it best when he disclosed that on the days that he spent the most time talking others out of their "crazy bullshit" (he actually used a few more colorful words) were those times when he was most brutally honest with himself.

Our clients introduce us to aspects of life that we could never possibly experience ourselves. In a single day you might hear about the realities of what it's like to work as a cocktail waitress in a strip club, prepare a sermon for a community church, run a board meeting, beg for money to support a drug habit, work on an assembly line, or (one of my personal favorite) rehearse as a circus clown. Because I began working as therapist when I was so young (21 years old), most of my clients were much older than me and talked about problems that I would eventually come to face throughout the rest of my life. I learned about the intimate details of what it's like to be a parent, a grandparent, to be fired from a job, to live in various parts of the world, to deal with a sick parent, and ten thousand (or a million) other life challenges that I would face on my own. I felt better prepared to deal with these struggles because, in one sense, I had already lived through them with my clients.

Parallel Processes

"Look, until such time that you are fully prepared to take the risk of reaching out to others, you are going to remain feeling isolated and frustrated by the lack of intimacy you say is so unsatisfying. I mean you complain—you complain a lot actually—that although we have such meaningful conversations in this office you haven't been able to seek out friendships to continue this kind of intimacy outside where it matters the most."

I didn't realize that I was actually talking to myself, not to my client, who was barely listening anyway. I have been disappointed most of my professional life by the contrast between what occurs in my office and what happens in my normal life when I'm not working. It's not that I don't have some very close relationships with family members and a few dear friends, it's just that the kinds of deep conversations I have with clients don't necessarily occur very often in daily life. There are all kinds of excuses for why this is the case: (1) I'm too busy, (2) my friends live too far away, (3) my friends and family members are too busy, and (4) I'm too busy. I guess I mentioned that one already. In other words, although I talk a good game, I haven't followed through on what I say is so important.

It doesn't seem that uncommon that I hear myself say something to a client (or classroom) and I realize that I am really speaking to myself. Just the other day I told a client that he was working way too hard to get certain things done, and I noticed him looking at me quizzically. Oops. That wasn't really his problem; rather, I had been musing about this issue to myself. I didn't exactly confess that at the time, feeling a little sheepish at losing perspective, but still felt grateful that something was brought to my attention that I needed to look at so it wouldn't distract me in session again (not to mention create unnecessary stress in my life).

As wonderful as it is to enjoy these gifts that accrue to us as a result of our therapeutic work with others, it is just as interesting how our own life experiences spark parallel processes in sessions. I am always looking for these examples that I might use when counseling or teaching or supervising (or writing); once we take on this mindset we can potentially discover metaphors and teaching examples almost every day. This morning, for example, I went out on the patio to find a baby bird, just a few days old, lying on the table squeaking. I saw its mother flying around but helpless to lift the baby back into its nest. At first I tried to ignore the situation, thinking that this was Nature in action, survival of the fittest. For all I know the siblings kicked this one out for being disruptive.

As the hours went by, I couldn't help but keep glancing outside and seeing the little one struggling, its beak open, calling for its mother. I realized in that moment how badly I wanted to save the bird, how I got into therapy in the first place because I wanted to save people, however doomed I've been to frustration because I don't have that power. But this time I thought I might! I climbed a ladder and placed the baby bird back into its nest, noting with satisfaction that the family is now (apparently) happily reunited. I say "apparently" because I acknowledge that things may not turn out as well as I hope.

In thinking about this episode it triggers for me all kinds of issues and feelings that I am trying to get my head around, mostly so I can use my own process as a means by which to help a client (or a reader). This sort of thing happens all the time in our line of work, which can become both a scourge—and a joy.

Conceptual Development

All of us are theorists and model makers in that we are continuously observing behavior, monitoring internal processes, making connections, analyzing data, searching for patterns, and ultimately, creating theories to explain what we believe might be going on. Eventually we thread together enough of these client-tailored and situation-specific theories to create some kind of operating model that guides our decision making and choice of interventions. These ideas may be linked to an existing theory we have chosen for our own, but often over time this conceptual plan is altered to suit our own needs and personal style.

Quite a number of prominent theorists in our field, William Glasser (reality), Albert Ellis (rational-emotive), David Scharf (psychodynamic), Laura Brown (feminist), John Krumboltz (behaviorist) among them, point to particular clients who were instrumental in clarifying their ideas and helping them to formulate alternative conceptions of how therapy could work (Kottler & Carlson, 2005). Despite what we may have heard, or been taught in graduate school, it is actually our clients who help us to refine our working models by providing real-time responses to what is most and least helpful to them.

Most theorists can recall certain seminal cases that changed everything for them. They were routinely proceeding along a familiar path, applying standard strategies that had been introduced to them long ago, when they found themselves completely stuck and at a loss as to where to go next. In other words, they reached the limits of what their current model could explain. Or, in other cases, they realized that what they were doing, what they had been doing for so long, no longer met the best needs of their clients or fit with their own evolving style. Or perhaps they were just bored with routines and longed for something different.

Most of my career I've been a big proponent of gently pointing out discrepancies between client incongruence or inconsistencies. I've believed that people stay stuck because they can get away with it, and my theory is that they will only let go of these dysfunctional patterns when they are confronted with their self-defeating nature. This has worked well for me, and especially for my clients, so my theory has become more robust over the years. Until recently.

Lately I've noticed in the last few cases that clients are less responsive to my "gentle confrontations," a model that has worked so well for me in the past. I've been thinking hard about what's different and I realize that *I'm* the one who is different: I'm older and more intimidating. I can't seem to get away with certain things that worked quite well in the past when I was younger and appeared less threatening. I now must revise, if not rebuild, a new model in light of input I'm getting from annoyed clients who are now telling me by their responses that they don't much appreciate my seeming lack of compassion. One client was so direct as to tell me that if I couldn't control my critical judgment she'd find someone else who was more understanding. This got my attention in such a way that I realized it was time to let go of my current conceptual model and rework it to better match my current functioning and client needs.

Skill Development

Clients become our greatest teachers in terms of guiding our increased competence in a variety of interpersonal skills that are most useful both inside therapy and in our personal relationships. They let us know when we are pushy or nonresponsive to their needs. With some individuals we learn to be so, so careful in how we approach sensitive topics, all the while we monitor their reactions carefully. We learn to confront people so diplomatically they hardly realize that we pointed out some contradiction or discrepancy. From so much systematic and intensive practice we develop incredible fluency in the ways we hear, listen, and respond in conversations. All in all, clients let us know when we are off base or on target. They provide instant feedback on whether they feel heard and understood. And all of this translates into greater mastery of those core helping skills that were first taught in graduate school.

We might remember, for instance, that reflecting feelings was one of the simplest skills that were introduced to us. At first we were leery that such an apparently "primitive" intervention would be of much use, especially when it was presented as a formula that we followed: "You feel_____ because_____." When we first attempted to practice this basic skill, it may have been with the expectation that our clients would become irritated and impatient: "I just said that! You don't have to repeat what I said. I may be suffering, but I'm not an idiot!"

Only later did we realize that although such reflections are indeed basic, and even the bread and butter of what we do, there is nothing we would ever learn that would be more challenging to "get right," meaning to respond to someone at a deep level in such a way that we truly captured the essence of one's felt experience. In such a way that paraphrasing or reflecting content could never touch, we aim for explorations into the disguised, hidden, denied, and disowned feelings that have barely ever reached awareness.

Although I selected this one reflection skill, there are so many others that can only develop with deep practice, the kind that helps us to refine our technique and deepen the accuracy of our interpretations, confrontations, or reframes. The reality after graduate school is that we rarely receive much meaningful feedback from anyone other than our clients. During ongoing supervision we merely report what we think happened in sessions, selectively including only those aspects that we feel are relevant—or safe to disclose. But the only person(s) who are actually in the room are our partners in the process as it unfolds.

Finally, one last example of how our clients influence and impact us is through the almost spiritually transcendent process of deep connection. There are times, admittedly rare, when we can almost read one another's minds. We feel the client's heart beating and soul fluttering. I don't mean to be flakey or unscientific, but it does sometimes feel like an ethereal state of higher order communication. Sometimes we just smile or nod at one another in recognition, as if to say, "Yes, we *do* understand one another in such a way that has not happened previously."

As we will explore further in the next chapter, relationships are almost *everything* in what we do.

Chapter 7

Relationships Are (Almost) Everything!

I've already discussed at length that the theories, concepts, strategies, and techniques we learned in graduate school, however important for our foundational knowledge and skills, have not been as important as our ability to efficiently establish and maintain effective relationships with those we help (and with our colleagues).

There have been all kinds of debates over the years about the optimal kind of relationship that should be developed with clients. Freud promoted a detached, hovering neutrality as the ideal for which we should strive in order to maximize transference effects and keep ourselves out of the fray. Carl Rogers proposed certain core conditions of warmth, unconditional positive regard, respect, genuineness, and caring must be evident in the helping relationship. Behaviorists advocated an objective structure for the therapeutic relationship, one that was focused on systematic, often prescriptive problem solving. Likewise, the strategic and brief therapists also preferred a more collaborative model, but one in which an authority position would be employed to empower interventions. This was in marked contrast to some more contemporary conceptions of the relationship, such as those designed by emotionally focused, feminist, narrative, and relational cultural, in which a far more egalitarian alliance is preferred. Other configurations for the alliance have their own distinct emphases, depending on whether they rely on attachment theory, systemic patterns, interpersonal relations, cognitive schemas, transference processes, motivational interviewing, or others. That's why the most effective and useful therapeutic alliances are so carefully tailored to the client's preferences, expectations, personality and characteristics, reactance/resistance level, cultural background, coping style, attachment style, spiritual beliefs, and the particular stage of therapy.

Despite continued discussion (and conflict) over which kind of relationship is best, we have come to somewhat of a consensus that the answer to this question depends on the individual client, presenting problem, therapist abilities, and pragmatic concerns such as the length of time and resources available (and what is permitted/encouraged) in your work setting. There are obviously some clients who do quite well in a permissive, warm, authentic form of engagement, while others would eat the therapist alive in such circumstances. Someone manifesting "borderline-ish" characteristics (manipulative, controlling, dramatic, exploitive, deceitful) or who has been actively abusing alcohol or drugs would respond best to a different kind of structure in the relationship in which boundaries are enforced consistently and clients are held strictly responsible for their behavior. Other clients, recovering from abuse and neglect, severely traumatized from withholding relationships in the past, might do better with a relationship that is far more comforting and nurturing. In other words, the relationships we create and negotiate with our clients hopefully depend less on our own preferences and instead are designed to meet the needs of a given case. It is thus the therapist's flexibility that seems to be key in constructing an optimal relationship at any moment in time, one that best meets the needs of the situation.

A Good Start

It is a curious phenomenon that even when credible and overwhelming research demonstrates fairly decisively that certain things are terrible for our health, this knowledge doesn't seem to alter behavior the way we imagine it should. For instance, we have known for decades that smoking and obesity will shorten life, if not lead to death, but that doesn't seem to inspire many people to alter their destructive patterns. Likewise, the knowledge that regular exercise prevents all kinds of aging and cognitive deterioration, reduces depression and anxiety, and improves daily functioning and life satisfaction doesn't seem to be enough to keep people maintaining their exercise programs over time. So it is the same in our field in which there is overwhelming evidence that the single most important factor in therapy that predicts success is the alliance that is established (Castonguay & Beutler, 2006; Duncan, Miller, Wampold, & Hubble, 2010; Falkenstrom, Granstrom, & Holmqvist, 2013; Lambert, 2013; Norcross, 2011; Stewart, 2013). It is estimated from various studies to account for far more of successful outcomes than any specific technique or strategy. Unfortunately, as I discussed earlier in relation to researcher and clinician biases, how robust the results might be depends, in part, on the initial allegiance of the investigators (Fluckiger, Del Re, Wampold, & Symonds, 2012).

It's ironic that many of those who most worship at the altar of evidence-based practice seem to ignore the evidence that the relationships they develop with their clients may be just as important, if not more so, than their empirically supported "treatments." Full disclosure: I am as guilty as anyone else of sometimes mistrusting that what I do in sessions is anything more than a sleight of hand. A lovely relationship is nice and all, but it also isn't nearly enough to make a significant difference in the lives of people who are so struggling to keep from drowning in their despair. It turns out that Carl Rogers was wrong: It is not a "necessary and sufficient condition" for change to occur, although it sure as heck is a good start.

Helping Relationships Empower Nonspecific Factors

We can all agree that therapeutic relationships are a means to an ultimate goal. The alliance exists purely as the vehicle by which to help capitalize on those factors that are most associated with lasting change, whether they occur in sessions or in the outside world. When constructed optimally, this alliance makes it possible to deal with aspects of existence that may previously have been denied or ignored.

Among the core ingredients of transformative change that have been identified by researchers and writers (Higginson & Mansell, 2008; Kottler, 1997, 2014; Lampropoulos & Spengler, 2005; Laska, Gurman, & Wampold, 2013; Miller & Rollnick, 2002; Tschacher, Martin, Pfammatter, & Pfammatter, 2014) both within therapy, as well as in the outside world, several common or nonspecific factors have been identified that are only strengthened via the helping relationship. Some of the powerful factors are as follows:

1. *Dissatisfaction with life.* Many of the most distressing symptoms represent signals that something is out of balance and must be addressed. Whether as depression, anxiety, loneliness, or general unhappiness, the negative emotional state draws attention to unresolved issues that are often ignored and usually not talked about very much. The safe and inviting relationships we create become the place to finally bring these problems into the open.

2. *New insights.* As mentioned previously, there are all kinds of ways that therapists promote new understandings and life lessons during sessions, almost all of which take place within an interpersonal context. It is never as simple as just introducing some novel idea, after which the client compliantly and enthusiastically accepts it. There are sometimes spirited discussions and heated debates regarding ideas that may be perceived as threatening—because they often are temporarily destabilizing.

3. *Hitting bottom.* We see people during their times of greatest desperation, when they feel like they've lost everything, including hope. There must be some level of safety and trust before anyone is going to risk letting his or her defenses down.

4. *Keystone behaviors.* The relationship is often used as leverage to persuade clients to take little steps toward ultimate goals. Such tiny, incremental movements often lead to dramatic transformations later on. In all the ways we can think of, we attempt to promote movement and do so through the trust we earn.

5. *Trauma.* Clients bring all kinds of life difficulties into sessions, including trauma, abuse, neglect, illnesses, grief, and losses. The relationship becomes a holding environment to nourish and nurture people during times of maximum vulnerability.

6. *Validation.* Affirmation and support often become the primary felt experience of clients, regardless of what brought them into sessions in the first place. Time and time again we hear their testimony regarding anything that we did for them beyond resolving their initial difficulties: They talk about feeling understood. What makes this so interesting is sometimes we don't feel like we understood them much at all, but it matters little as long as *they* feel validated.

7. *Storytelling.* If you were going to try to explain to a 5-year-old what you do for a living, you might very well say that you are a story listener and a storyteller. As mentioned previously, so much of what we do is honor people's stories within the context of our special relationship. Even more than that, we share stories with them, particularly those that are designed to entertain, enlighten, or reconfigure narratives in a significantly more functional way.

8. *Spiritual transcendence.* There is something about a therapeutic relationship, at least one that is extremely well developed, that seems almost magical. It is as if we can read each other's minds. There is a kind of intimacy that can never quite seem to be replicated anywhere else. Of course, it helps that there is minimal small talk, a promise of complete privacy and confidentiality, and a commitment to speak only about the most meaningful

and present issues of one's life. We often reach a transcendent, almost meditative trance state in which we are completely present in the moment. No distractions. Total investment. Deep listening. And complete immersion in whatever is happening in the moment.

Being Fully Present—Inside and Outside of Sessions

I'm not saying that we necessarily apply what we do in therapy to all our other relationships—alas, it takes far too much energy for that—but we have learned over time this amazing capacity for maintaining that kind of hovering attention when we are engaged with someone. We hear, feel, see, and sense things that would be inaccessible to mere mortal beings. We have developed that rare ability to fully connect with someone, almost anyone, and respond with remarkable presence that leaves little doubt that we are *there* with them.

Felipa remembered learning in her graduate program about the theoretical concepts of authenticity and genuineness, qualities that, while certainly admirable, seemed impossible to ever fully attain. "Sure, it all sounded good to me about being full present," Felipa admitted, "but they were just words that had no resonance. It wasn't until I started seeing clients that the true depth of meaning became far more clear to me."

Felipa spoke passionately about the magic she felt when she was most connected to clients. It is during those times that she is able to suspend critical judgments and completely clear her mind. It is also when she is able to get outside herself to leave her own past trauma and present problems behind. "I've learned that counseling isn't just a job or a profession; it's a lifestyle, a way of being. Just as my presence with and for my clients is the foundation for our work together, it is also what grounds me in my own life."

Felipa is also quite aware of how all of her relationships have been transformed since she began practicing her profession. If she feels inspired to work toward greater authenticity, genuineness, and presence when she is in session, then the same holds true for every other aspect of her life.

Who knew, or imagined, how much *all* of our relationships would become transformed as a result of training to become a therapist? Would we have proceeded anyway if we truly understood the "informed consent" warnings that may (or may not) have been mentioned?

Every fall semester I orient a new cohort of therapy students, and I feel it is my duty to tell them some things about their choice that nobody ever told me about the consequences of being in this profession. The first thing I tell them to get their attention is that becoming a therapist puts every relationship in jeopardy of a major shift. Then I warn them that if they don't bring their families, partners, spouses, and friends along for the ride, they will likely leave them behind.

It is certainly true that we have high standards for intimacy and personal engagement, given what we do for a living. We are used to getting to the point, talking only about meaningful issues, and especially eliciting and sharing deep feelings. Many of our acquaintances, friends, and family members persist in talking about football or basketball, endless gossip, the weather, recipes, their children's latest accomplishments, their annoying in-laws, fruitless attempts to lose weight or stop smoking, exasperation with some new technological advancement, passionate opinions about political figures (often those we despise the most), frustrations with colleagues not doing their fair share of work, or complaints about "the way things are" versus "the way things used to be." I could go on, but this is as familiar to you as it is to me. Furthermore, we admit that it is fun to talk about these things—to a certain extent. But we also often yearn to go deeper, much deeper, to enjoy the kinds of intimate connections we have with our clients extended to those people in our lives we love the most.

Tran, although from a traditional Vietnamese American family, is an extraordinarily emotionally expressive individual and therapist. He speaks from his heart. He wears his feelings visible for anyone to see. He feels everything with great intensity. He conveys passion and genuine caring in all his interactions. When pressed, he isn't quite sure how he turned out that way, considering his parents are so emotionally restrictive, even cold and withholding. He accepts and understands that they are the products of their culture and ancestral ways, but he is much less tolerant of his Chinese wife, who very much resembles the model of restraint that is idealized in his own cultural background.

Even since Tran began training as a therapist he has felt a gulf open up between him and his wife, Mei. As he has continued his work and development, he has noticed that things between them have become even more distant. Every time he tries to broach the subject with her, Mei immediately withdraws; even worse, she starts to cry but won't give voice to the tears except to tell him that it is best not to speak about these things. He has asked her, then begged her, to attend couples therapy, but she adamantly refuses. Although Tran spends his life helping others to work on these exact kinds of issues related to a lack of intimacy, he feels helpless to do anything to alter their own pattern.

"This is not what we agreed," Mei tells him, referring to the ways her husband has changed—and she is absolutely correct in her assessment: Tran is a completely different person than he was before he became a therapist. Even more alarming to him, many other family members, both Chinese and Vietnamese, feel estranged and disappointed because of these American ways that he has adapted for himself. Except it is not so much that Tran has become "Americanized" as he has become "therapistized." He has joined our exclusive club, with its strange rituals and demands that don't fit much at all with the usual ways the rest of the world might function in which discourse is dominated by small talk, evasions, manipulation, and especially a lack of intimacy. It presents all of us with a challenge of straddling both worlds, learning to become patient and accepting in our relationships with others outside of our office. It also puts pressure on us to try to recreate what we create during sessions in our other relationships. Some people really appreciate and love that opportunity; others flee screaming in terror.

In an ideal world, we would truly be able to translate what we know and understand about intimate relationships in all of our interactions. Even if that is neither possible nor perhaps desirable (given how exhausting that would be), we still have extraordinary opportunities to apply our knowledge and skills to many other contexts that would enrich others' lives, not to mention our own. This is certainly the case with regard to all the time we spend in groups and meetings, most of it squandered because of ineffective leadership and dysfunctional dynamics. This would perhaps be understandable if it occurred only in corporate environments in which the people in charge are not necessarily trained in interpersonal skills, but it is almost scandalous how often systemic dysfunction occurs in therapeutic settings.

Relational and Leadership Skills in Everyday Life

I can't stop watching the fingers drumming on the table. From where I sit, slouched in my chair, I have a perfect view of a horizontal slice of the people across from me. I watch their hands moving papers around, clenching, wiggling, dancing, searching for something to occupy themselves. Every so often I see the hands slip down into laps, where they believe they are secretly checking messages on their mobile devices. Everyone is checked out, bored out of their minds, watching the clock whose hands seem frozen in place.

The person running the meeting seems oblivious to what is going on. Or if he notices that nobody is paying much attention, he seems unable or unwilling to change what he's doing. And what he's doing is droning on and on about some issue that nobody cares much about. When he asks if anyone has any input, everyone studiously looks at their hands, everyone except one person who seems to have something to say about almost everything. I know this for a fact because my strategy for managing my own frustration and disengagement is to count the number of times she has spoken during the meeting. So far it's been 61 times, and we've only been in the room for roughly 90 minutes, which means that basically we have a dialogue going on between the leader and her, with the rest of us as spectators.

I've tried to insert a few comments on occasion, not because I have anything meaningful to offer on the subject but rather because I'm just trying to keep myself awake. But since I'm interrupted by the woman every time I speak, I decide to withdraw. Actually I'm pouting.

What's most curious to me is that everyone in the room—well, *almost* everyone—knows exactly what's going on but doesn't say or do anything to change the dynamics of the interaction. The truly startling thing is that everyone in attendance is actually a psychotherapist who spends his or her time supervising and teaching others. In some cases, they even specialize in teaching group therapy, yet they (or I should more accurately say "*we*") insist on remaining oblivious, or at least mute, in the face of obvious group dysfunction. We all allow this unsatisfying pattern to continue week after week. Certainly there is private grumbling and talk behind the scenes but apparently not sufficient annoyance to actually *do* anything to change the interactions.

We've all sat in meetings like this, or been part of various group functions, in which it is clear to anyone who is paying attention that what's going on is not particularly productive and, in some cases, is downright toxic. We live in a world of groups in almost every facet of our lives, whether at work or play, in scheduled meetings or impromptu social gatherings. Whether at dinner parties, family meals, business or neighborhood meetings, political events, parties, classes, consultations, sports teams, conference calls, or on social media, we are required to function as part of a collective.

Despite all the glorification of individualism and singular achievement, human beings evolved to function as part of tribes. What we may lack in strength, speed, and claws, we make up for with our division of labor and collaborations. We take care of one another as a community. We literally watch one another's backs. We have learned to hunt, gather food, seek shelter, build whole cities, and protect ourselves, through extraordinary and unprecedented interpersonal communication. We are among the most social animals on the planet, evolving cooperative strategies that may not rival those of ants or termites, but nevertheless form impressive alliances that allow us to control our environment and increase the probability of our survival. And all this occurs because of the groups we form and the ways those collectives work together toward a common goal.

In order for any group to function reasonably well, if not optimally, there must be some kind of delegated leadership. Ideally, this would operate in such a way that (1) trust and respect are created to maximize safety and encourage participation, (2) all voices are heard so that participants feel a commitment to the decisions and outcomes, (3) proceedings operate efficiently with minimal distractions and unproductive digressions, (4) everyone present remains and feels engaged and a meaningful part of the discussion, (5) consensus is reached on issues that involve compromises without sacrificing effective courses of action, and (6) people leave the group believing that it was helpful if not an enjoyable process. Actually, this description is not an ideal at all but rather what we should consider to be absolutely mandatory in any group of which we are a part.

Alas, sadly, this is hardly the reality that we face in our daily lives. Most meetings feel like a waste of time. Whatever decisions that are made rarely represent a consensus but instead are the result of a few people with the most power or the loudest, most persistent voices. And even those in leadership roles with extensive training and experience don't seem to apply what they know and understand to settings outside therapeutic contexts.

It has always been strange to me how someone, for instance, could stand before a room full of people who are obviously bored and yet continue with an agenda that is clearly not working at all. You look around the room and see people yawning, rolling their eyes, texting, doodling on pads, whispering to one another, even taking little power naps, and yet the speaker keeps going. Don't you wonder why it is that you can see all this unfolding, but the person in the front of the room, who has the best view of all, can't seem to figure out what's going on? Or more likely the case, the person is so locked into a structure that it feels impossible to change what is planned, even in light of overwhelming evidence that it is not working at all.

If there is a life skill that is more important than being able to read, decode, and lead groups, as well as promote more collaborative relationships, I'd like to know what that is. It is this knowledge, expertise, and interpersonal skill that make it possible for us to get anything done. It is what makes a great leader and teacher and therapist and supervisor but also an extraordinary parent or friend. It is what creates the most enjoyment in life, feeling part of a group of like-minded people who function in harmony and joy.

So, if you were leading the meeting that I am required to attend, in which participants are disengaged and bored, in which only a few people dominate the conversation and everyone else is (or feels) marginalized, in which discussions continue *way* longer than they should, meetings run over their scheduled time allotment, and any decisions that are made are rarely followed through with assigned action tasks, what would you do to change these patterns? This is a question you could apply to *any* interpersonal context, and it represents an excellent example of the disconnect between what we are supposedly well-trained to do versus what we actually apply in the real world.

Whether at work or play, whether engaged with a client, stranger, or best friend, our relationships are built and fortified through the stories we share with one another. That is how we create trust and intimacy. It is the way we connect experiences. It is how we teach one another about where we've been, what we've lived and known, and what we've suffered and learned. Most of all, it is how we tell people who we really are. In the chapter that follows we delve more deeply into one of the most important skills of any therapist, or for that matter, any human being, a crucial ability that was virtually ignored in graduate school yet provides the foundation for almost everything we do in the real world.

Chapter 8

Honoring and Telling Stories

Felicia was housebound for months. In actuality, she refused to leave her bed. Her family was understandably concerned, becoming more apprehensive as time went on with absolutely no response to their begging and cajoling. She was the matriarch of their family, a proud and stubborn woman in her seventies, who was used to caring for everyone else in her large extended family. Her son had died unexpectedly and she was so grief-stricken she refused to get out of bed. This had been going on for two months and in response to anyone who pleaded with her, she replied simply that it was God's will.

Rako, the therapist assigned to the case, visited Felicia in her home because she wouldn't leave her bed for help. He sat at her bedside and tried to learn more about what was going on. He pointed to the photograph of Felicia's son, sitting on the bed table, and asked her what he'd been like.

"He was my last hope," she said with a sigh. And then she refused to say anything further.

Rako tried everything he could think of to convince Felicia to reconsider her position, becoming increasingly frustrated. He used logic to challenge her assumptions. He talked to her about the health problems that could result without movement or exercise.

He reflected back to her what he imagined she must be feeling. He presented persuasive arguments for how she was hurting others, as well as herself. He tried to use the leverage of their relationship to get out of bed for his sake, because she was making him look bad. She smiled sadly but refused to budge. Literally.

"God will tell me when it is time to get out of bed," Felicia explained quite firmly, ending the discussion.

Rako nodded in understanding and just sat silently by her bedside. "I wonder if you'd like to hear a story?" he finally asked her.

The woman shrugged as if she could care less, one way or the other.

"There once was a man of great faith who lived alone in a big house not far from the Missouri River. It had begun to rain, day after day, sheets of water flowing into the bulging river, flooding its banks."

Felicia sat up in bed, puffed her pillows, and arranged them more comfortably behind her back. It was clear to Rako that she was listening carefully.

"The residents in the town were warned by the police, and by the local media, to evacuate the area because of the threat of severe flooding. Although her neighbors all followed the order, one woman refused to leave her home. This was where she had been born, where she spent her life, and she wasn't going to move come hell or high water.

"As the water level continued to rise, swallowing everything in its path, the police visited the woman's home to instruct her to leave immediately. She stubbornly refused, insisting that if indeed her life was in jeopardy, God would save her. She had been a servant of God her whole life."

As Felicia was listening to Jamie talk, she couldn't help but nod her head and smile in recognition. She knew *exactly* how the woman in the story must have felt.

"The rains continued, and with them, the flooding became even more severe, moving relentlessly across the area. The water had, by this point, started to creep up to the doorway of the woman's house, then seep onto the bottom floor. By this time, the woman had started to move her belongings up to the second floor, and she was found standing in her bare feet in puddles of water when the fire department arrived by rowboat to check on her.

"So, what happened then?" Rako's client asked. "Did she get out? Was she okay?"

Rako smiled and held out a hand to be patient as he finished the story. "The woman still refused to leave. She told the rescuers standing in her doorway that she'd be fine, that God would take care of her.

"The floods kept coming and the water kept rising, forcing the woman to retreat upstairs and eventually to climb up on the roof. She was balanced precariously on top by the chimney when a helicopter hovered overhead, signaling that they'd come to rescue her. But she waved frantically back, yelling that she was fine, that God would take care of her, that if she was truly in danger God would save her."

"So, then what happened?" Felicia asked. "Did God save her?"

Rako shook his head. "No, actually she died. The flood carried her away."

"Really?"

"Yes, she perished. But here's where the story gets really interesting."

Felicia leaned forward, listening intently.

"The woman arrived in Heaven and met God for the first time. "'Why didn't you save me?' she asked God. 'I've devoted my whole life to my unwavering belief in you. I put all my trust in you. Why didn't you rescue me?'"

"God shook His head sadly. 'But I *did* try to save you! First I sent the police to your house. Then the fire department. And finally I sent a helicopter. But you turned them all away.'"

Rako heard his client gasp in recognition. He had thought she might laugh at the story but instead she was sitting up in bed, wide-eyed. "That was a pretty good story," she said, then waved Rako away.

A few days later Rako arrived to check on Felicia and found, to his surprise, that she greeted him at the door and offered to make him a sandwich as soon as he walked in.

In reflecting on what happened, Rako realized that he'd learned an important lesson that had never been part of his education. "I learned that telling a story can be more powerful than anything I could ever do to help someone. I think it helps when it is a 'natural' story that arises from the conversation rather than one pulled out of a bag. I try to listen really carefully to my clients, as well as to myself, and sometimes I flash on a story that seems appropriate or relevant. I trust that this is sometimes exactly what a client needs to break through the resistance."

Therapy as an Exchange of Stories

If there is one aspect of being a therapist that was virtually ignored in graduate school—and most training opportunities since then—it is the role we play as storytellers. Yes, it is true that narrative therapies have brought increased attention to the power of narrative in constructing perceived reality. It is also the case that almost every other form of therapy makes some attempt to help clients alter the stories they tell themselves (and others) about their predicament. Cognitive therapies challenge the stories embedded in self-talk. Ericksonian therapy introduces metaphorical tales. Solution-focused therapy reframes the stories that clients bring into sessions, reshaping them into more manageable problems. Psychodynamic therapy explores the stories from the past that shape present symptoms. Feminist and constructionist therapies look at the ways that culture has colonized clients into adapting certain stories about who they are. Every conceptual model has its own language and approach to the ways that experience is interpreted not so much by what actually happened as the stories we tell ourselves about those experiences.

And yet nothing quite prepared us for the reality that therapy is really all about the exchange of stories, those we hear and those we tell (Kottler, 2015). If there is one skill that was most neglected, if not completely ignored, during our training, it was how to become fabulous storytellers, the kind who can spin tales designed to persuade, influence, and move clients through the subtle processes of vicarious identification and the underlying neurophysiological effects sparked by mirror neurons.

Stories Are Real—and the Means by Which the Brain Learns and Remembers

There are a series of research studies investigating the architecture of the brain, especially as humans adapt to their environment and cement critical learning that is necessary for survival. It is primarily through mirror neurons that not only empathy has evolved as a way for us to relate to others' experience but also to enjoy the benefits of vicarious learning (Hess, 2012; Iacoboni, 2008; Marshall, 2014; Nigham, 2012; Rizzolatti & Craighero, 2004). In other words, we can have all kinds of adventures, take incredible risks, live in a hundred other countries, experience a thousand other lives, slay dragons, fight wars, have affairs, hit a home run in the World Series, catch serial killers, meet aliens, travel in space or under the sea, and get inside the minds of the greatest thinkers who have ever lived—all without ever leaving the safety and comfort of a chair.

The brain is primarily a storied organ that has evolved in such a way that memories, actions, events, experiences, even dreams, are converted from fragments and images into relatively coherent narratives that are stored and later retrieved (Elder & Holyan, 2010; Gottschall, 2012; Herman, 2013; Hsu, 2008). This is what allows us to access a whole assortment of lessons, past history, and collective experiences so that we may more effectively navigate the dangers of the world. It is also the foundation of so much of what we do in therapy when we relate or create stories that help clients develop new understandings about themselves and the world (Bergner, 2007; Cronin, 2001; Greenberg, 2008; Ingemark, 2013; Kottler, 2015; Polkinghorne, 2013).

Although we were exposed in graduate school to all kinds of basic concepts and fancy techniques, the single most important set of skills are those we actually use more often in the real world—using stories to sidestep client resistance and peak their interest in such a way that they find it difficult to ignore the lessons presented. Recently I was trying all kinds of ways to explain to a client that it wasn't in her best interests to continue waiting for her "friend" (she wasn't allowed to refer to him as a boyfriend) to let go of his dependence on his ex-wife and commit to a new relationship. She was only involved with him to the extent he would permit, which included all kinds of barriers and rules. She was not allowed to meet his children. She could only see him when *he* decided he was available but never when she was interested in doing so. It seemed fairly obvious (at least to me) that this relationship was going nowhere and that it was a source of endless anguish that was going to continue indefinitely.

Each time I tried to broach the subject of renegotiating the terms of this relationship, or at the very least, expressing her dissatisfaction with the status quo, she would become angry with me and accuse me of not being very understanding. I suppose this was true. So I had no choice but to back off, even though she would continue to relate examples of how she felt neglected and abused. As I listened to her, I would feel more and more helpless and frustrated, echoing her own unacknowledged feelings.

Finally one day I began the session by telling her a story of a time in college when I was involved with a woman who pulled all the strings. I was at her beck and call but was so smitten with her I felt powerless to do anything other than cater to her whims and unreasonable demands. It wasn't just the relationship that was the problem but that I also noticed contagious effects on the way I felt about myself—essentially unworthy of being with someone who valued me in any other way than a slave. I related to my client how I never found the courage to end the relationship but got dumped when my girlfriend replaced me with someone else who was even more compliant.

"So, what are you saying?" she lashed back at me, "that I'm going to get dumped, too?"

"Not at all. On the contrary, I'm saying that I *do* know what you might be going through and my impatience with you that you've noticed and pointed out is partially related to my own wounds that I still carry. I believe there is a way that you can do far better than me and perhaps even renegotiate a different relationship with your friend. I think you can learn something from the mistakes I made when I accepted that I never deserved anything different or better."

This sort of self-disclosing story is risky in some ways because the focus is taken off the client and put on the therapist. You might feel the same way in parts of this book when I share some personal experience that you find self-indulgent or find yourself wondering, "Why are you telling me that?"

In this case, however, the main point of the story was to earn back my client's trust. She had been right on target when she accused me of being impatient and not understanding what she felt. I can't tell you the end of this story quite yet because it is ongoing, but I will tell you that it did make a huge difference in our relationship. I happen to know this because she may have "forgotten" so many other things I brought up in sessions and tried to teach her, but she never forgot this story, which she brought up several times afterward. It became a turning point in the connection we felt to one another.

There are so many other ways that a story could have been brought into the session that was configured very differently. I could have created a metaphor to more indirectly address her issues, perhaps a tale of a spurned princess who was kept locked up at night in a castle even though she was allowed to roam free for several hours a day in the most luscious garden accompanied by her true love. I could have introduced a story of someone with a similar predicament who chose not to complain about the situation but instead just accept things as they are. The options are endless, but the point I wish to make is that this is really what we do so much of the time, think of ways that we can touch our clients, persuade them to do things that they wish to avoid, and do so without encountering resistance.

Features and Functions of Storytelling in Therapy

We hear stories, read stories, and digest stories in dozens of different ways every day. We read books, watch movies and televisions shows, plays and operas. Even song lyrics tell stories of love and disappointment, triumph and tragedies. The most memorable speakers we've ever heard—and most skilled therapists we know—are consummate storytellers who can regale a listener or audience with a particular tale that is captivating and powerfully memorable. Just consider the stories that have most impacted your own life, those that may have even guided you to your current profession. Review the stories of your childhood that haunt you to this day, whether from books, television, films, media, or family anecdotes. Inventory those stories that have been most enduringly influential, and they were likely those that had certain features that we would try to replicate in sessions to maximize their effects.

How Stories Operate in Therapy

- Captures attention and interest through provocation and intense stimulation
- Follows natural structural and functional properties of memory
- Presents "coded" information in efficient package
- Provides a different form of "direct experience" through vicarious identification
- Evokes strong emotional reactions that inspire, motivate, or ignite passion
- Induces altered states of consciousness and hypnotic inductions through immersion in narrative
- Resonates with cultural and historical traditions within community, tribe, and social/political/environmental context
- Bypasses resistance and defensiveness through subtle introduction of concepts and ideas
- Appeals to multiple dimensions of complexity and cognitive processing
- Facilitates recognition of patterns across life experiences
- Provides a digestible and palatable meaningful diagnosis that is also destigmatizing
- Introduces overarching, organizing scaffolds to understand phenomena and life experiences
- Presents a canvas upon which clients can create their own work of art to capture their experiences

- Introduces alternative realities (fantasy) that facilitate creative thinking
- Teaches significant adaptation and problem-solving skills through vicarious experiences
- Presents alternative pathways and options for viewing problems and their solutions
- Accesses unconscious processes
- Externalizes problems
- Provides opportunities for rehearsal of new behavior through surrogates
- Self-disclosures reduce power imbalance and humanize the therapist in addition to modeling deep sharing
- Reveals courageous tales of survival and achievement that may be inspiring
- Promotes restitution, renewal, and redemption when stories are recast in own life narrative
- Holds staying power that haunts clients in ways that direct advice or information can't touch
- Assists in existential search for meaning of life path
- Fosters higher level of moral development and ethical decision making
- Creates "secret" passwords that act as reminders and reinforcements of prior insights
- Provides adjuncts to sessions that support lessons learned or challenge dysfunctional beliefs
- Leads to critical evaluation of parallel issues that might otherwise feel threatening
- Promotes wisdom, tolerance, and flexibility in thinking about self, others, and the world
- Becomes a contagious narrative "virus" that reproduces and is transmitted to others
- Encapsulates the mystery of change, including features and processes that we will never fully understand

Each one of us has our own priorities, assumptions, values, goals, and styles that we employ in our therapeutic work. Likewise, each client presents a different set of interests, needs, complaints, and expectations that we attempt to address. Given that they also have different and unique cultural backgrounds reflecting their gender, ethnicity, sexual orientation, religion, and other influences, plus distinctive personalities, we adapt storytelling in various ways. For those therapists who identify as narrative therapists, stories might be introduced to externalize problems. Existential or person-centered therapists might employ more personal stories to emphasize their authenticity and genuineness. Cognitive therapists tell stories that emphasize and reinforce personal control over thoughts and feelings. Spiritually based therapists, and those influenced by indigenous practices, present stories that honor the mystery in human experience. And although it might seem as if these functions are restricted only to particular theoretical orientations, the reality is that we are all a lot more flexible than we might believe or claim to others.

Lest you feel some question and doubts about the power that stories can have on individuals, or even events on a global scale, there have been many instances in which a particular book or story has actually changed the world (Downs, 1983). Consider the ways that stories from the Old Testament, New Testament, Torah, Koran, and other religious volumes have been so influential in shaping beliefs and values. Machiavelli's *The Prince* helped free Italy from oppression. Thomas Paine's *Common Sense* helped launch the American Revolution, which, in turn, inspired the French Revolution. Thoreau's *On Civil Disobedience* inspired Mahatma Gandhi. Harriet Beecher Stowe's *Uncle Tom's Cabin* helped spark the American Civil War. Upton Sinclair's *The Jungle* led to union rights, and Rachel Carson's *Silent Spring* pushed for environmental activism. The list goes on and on.

One intriguing aspect of the power of storytelling is that the stories themselves don't necessarily have to be accurate or true. There have been many biased and slanted reports in the media, rumors and innuendo, urban myths, even fabricated stories that have no basis whatsoever in reality, yet they still exert tremendous influence on public opinion and behavior. Wars have been launched as a result of nothing more than gossip. Likewise, the stories that are told in therapy—by therapists or clients—may not really be as they seem. That may seem obvious and yet the whole premise of helping and healing, at least as we were originally taught, is based on a degree of mutual honesty and authenticity.

When Stories Deceive, Manipulate, Exaggerate, and Lie

Among the aspects of therapy that were almost never mentioned in graduate school, but nevertheless becomes a salient issue during clinical practice, is that what we sometimes hear and see in sessions is not necessarily an accurate representation of what is true and real. I'm not talking about unconscious distortions, defense mechanisms, and things that clients "forget" to tell us, but rather deliberate misrepresentations and outright lies that are far more common than we could imagine. Some clients, as a function of their psychopathology, or just plain orneriness, tend to leave out significant information, minimize or hide things, exaggerate complaints, or sometimes create whole fantasy worlds to mislead or entertain us.

We are quite aware that the stories that people tell about themselves are often biased and skewed, often having little correlation to what may have actually happened (Newman & Strauss, 2003). Spence (1984) was one of the first writers to speak eloquently about all the levels of translation that take place during a therapeutic encounter. The client tells a story that is not remembered completely accurately in the first place. Then once converted into language, there is considerable information lost, exacerbated by the therapist hearing what was said in another limited and slanted way. These stories may help construct the sense of self and create meaning, but that doesn't mean they are even remotely reflective of actual incidents and experiences (Adler, Wagner, & McAdams, 2007; Bruner, 1990; McAdams, 1993, 2006).

What's interesting about all this is how much we depend on the stories presented to do our work. When a client tells us that he is depressed because of a job loss, or traumatized because of battle fatigue, or anxious because of early abuse, we tend to believe what we are told and operate accordingly. And according to narrative, constructive, and postmodern therapists, it may not matter all that much if the events described really happened as they were related or whether the client just *believes* this is the case. After all, there is no absolute truth with respect to human experience and memory, certainly in a way that it can ever be verified as "facts" (Gergen, 1991; Hansen, 2007; Mahoney, 1991). There is also a kind of "storytelling effect" that is part of any recollection, retrieval, and sharing of a narrative, one in which what is remembered changes shape over time, with each telling, making it difficult to distinguish between fact and fiction (Birch, Kelln, & Aquino, 2006; McGregor & Holmes, 1999).

Perhaps it shouldn't be all that surprising that clients deceive us or lie considering that such behavior is so common in everyday life, estimated to range from a dozen to over 200 times per day (Ekman, 2009). People lie a lot. They tell little white lies and big whoppers. They make stuff up to inflate their ego or increase their status. They lie to hide things that might be shameful or embarrassing. They lie to protect others. They lie sometimes because it is fun to fool people (especially therapists!). They lie because they can't help it. They lie every hour of every day—to others but, most of all, to themselves. So it shouldn't be all that much of a shock to discover that our clients are lying to us some (or a lot) of the time.

And believe me, there are some doozies. In a previous project, I (Kottler, 2010; Kottler & Carlson, 2011) asked experienced therapists to share examples of times in which they were hoodwinked, and the cases they related were both hilarious and disturbing. One client actually stole his therapist's identity; another took on the identities of various law enforcement personnel so he could visit crime scenes (and he actually helped solve crimes!). Another client was working on end-of-life issues as she was dying of a terminal disease and was confined to a wheelchair—only the therapist saw her walking around town perfectly healthy. The therapists described instances in which their clients faked symptoms, pretended to be someone they were not, and in some cases, hid all kinds of crucial information that would have actually helped them to recover.

There are a lot of different diagnoses we use to describe clients who tell less than accurate stories about themselves. There are various personality disorders (borderline, histrionic, sociopathic) that fit that description, as well as degenerative diseases (Korsakov syndrome) and factitious disorders (Gander or Munchausen syndrome). But in most cases there is nothing more complex going on than the client fears shame or humiliation or doesn't trust the therapist or wish to disappoint him or her.

When clients are asked afterward why they chose to lie so baldly to their therapists, often compromising their own treatment, they offer explanations such as the following:

- "I don't really trust you yet, and I'm not even sure you can help me."
- "I was kind of embarrassed to talk to you about certain things because I thought you'd criticize me like everyone else does."
- "I thought it would come out wrong and you wouldn't understand."
- "I know this sounds weird but you seem to know so much all the time and it felt good to fool you."
- "I don't know why I did that. I think I just wanted to hide for a while. It felt good to pretend that things were different than they really are."

Perhaps in one way it makes perfect sense that clients would tell stories that don't necessarily present complete accuracy. The main issue is what sense we make of the behavior, as well as what to do about it. It's hard not to take it personally and feel like we were somehow duped because of our naïveté or incompetence (which could sometimes be the case). Our job is to work with the story, whether partially fictitious or not, to help the client save face, and look at the deception in the context of the particular relationship.

Therapeutic Use of Stories

The best conversations in general, and therapy sessions in particular, involve an exchange of stories in which participants honor and respond to one another's narratives, collaborating in a sense on a shared consensus. The client begins by telling a story in which he is the victim of circumstances outside of his control: "I don't really need to be here but my parents told me that unless I come to see you I can't live with them anymore. Sure, I've got a few problems but no more than anyone else."

"I see," you respond, realizing in that moment you can't work much with that version of the situation. "So, what you're saying is that the real problem is with your parents. They have a different set of expectations regarding what you should be doing."

"You could say that," he says with a shrug, not sure where you're going with this.

"I recall feeling something similar when I was your age and that led to a lot of conflict at home, at least until I was willing to move on and establish my own independence."

And so you are off and running, presenting alternate perspectives that may or may not be embraced, but at least there is a dialogue regarding other possible ways of looking at things. It is at this point that a therapist could guide things in a variety of different directions but regardless of where the session heads it will involve each participant sharing a story that is designed to persuade the other one to jump on board.

First and foremost, therapists of every style help their clients to tell their story—and do so in a way that they feel fully understood. In today's current climate of distracted attention, anyone is fortunate to complete a sentence without being interrupted by a text, call, or intrusion. It has become rare that people have the opportunity, much less an attentive listener, who will devote complete attention to the conversation. Mobile devices have become so commonplace and ever present that clients are starved for undivided attention. Even when troubled and in excruciating pain, seeking the care of a health professional, the average patient has less than 20 seconds to tell her story before being interrupted by the doctor, and only 2% will ever be given the chance to eventually finish. And as if that isn't frustrating enough to not feel heard, less than half of patients leave the office visit confused about what the doctor recommended (Levine, 2004).

Helping clients to tell their stories is certainly cathartic, and almost always revealing, but it is usually not nearly enough to transform their versions of events into a far more self-enhancing internalized narrative. One definition of trauma is that it represents a "disordered story," a series of fragmented, distorted memories that have yet to be fully processed and remain stuck in a recursive, haunting loop (Cummings, 2011; Joseph, 2011; Neimeyer, 2012). During such traumatic experiences, brain functions associated with memory and language are shut down, leading to intrusive re-experiencing of the events as well as distorted recall. Clients are unable to form coherent narratives, much less tell their stories.

Our job is often to help clients refashion a different story than the one they've been telling themselves (and others), a narrative in which they abandon the role of victim and instead become a courageous survivor who has developed greater resilience and adaptive skills. This is consistent with much of the current practice in narrative and constructivist therapies developed by Michael White and other colleagues.

So, let's be clear: We don't just listen to clients' stories; we also *do* something with them. The particular response or action we might take certainly depends on desired goals, as well as theoretical orientation, but there are still some relatively universal applications of storytelling in therapy, few of which were part of our original training.

"There Once Was a Frog": Use of Metaphors

Metaphors have been an integral part of teaching, writing, mentoring, and therapy ever since conversations were first used to instruct or heal people. We think in metaphors and employ them in all kinds of ways to capture complex ideas. Although every system of therapy utilizes metaphors in some form, it was probably the Ericksonian therapists who contributed a systematic framework for creating those that are programmed to be maximally influential (Lankton & Lankton, 1989). Many other writers (Burns, 2005, 2007; Gordon, 1978; Lakoff & Johnson, 2003; Malhotra, 2014) have also described ways metaphors can be incorporated into therapy to enliven sessions and access unconscious processes.

Raise your hand if you were taught how to utilize metaphors with clients.

I'm guessing that might not have been included in the curriculum, even though it is such a significant part of the most complex, deep work that we do with clients and such an integral part of some forms of brief therapy. Perhaps one reason why it isn't usually included in the first place is because of the difficulty in teaching people how to create useful metaphors. Another reason is that the best metaphors often emerge in the moment, a co-created story that includes the details and descriptions most relevant to a client's needs. Yet every experienced therapist also creates and collects a whole catalogue of time-tested stories that can be plugged into a conversation as needed. It is as if we each have a "playlist" of favorites that fit any situation or mood (and this was a metaphor in itself).

"That Reminds Me of a Time": Self-Disclosure

Not every practitioner would use much self-disclosure, concerned that it might breach boundaries, pollute transference processes, or simply take the focus off clients who are already used to not getting much attention in their lives. Indeed, therapists talking about themselves is among the most common ways that our narcissism rears its ugly, demanding head. There are those among us who use their position to tell endless stories of their triumphs and greatness, all the while they reinforce their clients' own sense of relative worthlessness. I suppose that's why I often tend to focus on telling stories that feature my doubts and imperfections.

I remember sitting in lectures or supervision sessions listening to mentors sing their own praises, share stories of their miracle cures, present seeming impossible cases that they managed to figure out and work through because of their singular brilliance. I recall so many workshops I've attended in which the presenters show videos of these hopeless, intractable cases that I can't imagine doing much with myself and then—Voila!—they apply some newfangled idea or technique they are selling to the audience and there is an instant resolution. The stories they tell are designed to support and reinforce the idea that they have discovered the "true path" and that what I've been doing until this point is obsolete, if not evidence of my incompetence. Then I'd go back to my office and try whatever was introduced and it would almost never work out as advertised. Naturally I blamed myself for my own inability to master what was supposedly a foolproof system.

Notice your own reactions as you read this example. I just told a self-disclosing story, completely accurate, that (hopefully) resonated with your own experience and validated your own frustrations with aspects of our profession in which we laud our successes but rarely talk about our doubts. When was the last time you attended a workshop in which the presenter showed a video of the approach failing miserably and the client becoming furious, threatening to sue the presenter for incompetence?

Of course, by revealing my own doubts and uncertainties, I risk losing credibility, which is why we have to be very careful about the personal stories we share, especially those that reveal our humanness. Sometimes that can often be too much of a good thing. And that is also why self-disclosures must always be used judiciously, briefly, and only when we can't think of another way of getting a point across.

"I Knew Someone Who Had a Similar Problem": Teaching Tales

Whether based on films we've watched, previous clients we've seen, friends we've known, articles we encountered, or books we've read, we often encourage and support clients by telling them about cases similar to their own in which creative or alternative solutions were created to resolve or mediate the difficulties. Even with respect to severe emotional disorders, there is a whole catalogue of literature describing first-person accounts of struggles such as William Styron's *Darkness Visible*, Sylvia Plath's *The Bell Jar*, Kay Jamison's *An Unquiet Mind*, Sylvia Nasar's *A Beautiful Mind*, Austin Burrough's *Running With Scissors*, and so many others.

They may not all have happy endings, but they do help clients feel like they are not alone in their struggles.

One of the advantages of group therapy is the universality that develops over time in which clients feel like they are no longer alone in their struggles. We attempt to generalize and re-story individual concerns in such a way that almost everyone can relate. "When you say that what you want to work on in this group is to lose weight and improve your body image, what you are also saying is that there are aspects of your life that you don't feel in control of. Others have said that they wish to feel more in control of individuals in their family, their work situations, or addictions that have remained persistent. So even though there might, at first, seem to be quite different problems, you all share this commitment to face aspects of yourself that have been a problem for some time."

This might be a stretch, but it does build connections between people and help them to realize that although they may be troubled, they don't need to feel shame about being the only ones. During individual sessions, without access to others in the room, we attempt to bring in universality by sharing stories about others who have faced similar struggles. Sometimes this introduces creative ideas for resolving the difficulties, but at the very least it encourage hope.

"Instead of Him Hurting Your Feelings, Don't You Mean You Overpersonalized What He Said?": Reinterpretations

Therapists of most orientations utilize alternative interpretations of client stories, even if they are configured in different ways. Cognitive therapists and rational-emotive therapists, in particular, focus on challenging the ways that clients talk to themselves internally, just as they correct the language that is used to describe events. Whereas this approach might work to help internalize control, other approaches such as narrative therapy would work in the opposite direction to offer another interpretation of experience in which symptoms are *externalized* instead. Strategic and brief therapists, who may seek to avoid interpretations altogether because of a belief that insight isn't all that necessary or even useful, nevertheless use reframing as their preferred means to reshape the stories that clients tell themselves.

"I have a terrible temper," the client says with a helpless sigh. "I just can't help it. All the men in my family are this way."

This client was referred by the courts because of repeated altercations that have led the police to intervene. He genuinely wishes he could change this pattern but believes that this is an ingrained trait that is impervious to any shift. When challenged about the validity of this assumption, he has mentioned a number of excuses, that his family has both Irish and Italian roots and that he was born with a bad temper, and then proceeds to relate story after story of how he used to throw temper tantrums as a child.

This self-diagnosis is likely to be reframed: "When you say you have a bad temper, I think you mean you express feelings fluently."

The client's puzzled and resistant response to this interpretation invites the therapist to elaborate on an alternative way of looking at the behavior, one in which potential control is indeed possible and that he is not really a helpless victim of his genes.

"That Reminds Me of a Book (or Movie or TV Show) You Might Find Interesting": Bibliotherapy

Virtually all therapists recommend books to their clients, whether self-help volumes or fictional tales (Norcross, 2006). Ironically, the books that are specifically designed to provide guidance for various troubles aren't nearly as impactful as reading novels in which people suspend disbelief, quiet their critical voice, and experience high levels of emotional arousal that cement memories and help with vicarious identification (Burns, 2008; Djikic, Oatley, Zoeterman, & Peterson, 2009; Levitt, Rattanasampan, Chaidaroon, Stanley, & Robinson, 2009; Mar & Oatley, 2008; Paul, 2012; Strange, 2002). Furthermore, the enduring effects of fictional stories become magnified over time, whereas nonfiction and self-help books often lessen their impact (Appel, 2008; Appel & Richter, 2007; Mar, Oatley, Djikic, & Mullin, 2011). Fictional stories, whether made up on the spot or recommended in the forms of books, serve a number of adaptive functions.

Adaptive Functions of Fictional Stories
- Provide vicarious experiences and alternative possibilities
- Supply strategic data without risk
- Prepare defensive responses against perceived threats
- Interpret hidden motives and innermost thoughts
- Train cognitive flexibility
- Encourage reflection of deep issues
- Promote empathy and identification with others' experience
- Spark emotional arousal that aids memory retention

The powerful and persuasive effects of fiction are not just confined to books. Many therapists are quite aware that films can have equal impact if not become even more emotionally arousing (Hesley & Hesley, 2001; Schulenberg, 2003; Solomon, 2001; Wedding & Niemiec, 2003; Wooder, 2008). A therapist might recommend watching Denzel Washington in the movie *Flight* for those struggling with alcoholism or addictions. *Silver Linings Playbook*, *A Beautiful Mind*, or *Girl Interrupted* might be prescribed for those suffering severe mental disorders. Likewise, certain television shows highlight particular themes that arise during sessions and bring fertile areas of discussion into the light.

What this means for the practice of therapy is that rather than recommending only self-help books to our clients, we should be thinking more creatively about utilizing fictional stories that operate far more subtly and activate emotional processes. Instead of only suggesting that a client read some volume on stress management, we could also mention particular novels that feature protagonists who are suffering from similar problems in their lives. The vicarious identification that often takes place can be just as healing as anything we could do in session. In fact, many people, when asked about a particular life event that transformed their life, often point to a particular book that was instrumental in sparking quantum changes that last until this day (Kottler, 2013, 2015).

Consider the impact that a story has had in your life and perhaps even the trajectory of your career. This could have been a fairy tale, myth, or legend you encountered as a child. It could have been sparked by a comic book, puppet show, song lyrics, play, opera, documentary film, movie, television show, short story, novel, or a story told to you by someone else. Regardless of its source, this story continues to haunt you to this day and is perhaps in some way responsible for who you have become.

Just as revealing, what is a story that you frequently tell someone new that you meet, someone who you want to truly *know* you? Likewise what is a story that you frequently find yourself telling clients to illustrate some favored idea, to inspire, motivate, or support them in some way? This could include a metaphor, teaching tale, self-disclosure, or other anecdote.

Developing the Capacity to Become a Better Storyteller

Considering that we were never taught how to tell great stories in graduate school, and there are few opportunities to learn how to do this at professional conferences and therapist workshops, this is one of those skills that requires systematic study and commitment on our own. The task begins with expanding interests to include more great fictional novels into our weekly diet. I've often wondered whether if we really want to advance our development we should limit the number of books we actually read in the field (like this one) and instead read more novels.

I must confess that I've become frustrated and impatient with many of the articles and books published in our discipline, and it is rare that I find something enduringly useful. Perhaps I should admit that this might reflect my own limitations rather than representing an indictment of the quality of works. Nevertheless, I make a point to read a novel each week, and I find more than anything else at this later stage in my career that this is what empowers my therapeutic work and sparks my creative imagination. It is true that I suspend my critical judgment and enter an alternative world of fiction where anything is possible. But it is also the case that I get some incredible ideas for how to tell more persuasive stories myself.

There are a number of resources that are especially useful for studying the features of best-told stories, that is, those that are most persuasive and memorable. Some of these are classic studies of the subject, including those by Bettelheim (1976) about the power of fairy tales and Rosen (1982) deconstructing the operative features of Milton Erickson's hypnotic tales. In addition, there have been additional contributions to help guide therapists in their further development as storytellers (Burns, 2001; Gottschall, 2011; Hoyt, 2013; Lankton & Lankton, 1989; Mehl-Madrona, 2010; Roberts & Holmes, 1999; Spaulding, 2011; Zipes, 2006). In a later chapter we will discuss how some of the ideas can be applied to doing presentations and or speaking to audiences, but for now we'll review a few of the most important components of any storytelling enterprise, regardless of whether you are talking to a client, a large group, or your own family members.

Be Dramatic, Passionate, Flamboyant, and Expressive

As a rule, we have been taught to present ourselves as calm, collected, measured, and soothing. Our voice is softly modulated, our manner controlled. Yet in the real world the best storytellers are crazily dramatic. They act out the action, pantomime gestures of characters, and get totally into the roles that are played out. They use their voice, body, facial expressions, gestures, movements, sound effects, props, even costume changes, to make the story come alive.

I've been privileged to have some incredible editors during my career as a writer; some of them served as muses and editors for some my favorite writers of dialogue like Tom Robbins, Hunter Thompson, and John Cleese. What I learned along the way is that it is far better to "show" what is happening than "tell" it through narrative. This is accomplished primarily through dialogue, that is, using conversations in various voices to illustrate the character traits or actions that are described.

I could describe to you how confused and overwhelmed I felt seeing a client who is decompensating and experiencing a breakdown, or I could *show* you what happened.

"Last week you were saying that you were having a hard time after losing your job and wondering how you would support yourself."

She nodded her head. At least I think she did. It was hard to tell because she was staring over my shoulder at the blank wall, seemingly fascinated by its emptiness. "Oh, yeah," she barely whispered. "Guess so."

"I'm sorry. I couldn't quite hear you."

"The refrigerator." She said this word forcefully, enunciating each syllable carefully: re-fridge-er-ate-tor.

"Excuse me?"

"Never mind," she answered. She started shaking her head back and forth, back and forth, almost vibrating.

And so continues a very bizarre, unpredictable conversation in which you can easily place yourself in my chair and wonder what you would do in a similar situation. If I do my job well as the storyteller, the scene comes alive for you, as if you are *there*, in the room.

Access All the Senses of Sound, Smell, Sight, and Touch, Placing the Listener in the Story

One reason why great stories are so powerfully influential is because they make the reader or listener or viewer feel as if she is actually experiencing what is happening. While doing research for a book about entertainment violence, I studied many of the theories and investigations why people are so attracted to stories of serial killers, murder, catastrophes, apocalypses, alien invasions, vampire stalkings, and zombie attacks (Kottler, 2011). It turns out that when fully immersed in a film or book or true crime story, it is as if what is unfolding is absolutely real and we have actually entered the story as an active participant. This is one reason why interactive video games are increasingly popular and why there is such endless enthusiasm for stories about zombie or alien invasions. When watching a particularly riveting film, for instance, your heart is pounding, real tears are aroused, and for a few hours it feels like you are inside the film being chased or doing the chasing. Then, when the lights come on, you survived!

You had the opportunity to really feel what it must have been like to defeat a villain or recover from some crisis, all while sitting comfortably in a chair.

My whole interest in this subject emerged from my own guileless ability to enter into stories as if they were real. I had been zipping through a wonderfully engaging series of zombie apocalypse novels, and the stories were so well told that they truly came alive for me. I could smell the decay of putrid bodies. I could see and hear what was happening. I was so haunted I could barely sleep at night, but I still couldn't put the books down.

Then one day, as I was going for my usual morning run, another runner approached me to offer a high five to celebrate our dedication to fitness on such a beautiful day. Although at first I was delighted by the expression of camaraderie, which so rarely happens among runners, I then started thinking that maybe he has just passed along an infectious virus. I knew this was insane. I knew my overactive imagination was working overtime, but I still kept wiping my hand on my shirt, whispering to myself not to touch my face until I could get home and sterilize my hand. This is the power of a well-told story. It haunts us. It infects us. It won't let us go. It moves us emotionally, stimulating intense experiences that feel as real as anything we live in daily life. And that is the kind of stories we want to share with clients so they are maximally affected by the lessons we offer.

Customize and Adapt the Story to the Specific Context to Make It Personal and Relevant

One mistake that therapists and all storytellers make is to tell the same story the same way, no matter who is in the room. We are guiltier of this than most because sometimes it feels like we are a jukebox in which clients put in their quarter (meaning trigger some programmed lesson plan) and we recite from rote memory the standard version of the story.

I've always wondered how actors on Broadway or elsewhere can perform every single night—plus two matinees on Saturday—and do so for months or years and yet still maintain their passion and energy, pretending it is the first time. But I suppose because they are actors they are good at pretending. As for therapists, our well-worn stories feel stale after a while. We either need new ones or it is absolutely crucial that we at least adapt them to serve the moment.

Include Something Novel That Catches the Client by Surprise

Some of the best stories throw the listener for a loop. It is the unexpected that most captures interest and is logged into memory—and for good reason in that it prepares us to tackle new challenges and deal with situations that may test us in the future. When a film like *Memento*, *Pulp Fiction*, or *Time Traveler's Wife* plays with the sequence of events, beginning in the middle of the story and moving backward or forward, it requires a different kind of focused attention to thread the narrative together.

Memorable stories are usually those that stick with us because they are different than others we have heard. It is novelty that stimulates interest and provides surprises and shocks to the system that makes for enduring memories. Even good jokes are effective because they lead the listener in one direction and them turn things upside down for the punch line. If we can create any kind of similar unexpected twist in the plot, we increase the likelihood that the story will have an impact—if for no other reason than because it is strange or has no real closure.

Present a Conflict or Problem With Which the Client Can Identify

Stories offered in therapy are usually intended to invite clients to imagine themselves in the role of the protagonist. It is thus important to create a protagonist, as well as a plotline, that makes it relatively easy for the client to identify (like the story that began the chapter). On the one hand, it is useful to engage the client's curiosity and wonderment, asking, "What does this have to do with *me*?" On the other hand, it is a good idea to preserve enough mystery and ambiguity in the narrative so that the client can fill in the blanks and personalize it in the most relevant way.

Ericksonian therapists, of course, are famous for telling stories that are deliberately as obtuse and mysterious as possible. Steve Lankton, one former student of Milton Erickson and a leading proponent of metaphorical storytelling, once explained to me that he was pretty sure that a lot of time the great master had no idea where his stories were going or what they were intended to do. Instead, the stories needed to be just a little bit relevant to the presenting issues in such a way that the client would create the meaning.

Regardless of the setting in which a therapist works, whether in private practice, an inpatient facility, substance abuse agency, school, university, or standing in front of an audience, it is often through stories that we teach clients about possibilities for the future, as well as to imagine a different reality. In the next chapter we explore more about the realities of clinical practice, discussing the ways that clinicians flourish in both private practice and the public sector.

Chapter 9

PRIVATE PRACTICE AND/OR PUBLIC SERVICE?

Each year I greet a new cohort of 60 eager, hopeful therapy students with stars in their eyes and visions of a lucrative future. More than three quarters of them imagine themselves in private practice, picturing clients lined up at their door, six-figure incomes at their disposal, and all the freedom they could ever wish, working their own schedules and answering only to themselves. They may admire their brethren who desire to work in the public sector, or work for some advocacy organization, but they also view them as naïve idealists who may very well end up in poverty themselves.

Those who plan to work in homeless shelters, community agencies, substance abuse programs, charities, government service, and similar settings likewise view the aspiring private practitioners as misguided. They believe passionately that for too many years psychotherapy has been a luxury for the affluent "worried well." And they are not far wrong. But both sets of aspirations have an important place in our field, and the set of expectations that each group holds is often just as unrealistic as the other.

The reality is that some of the most satisfied members of our profession have had the opportunity to traverse both domains. They feel a strong commitment to issues of social justice. They believe they have a responsibility to serve underserved populations. They take their roles quite seriously as advocates on behalf of the dispossessed and marginalized. They may often work, part time or full time, for community agencies, NGOs, schools, or the mental health system. And yet they also revel in the opportunities they've created to work in their own way, at their own pace, in the private sector.

Originally I had planned two separate chapters for this subject of the book, one devoted to the pragmatic aspects of launching and maintaining a private practice and the other focused on ways that therapists can change the larger world by their involvement in social justice and advocacy. But these are not necessarily different paths as much as they are compatible partners. Each professional activity complements and empowers the other, just as clinical practice informs teaching, and mentoring and supervising others makes us more effective as practitioners.

In the first part of this chapter we examine some of the realities of work in private practice that were hardly mentioned in graduate school. This includes not only the joys and satisfactions of this work but also some of the hidden or neglected challenges that make this lifestyle difficult in some ways. In a similar vein, we hear so many lectures and so much scolding about becoming more actively involved in social justice but rarely hear much about how frustrating and overwhelming these efforts can be, especially if the goal is to sustain progress over time in communities without much support. Consistent with the theme of this book, we discuss both subjects with an emphasis on practice in the real world.

Some Realities of Private Practice

There are two main reasons why therapists choose to go into private practice, both of them based on somewhat unrealistic expectations. The first is the fantasy of unbridled freedom, of working as a self-employed professional, responsible only to yourself and your clients. Just think of the possibilities—setting your own hours, working as little or as much as you like. Unfortunately, it doesn't take very long to figure out that if you want to succeed, you have to see people when they are available, which often means working late into the evening, Saturdays, lunch hours, and random hours during the day.

"I have young children," explained one therapist about her motivation for choosing private practice as her preferred option, "so I thought it would be a perfect match, schedule-wise. I wonder how I could have been so clueless."

She is talking about the reality that although she gets to spend time with her children in the mornings before they head off to school, most nights she doesn't get home until they are ready for bed. "I try so hard to be disciplined and not see people after 7 PM, but that's the time when people get off work and the hours that are most in demand."

The second motivation for private practice is based on illusions of generous financial rewards, if not enormous wealth. Ah, the possibilities are endless. Figure an hourly rate of $100 or $200 per hour. Multiply that by 8 clients per day, 5 days a week, and it seems like you hit the jackpot.

But of course that doesn't take into consideration that it is rare indeed that anyone sees 40 clients a week at full fee. It is far more likely that clients cancel, referrals slow down at times, and many on the caseload are being seen at significantly reduced fees. And then there are all the overhead expenses for an office, billing service, support staff, payments on equipment, legal and accounting fees, medical insurance, malpractice insurance, disability insurance, and life insurance. Oh yeah, there are also retirement contributions if you have anything left over.

Yet among all the things I never realized when I worked in private practice full time is that there are no paid vacations. During a period of 10 years, I rarely, if ever, left town for more than a long weekend because I was unable (or unwilling) to let go of a week's or month's income. Once I added the price of two weeks of lost salary to the price of a trip, it was so exorbitant that I managed to squeeze most of my clients into two very long days and then take off for a few days. Or on a smaller scale, a friend would invite me to lunch and I'd figure that losing that two-hour block of time would cost me several hundred dollars—plus the cost of lunch—so I'd usually decline and stuff a sandwich down my face during the 10-minute break between sessions.

Does it have to be this way? Of course not! And those therapists who are flourishing in private practice and love their jobs are those who are able to enforce strict boundaries on their time and plan in such a way that they do lead a healthy and balanced lifestyle.

"I'm not in this for the money," one therapist explained. "In some ways, I was better off before when my employer was putting away retirement for me and paying my health insurance. I can't seem to save anything, and we are always short of cash."

Yet in spite of some unexpected financial challenges, this therapist absolutely loves what he's doing and can't imagine doing anything else. One reason for this is that he keeps his priorities clear. "One rule I've had, and stuck with no matter what, is that I won't work evenings past 6:00 p.m. I won't work Fridays and weekends."

Sure, that's reduced his income and limited the referrals he can take. But he decided that his time with family and friends, as well as his freedom, are more important than anything else.

Enjoying Freedom of Choice

There is no doubt that one of the main attractions of private practice is the freedom to control who you see, when you see them, and pretty much how you decide to work with them. Compared to the bureaucracies and political maneuverings contained within most community agency settings, private practices are downright staid. That's not to say that all human conflicts are eliminated, but they are significantly reduced, if for no other reason than that people are not really required to work together very much. Furthermore, you do have the option of setting your own hours, if you are prepared to live with the consequences.

If freedom means having choices, having the power to control what you do and how you do it, then private practice truly provides more opportunities than any other setting. It is ironic, however, that although private practitioners *can* have more freedom than colleagues who work in organizations, often they don't as a practical matter. As illustrated earlier, they may, in fact end up working longer hours for less compensation.

Not everyone is right for independent practice. It takes a certain disposition, a particular mindset, a set of attitudes, maybe even certain personality characteristics, to be successful. Some of the most satisfied, and also the most miserable, therapists I know are operating in this setting. For some, there is a perfect match between the requirements of the job and the things they love to do. For others, illusions are quickly dispelled by the realities of what is involved on a daily basis, tasks that often have little to do with what you were originally prepared for.

What does it take to flourish in private practice with the inherent uncertainties? For one thing it requires a willingness, if not an eagerness, to embrace the unknown. There are some weeks in which there are more holes in the schedule than there are filled appointment slots and other weeks when things are so packed you can barely catch your breath. It is hard to turn away new referrals, no matter how busy you are, because of the fear that they may dry up all of a sudden. Income can fluctuate wildly, week to week, and season to season.

For those who crave stability and predictability, private practice can become a nightmare. It requires self-discipline in all kinds of ways, controlling schedule hours, saving money, setting limits, being self-reliant, making sound business decisions. Many of the qualities can be learned over time, if you have the right training and supervision. The problem is that most of this stuff you didn't learn in graduate school but must teach yourself on your own.

What They Didn't Tell You in Graduate School

There have been many debates about the responsibility of graduate school to prepare professionals for success as entrepreneurs and small business owners. This is true as much for lawyers and physicians as it is for therapists. There is so much in the curriculum that is already mandated by state licensing boards and accreditation bodies that there is hardly any time to cover luxuries beyond basic professional practice and clinical skills. Yet if there is one consistent complaint by alumni, it is that graduate school didn't provide even rudimentary preparation for launching and maintaining a successful private practice. There is some question whether that should even be the role of professional training, given there is so much need for clinicians to work in the public sector and serve people who would never, ever schedule an appointment on their own. That's why there are books such as this one, and workshops specifically designed to cover some of the more pragmatic business and marketing skills of this specialty.

The Hook

The object of the first session is to get the client to come back for a second one. In the parlance of sales experts, if you can't close the deal in the first contact, you lose the customer. This is actually true with respect to any therapeutic contact but becomes even more salient for those who earn their living by getting clients to return as satisfied customers. By contrast, those who work in schools or the mental health system are used to dealing with long waiting lists and an unlimited client population waiting for services.

I was one of those therapists who was completely unprepared for the real world. After quitting a salaried positioned I moved back to my home state to begin a private practice, with stars in my eyes and the fantasy that all I had to do was open an office and clients would flock to my door. I was the sole support of my family at this time and desperate for income. Alas, referrals weren't materializing as I expected. After a few months I still had only a handful of clients and yet I had endless bills to pay. One of my four clients dropped out (or I'd like to think he was cured) when I received a call for a new referral bringing renewed hope.

I paced restlessly until I heard the outside door close softly. I peeked into the waiting room and, sure enough, there she was. I rubbed my hands together in glee, I really did. Just as I had been schooled in the outpatient clinic where I had completed my internship, I greeted her politely and gave her an intake questionnaire to fill out—you know, the usual stuff: billing information, presenting complaints, history of medical problems, medications she was taking, and so on. I told her I'd return after she was done. She nodded nervously as she scrutinized the pages.

I went back to my office, already calculating that if she could afford my full fee, maybe I could pay my phone bill on time. Maybe she would even need to come twice per week, I fantasized.

After what I estimated was plenty of time, I returned to the waiting room, only to find it empty. Primly perched on the chair where she had been sitting was the clipboard, but the client was nowhere to be seen. I giggled hysterically with an instant image of a spaceship that had sucked her out through the ceiling. How had she sneaked out without my hearing a sound? I mumbled to myself in shock. Scrawled across the front page of the form was written: "Sorry. I couldn't go through with this."

I was crushed. Devastated. I wanted to cry.

I vowed in that moment I would never let a client escape my grasp again, at least not without having had the chance to sell my services first. The lesson I learned was one I could never have imagined from graduate school, or even after years working in public agencies: If I wanted to survive, I had to become an expert at convincing people to return for more therapy.

Indeed, as the story illustrates, there is an altogether different mentality in the approach taken by a private practitioner. Whereas the therapist in an agency might communicate: "Look, this is what I do and how I do it. If this fits for you, great! If not, go elsewhere because there are plenty of others who want this time slot." Under such circumstances, you might even feel grateful when certain clients don't return. Not so with private practice, where a different sort of message comes across: "What is it that you want? Whatever it is, I can probably do that. If not, I learn very quickly."

How to Run a Business

The actual task of doing therapy with clients represents about half the work involved in being a private practitioner. That means that graduate school prepared us to do very little that is actually involved in the daily work. What a shock to find yourself completely ignorant of what is involved in negotiating a lease, selecting a billing system, managing an office, or planning a marketing campaign. Who would have thought that your primary professional identify would change from that of healer to entrepreneur?

A number of manuals and guidebooks have been written for newcomers to the private practice scene, instructing them on the intricacies of office design and management, marketing strategies, billing procedures, managed care policies, and so on (see, for example, Brennan, 2013; Clement, 2013; Hodson, 2012). All of them hope to make up for holes in the education of most practitioners because a completely different mindset is required to think like a marketing specialist and business entrepreneur rather than as a mental health professional. I'm not saying that the roles aren't compatible, just that they sometimes present a conflict of interests. Instead of the usual posture of modesty and restrained dignity, one must become self-promoting and product driven. To succeed at this enterprise, you have to learn to enjoy the tasks associated with public relations and marketing rather than seeing them as an onerous burden.

Every week will challenge you to make decisions, *informed* decisions, about how to spend your advertising budget, which referral sources are most likely to pan out, whether to incorporate yourself or remain as a solely owned business, how to handle a conflict between staff members. Once you are on your own, you must also deal with things that come up on a regular basis, either as challenges to be faced or opportunities to be exploited. You may never have served as an expert witness before, but you may be asked to testify in a custody dispute. You may be approached about putting together a stress management program for a large company. Each of these invitations can be exciting or anxiety provoking, depending on the support system and resources you build around you.

The Reasoning of the Private Practice Mind

It is a strange, wonderful, and also sad feeling to have clients tell you they've gotten what they need and are ready to quit. The assortment of reactions that may go through your mind in that moment of revelation is staggering: "Well, good for you!" you think initially. "I'm so proud of you and what you've accomplished. I'm pretty proud of me, too. I did a good job here."

Then, a creeping voice might whisper indignantly: "What do you mean you're quitting?" We just got *started*. We haven't even made a dent yet in all the issues you've got to resolve. Running away from your problems isn't going to help."

I can't help but compare the differences in my own thinking when I was working for public agencies versus private practice. At various agencies I had so many people waiting for assistance, and so much pressure from administrators to serve as many as possible in the most efficient period of time, that "losing" a client for any reason—success, premature dropout, whatever—felt like a relief. Then I recall times we spent in case conferences at a group private practice when so much of the discussion revolved less around treatment plans and more about how to keep clients returning, even when their initial complaints were resolved. I always felt a little guilty about this type of thinking, wondering if I'd lost my perspective. I couldn't be sure whether we were persuading clients to continue their therapy because it was for their own sake or our own good.

So Alone

Most of us were attracted to the practice of therapy in the first place because of a love for people. We enjoy being part of a profession where we spend our days involved in intimate conversations and interpersonal connections. We have been highly trained to do just that—to relate to others effectively, to listen compassionately, articulate complex ideas, and create memorable encounters. Furthermore, we enjoy the camaraderie of being part of a larger professional family, one whose members have similar values. We like swapping stories of victory or defeat, of trading gossip and exchanging ideas. We are intrigued by intellectual debate and drawn to emotional expression. Above all else, we are people-oriented in the ways we perceive the world. We are nourished by our interactions with others and sustained by the support we feel.

In graduate school, many students may have enjoyed feeling part of a special club. It may have felt good to be under pressure in the company of like-minded compatriots who shared our dreams and watched our backs. On a small scale it may have felt like being part of a combat unit under fire, bonded together in foxholes dodging incoming mortar rounds in the form of exams, assigned papers, and skill assessments.

Graduate school was designed to prepare us to be team players. Over and over we got the message that this sometimes inexact science of helping requires continual consultation and reality checks. Bouncing ideas off others, testing hypotheses, and challenging assumptions are the lifeblood of our work. Supervision and cooperative case management are imperative in a field where personal biases and distortions can so easily lead us astray. In addition, the emotional toll this work takes on our psyche is brutal. Continually, we are bombarded by assaults on our ego. In almost every session we must confront the most frightening human issues—of death and meaninglessness and loss of control and infidelity and a thousand others. By definition, our job is to listen to stories that no one else will hear and wrestle with themes that are so terrifying they threaten to eat people alive. Throughout all these challenges the one thing we can count on most is the support of our peers.

What a shock it is for the private practitioner to adjust to the isolation of such a solitary activity. Whereas clients definitely prefer the perfect solitude and protection of their privacy, for the clinician such seclusion can be suffocating. There are therapists whose whole days are spent only in the company of their clients. Besides a few quick conversations with officemates, a few phone calls, e-mails, or texts into the outside world, virtually every minute is spent ensconced in the psychic bunkers of clients' lives.

Even those in group practices often find themselves famished for human companionship. Whereas in community agencies, staff members are required to attend meetings, in-service workshops, and case conferences, independent therapists may participate infrequently except when mandated to accrue continuing education credits. "I keep saying I will meet with a few colleagues on a regular basis," one therapist admits sheepishly, "but something always seems to come up. It amazes me how my friends in university counseling centers and mental health centers actually get paid for sitting in meetings. For me, the meter is only running when I've got a client who is talking."

There is also a "foxhole mentality" to many clinicians in the public sector, a feeling of being unappreciated and underpaid for working with the neediest clientele. It becomes a major priority to spend time together over breaks, in the hallways, after work, bolstering one another's spirits. In private practice, there is the same need but less opportunity (or at least less motivation) to get together in similar ways.

It may indeed be true that isolation is one of the greatest challenges for those working in the private sector. It's so easy to neglect the need for social nourishment. It is so easy to forget to take care of yourself.

With this potential for burnout and isolation clearly in mind, seasoned practitioners follow several proactive measures to encourage social contact with others. They schedule regular breaks during the day—no matter what comes up—whether making plans for coffee or lunch, going for a walk or workout, or just spending an hour relaxing, meditating, or staring out the window. They get actively involved in local and national professional organizations, just as much for networking and social support as any other altruistic motive. They join book clubs to talk about ideas completely unrelated to work. They go to workshops less for the content presented than for the opportunities to meet new friends. They diversify their interests and study things far afield. They also diversify their professional activities so they don't just sit around in their offices all day.

These examples sound good in theory but take considerable resolve to stick with over time. It's important to face the reality that in spite of how appealing these ideas sound, you will probably not do them. If you don't believe me, go talk to some veterans and ask them how often they take time out from schedules to nourish themselves. It is true that some therapists do, but not nearly enough of them. Scare yourself with the consequences of not reaching out to others—that you will become a burned-out shell of a person who feels isolated from the rest of the world.

Commitment to Change the World

If private practice offers some distinct privileges, as well as special challenges, so too does public advocacy but in very different ways. It has been made abundantly clear by our professional organizations and ethical codes that therapists have a moral responsibility, if not an obligation, to reach beyond the confines of their own practice to make a difference in their communities and the larger world. That all sounds good, of course, but the truth of the matter is that very few therapists actually sustain their efforts over a long period of time. We might take on a few pro bono clients, or volunteer a few hours a week, post a passionate plea for some cause on social media, or even begin some project that is meaningful, but realities and other obligations often intercede. We get distracted or waylaid; sometimes just burned out from frustration at all the obstacles that stand in the way. This doesn't necessarily reflect a lack of interest but rather a shortage of time and energy.

Therapists get involved in social justice work, outside the scope of their usual practice, for a variety of motives that go beyond altruism. There are often intensely personal reasons for undertaking these difficult jobs, given that they take place in less than comfortable environments, with clientele who may be resistant or feeling hopeless, and with very limited resources. Although this may be the most rewarding work imaginable, let's face it: It is also the most overwhelming and difficult.

I've been working for the past 15 years on a project in Nepal with lower caste girls who are at greatest risk to be trafficked as sex slaves because of abject poverty, neglect, or abandonment by one or both parents (Kottler, 2013; Kottler & Marriner, 2009). This is no doubt noble work: We assist over 300 children, ages 5 to 25 years, who remain in school and out of harm's way because of our mentoring and support. People tell me all the time how great it is that we undertake this project to help those who would otherwise be condemned to a life of torture, misery, abuse, and premature death (the girls, some as young as 11 years old, would be raped in Indian brothels a dozen times per day and have a life expectancy of 5 more years). They envy what we are doing and say that we are so lucky to travel so often to such an exotic and beautiful place deep in the Himalayas or the jungle. But I should perhaps be clear: This was never my goal or my intention to do this work. I was "trapped" into becoming involved when I first discovered that girls were "disappearing" in their villages, being sold or kidnapped into indentured slavery. Who could stand by and watch this happening without doing something to intervene? It was never, ever a choice.

The easy part was reaching into my pocket for the few dollars it took to save the very first girl at risk and keep her in school. After all, she was pointed out to me in the schoolyard, just 12 years old, and would be "disappeared" next because her father abandoned the family and they couldn't afford to support all the children. The boys are allowed to go to school, but girls are considered worthless, a burden. What would *you* have done?

But what if you were told that unless you return to this remote village to check on her and hold others accountable she would be disappeared anyway? And, by the way, it takes 5 days of continuous travel and thousands of dollars just to get to this place. Add to this expense, commitment, and inconvenience that the villagers resent efforts to help these "worthless" lower caste girls and that the facilities and accommodations you are staying in are—let's say—rather basic with squat toilets and cots for beds. You spend 6 hours each day walking up and down Himalayan peaks or along rice paddies, conducting home and school visits. It is no wonder that members of our team break down emotionally and physically after a few weeks, myself included. But the real problem is that our volunteers get involved for a year, or two at most, and then move on to the next enticing adventure. They'd "done" Nepal and raised a bit of money, but they've got other plans and new ideas they want to pursue. Meanwhile we have 300 children in more than dozen villages whose very lives depend on our continued help. This is so, so hard to do over the long haul, to stick with it, even though it doesn't feel any more like it is much of a choice.

So why do I do this? Why does *anyone* do this kind of work, whether in their own community or in some far-flung place on the globe where people are suffering? For those of us who work in the private sector, or in public institutions that serve largely middle-class clients or students, there is often a hunger felt to reach out to those who would never, ever otherwise receive any help.

Here are some examples of what therapists actively involved in social justice projects often report, beginning with a professional who specializes in career counseling: "I see clients every day in my office but, in some ways, I am replaceable; there are so many others who could do what I do. Maybe I've been doing therapy for too long, but sometimes I wonder if I'm really making much of a difference in the world helping people adjust to their everyday lives. I'm not saying that isn't useful and important but what I do at a local homeless shelter on weekends makes everything else pale in comparison."

Another therapist feels a spiritual connection to her work in the field. She travels several times a year to Southern Africa to volunteer to work in schools with children who have no access to counseling. "I love my job, don't misunderstand me. But I find myself counting the days until I return to Africa. The trips replenish my spirit and help me feel closer to a Higher Power. I think that, in some ways, I get as much from these visits as the children."

Some practitioners point to the ways they learn so many new things from their service projects that reenergize them in so many other ways. "It's not that I'm exactly bored with my job—okay, I *am* a little tired of doing the same things. I think that's why I started looking for other volunteer opportunities and then started this project on my own to work with women in a shelter. Boredom isn't exactly my problem anymore. I'll say that for sure!"

Just as this therapist admits she reached out for a service project as much for her own stimulation as any altruistic motive, other therapists confess that they get overinvolved in other activities as a way to avoid or hide from their own issues. Helping others, especially in needy areas, is indeed an excellent distraction from dealing with difficult personal problems. There is also some evidence that such volunteer service accrues considerable other advantages.

It turns out that those who are involved in selfless, altruistic acts enjoy a number of health benefits that have been supported by research (Brehony, 1999; Fredrickson, 2003; Kahana, Bhatta, Lovegreen, Kahana, & Midlarsky, 2013; Kottler, 2000; Post, 2007, 2011; Walsh, 2011; Warneken & Tomasello, 2009). Some of these positive consequences include (1) greater sense of well-being and life satisfaction, (2) broadened perspective and worldview, (3) increased sense of purpose and meaning for life's mission, (4) improved feelings of affiliation and sense of belongingness, (5) experience of "helper's high" with elevated oxytocin and vasopressin, (6) higher status, respect, and trust within professional and local community, (7) renewed faith and spiritual transcendence, (8) feeling of redemption to use own pain and life experience to help others, (9) release of guilt in paying some perceived debt, (10) opportunity to reinvent oneself in new and more creative ways, (11) leaving a legacy, and (12) simply expressing acts of selfless love. There have also been studies, which were cited earlier, that demonstrate how altruistic activities actually reduce chronic pain, provide immunities to disease, and significantly increase life span. Given these benefits, it is no wonder that so many of us give away not only our time and energy but a part of ourselves.

It has been a curiosity among evolutionary theorists to explain why anyone would give away money, time, or resources to others who are not related kin. How does that increase the likelihood that our own genetic material will survive and flourish? It seems that evolution has been far more "intelligent" than we could ever imagine in that we are actually programmed not only for individual evolutionary fitness but also to benefit the larger communities of which we are a part. That is why among so many other species animals will sacrifice themselves for the herd or flock, even if there is no

direct biological connection to brethren or even the hope of reciprocal favors.

Some Challenges in the Real World

Advocacy and social justice projects are sometimes overromanti-
cized. The stories people tell about their adventures are similar to
other travel experiences in which the burdens, obstacles, inconve-
niences, and discomforts are minimized in favor of the glorious lessons learned and humorous or poignant anecdotes. When seeking to
inspire people to become more actively involved in service, I tell the
story of strolling along a Himalayan mountainside and discovering a
shoeless young girl on the side of the trail who shyly looked up at me.
She was filthy and hugging herself from the cold, dressed only in a
tattered shirt several sizes too large. Those among my team tried to
speak to her, but she remained mute, her eyes fixated on the ground.
We eventually figured out that she had been abandoned, or perhaps
her parents had died as porters on one of the Everest mountain
expeditions. In any case, she was starving and traumatized.

We brought the girl to the nearest village and found a childless
couple who agreed to care for her after we promised to provide
financial support for her to attend school. It was one of the most
remarkable and satisfying experiences of my life: I have never felt
more useful. I actually remember thinking to myself that I could
die in that moment and feel perfectly content that my life was completely redeemed.

A wonderful story, isn't it? If only the reality matched the story.

Here's another version of the story. I wasn't exactly "strolling" up
the mountainside; I was stumbling along, dizzy from oxygen deprivation and utterly exhausted after climbing a steep ridge and
crossing not one, but two, rickety suspension bridges swaying over
a gorge. Did I mention I'm afraid of heights?

Secondly, I was hardly composed and rational when I met the
little girl: I was out of my mind with confusion, fear, and overwhelming sadness. Twice I had to excuse myself and go behind a

large rock to muffle the sounds of my sobbing. I completely lost control of myself and it scared me that I was so emotionally flooded. I felt ashamed. Did I mention that I was overwhelmed?

Thirdly, this was hardly an orderly and calm conversation with the village elders regarding what to do with this lost child. I don't understand a lot of the Nepali language, but I could grasp enough to get that the residents were not altogether pleased with our meddling in their affairs. There are hundreds of lost children wandering around this region, many of them orphans of porters who have fallen into crevasses or died in icefalls or mudslides. Just a few months earlier two of the children we support in this region died with their families, swallowed in an avalanche that wiped them off the face of the mountain in less than a minute.

In addition to my physical exhaustion and emotional overload, I had been sleep deprived throughout the previous week, unable to stay in bed for more than a few hours because of overstimulation and the need to empty my bladder from drinking so much water to keep altitude sickness at bay. I was also having stomach and digestion problems.

There were inevitable conflicts among the members of our team. We were not a high-functioning group during this particular visit—too many inexperienced volunteers with too many strong opinions that reflected their ignorance and cultural insensitivity. As their leader, I was being too heavy handed and autocratic in an attempt to bring them together into a more cohesive unit.

I could go on and on about all the hardships and challenges we faced, most of which I tend to "forget" or leave out of the stories I tell about our experiences. I know I'm not the only one inclined to do this—and that is partially what leads to unrealistic expectations for what these service trips are like.

Besides the personal challenges involved in public service projects, there are some other realities that must be considered. So many of the efforts on the part of therapists and other volunteers become token efforts that aren't sustained over time. Volunteering for a weekend, or spending a few weeks on an assignment, are better than nothing at all but sometimes not *that* much better.

"We appreciate you coming here and all," one resident of a homeless shelter said to me as a group of us arrived for a few days of volunteer work, "but ya'll come and go, feel good about yourselves, and then go back to your own lives." This is true, of course, but it also signals one of the main problems when we get involved in a project for a short period of time and then move on to something else. And we aren't the only ones with a short attention span.

Nowadays, people wear bracelets or pins proclaiming their affiliation with a particular cause. They post announcements on social media bringing attention to issues that are dear to their hearts. But often this becomes all talk and little action. There's a difference between really doing good versus feeling good. And sometimes I wonder if dabbling in social causes or service projects really instills much hope rather than greater despair when there is precious little follow-through over time.

Mahatma Gandhi was once asked for an inspirational message by an admirer as he was about to board a train. Gandhi looked down from the train to the man standing by the track and said, "My life is my message."

Isn't that what any of us would want?

PART III

✦

*Ongoing Personal and
Professional Development*

Chapter 10

UPGRADING YOUR PRESENTATIONS

One of the things we learned in graduate school is that many instructors, presenters, workshop experts, and other lecturers are often not very engaging or persuasive in their skills. They talk too much, fail to make adjustments, rely too much on distracting slides, and seem to forget that the essence of effectiveness is related to making a strong connection with the audience. And these were the models that we were supposed to emulate. We actually received negligible guidance in how to connect with audiences larger than a few clients in our offices, even though this is an important part of our jobs in the real world. We are often called upon to speak to groups, conduct workshops, give presentations, and address large audiences. This is a very different kind of "therapeutic" encounter, one for which we were singularly unprepared.

Unfortunately, many therapists—and for that matter, many professional teachers and instructors—are not all that skilled doing presentations. They drone on and on, even though anyone looking around the room can easily detect that people are nodding off. They fail to connect with their audience in any kind of intimate or meaningful way, believing (just as we were taught) that as long as the content is covered that somehow it will magically be heard, understood, and retained.

There's been a lot of research demonstrating clearly that the human attention span, while sitting passively, has certain limits. The average amount of time that most people can sit still and remain reasonably engaged while listening to someone else is about 20 minutes. That means that anyone who is presenting, reporting, or lecturing to a group that is over that time limit is basically talking to himself or herself. Once the innumerable slides begin clicking across the screen, listeners almost completely check out. That's why the CEOs of many major companies—Amazon, Google, even the Department of Defense—now forbid people to use PowerPoint or other slide presentations at meetings because they stifle meaningful conversations and effective decision making. Once the lights are dimmed and the slides come on screen, people go into a lethargic trance.

This chapter discusses some of the secrets of impacting large and small audiences in powerful ways. It offers a number of suggestions for upgrading presentations and applying therapeutic skills to beguile and influence larger groups. Some of the most impactful talks of all time have certain features that command attention and maximize learning processes. Many of these attributes have been standardized as part of TED Talks (Donovan, 2012; Karia, 2012; Stanton, 2012) or described in resources that are designed to help professional speakers improve their performance (Duarte, 2010; Gallo, 2014; Reynolds, 2012). We will review some of the most important ingredients to help adapt what you do in therapy to a different arena.

It's Harder Than It Seems

As you may have noticed, most university faculty receive virtually no systematic training in the art of teaching. The assumption in the academic world is that expertise in one's discipline is sufficient preparation to teach content to others. Likewise, it is assumed that because therapists are good talkers, it is a small matter to generalize those skills to a larger audience. Although it is true that public speaking does require abilities that therapists certainly have in abundance (fluency, flexibility, spontaneity, confidence), there are also many other qualities that may not be part of our repertoire.

At an international conference attended by representatives from two dozen countries, the schedule was packed with offerings by therapists—research papers and theoretical models, as well as more practical sessions. The presenters were brimming with confidence. Many of them were university faculty; others were seasoned veterans and supervisors. All of them were articulate, verbal, and like most therapists, used to speaking persuasively.

With such expertise and experience, you would expect that the quality of the presentations would be at a very high level. Most of the programs, however, were disorganized. Others, rich in content, were difficult to follow because the presenter's style was tedious. Even more amazing for a group of professionals who are supposed to be experts at helping people learn, they violated most of what is known about the rudimentary assumptions of learning and remembering content. Unfortunately, the quality of the programs at this conference was not much different from those offered elsewhere.

Interestingly, all of us are expert critics of other people's work. We sit in the audience muttering to ourselves about how boring a speech is. We whisper to friends about how superficial the ideas are, or about some irritating mannerism of the speaker that interferes with our attention. While watching others in action, we seem to have little trouble identifying all the things they are doing wrong, all the things we would do differently if we were in their place. So why don't we?

The answer is that we might recognize a lousy presentation when we see one but that doesn't mean we can construct one of our own that is informative, engaging, and influential. After all, clients come to us in the first place because they can't see things in themselves that we recognize with little trouble. The same holds true with our own work before large audiences: We may be making some serious miscalculations and errors in judgment, but who will tell us if we don't ask?

Subjecting Ourselves to Critical Scrutiny

Being sought out on a daily basis by people in need of our therapeutic services produces feelings of competence and acceptance that strengthen us for more difficult challenges. Observing clients improve from our efforts is rewarding and gives unquestionable purpose to our work. It is frustrating, however, during those times when we say such insightful things, pleased with our streak of brilliance or eloquence, and then recognize that our client never even heard us! We look around, waiting for applause, or at least some acknowledgment that our witticism or offering was heard, and we see the client staring off into space. At least when we are talking to a larger group, there is a greater likelihood that *someone* will understand what we are saying.

Indeed, speaking to a larger audience provides many of the same rewarding feelings you get from doing therapy, only on a larger scale. There is a whole room full of people who find value in your knowledge and ability to communicate. It is such a kick to stand there before twenty or a hundred people or more and *know* that you have them in the palm of your hand. They are with you. They are laughing at your jokes. You can see by their faces that they are really understanding what you are saying. Even better, they are finding the ideas useful. Some people are looking thoughtful: You can practically see the gears turning in their brains as they personalize some concept you have just introduced. Others are so animated, practically levitating with excitement and energy that you helped generate. A few others are looking puzzled, disturbed, or even upset, and that's okay, too, because it means that you have provoked something within them.

In addition to the personal satisfaction that comes from public speaking, you are also able to create wider recognition and acceptance of your practice, ideas, and abilities. These conditions bode well for a greater sense of success, which is good for your mental frame of mind as well as your economic status. Better business, greater therapeutic success, and a massaged ego: That's a pretty good deal for doing presentations, and I haven't even mentioned that it could be lucrative.

What Makes a Presentation Memorable?

Good presenters are asked to speak again and again because they communicate meaningful information that others can incorporate into their daily lives. If you think about the best presentations you have attended, it is likely that they had certain elements in common. What made this experience so memorable was hardly that it was chock full of things you didn't know, nor that it was meticulously organized and impeccably delivered. Certainly these are laudable qualities of a good talk or lecture, ones that we should all strive for. Yet what most often makes a presentation so meaningful is that it touched you in a profound way. It may have reached your head, your heart, or even your soul, but on some level you walked out of the room a bit different. And that is the goal in any professional context: to impact an audience with the same power and influence that we exert with our clients.

Reading the Audience

It is amazing how often professionals who are supposed to be experts at promoting learning seem to forget the most important principles when they are outside their offices. During the past few decades, for example, increasing attention has shifted away from the presenter to how the learner is reflecting on the information and process of the presentation. Good presenters are thus intimately connected to their audience: They *know* what they are thinking.

This is, of course, no different than our work with clients. The problem is that whereas when we are working with clients we suspend a formalized lesson plan in lieu of responding to "teachable moments" as they arise, when we are speaking we often become overinvested in our agenda so that we fail to make necessary adjustments according to how people are responding to what we are doing in any given moment.

The most common mistake that speakers make is that they become overly focused on their notes and slides, neglecting to pay attention to the audience. It does take a degree of courage to go with the flow and abandon one's agenda at times, but that is, after all, what we do during sessions no matter how much we have prepared.

Telling a Story

As we've already covered in a previous chapter, stories are the glue that hold any conversation or presentation together. All of the memorable and impactful talks begin with a story, one that holds the main points to be covered but does so in an engaging way. The stories should be relatively brief but also dramatic to hold attention and pique curiosity about what follows.

If you go online and review some of the most well-received TED talks or presentations on YouTube, you will notice immediately that they have certain elements in common (Gallo, 2014). They are always under 20 minutes. They are emotionally evocative. The style of the program, or its content, is novel, teaching some new idea. And they always begin with a story, one that is crafted to emphasize the novelty and strong feelings that keep people interested and engaged.

Creating a Context

We are already quite aware that each client or family we see requires different kinds of treatment, regardless of the presenting issues. Some people respond well to direct confrontation, others to gentle and gradual questioning. Some enjoy playfulness and others prefer getting down to business. Some are patient and others in a hurry. We have learned to adjust what we do, and how we do it, depending on who is in the room and how they are responding to our actions. If one thing isn't working, we (hopefully) stop doing that and try something else.

The same policy applies to speaking to larger audiences, even if many presenters don't seem able to make that translation. Everything we do, in any situation, is contextual. What kinds of humor are introduced, what sorts of activities are arranged, what types of stories are told, what language is used, what content is settled on, and what slides are shown all depend on what the audience will find most suitable and relevant to their lives. This may seem rather obvious, but how often have *you* sat in a room with someone speaking and wondered why the presenter seemed so clueless about what you were most interested in hearing about?

Teaching Stuff

One of the misguided expectations that inhibits therapists in their speaking efforts is the belief that their job is to tell people things they don't already know (this is also true for those who feel blocked in their writing). Indeed, people do buy books and attend lectures and workshops because they think the expert will tell them something new. Disappointment sets in once it is realized that what is being heard (or read) is not that novel or is just another variation of a familiar theme.

Actually, in most situations, the job of a presenter (or writer) is not so much to supply some amazing new insight or content, as much as it is to stimulate constructive thinking and reflection in the audience. As one veteran attender of hundreds of workshops remarked: "I've been in this field a long time, so long in fact, I am no longer surprised that what I hear is something I once heard before in a slightly different form. No, what I'm looking for is someone to get me to think in new ways, someone to stimulate my brain and heart. How does someone do that? Gee, I'm not really sure or I'd be doing that myself."

After further dialogue with this therapist, it is apparent that she *does* know how to stimulate growth—she does it every day in a different context. So do you. But the hardest thing to do is to find an authentic speaking voice, one that presents content in a personally unique way.

People attending presentations do expect to learn something new, and our job is to teach them some idea or concept that they may not already know. But the trick of a good speaker is to be able to present even familiar material in such a way that it feels fresh and fleshes out new facets that had never been considered before.

Getting People Actively Involved

The best therapy is the kind that motivates and inspires clients to actually do some things to improve their lives. Talk is not nearly enough if it isn't converted into action. Likewise, audiences are already oversaturated with experts telling them things that are supposedly life altering. Radio, television, books, magazines, web-sites, celebrity spokespersons, international authorities, and authors all claim to have found the answers that lead to a perfect body, career, mate, or hair color. A lot of the ideas actually sound pretty good when we hear or see them, but very few of them stick for very long.

It is rather daunting to consider that you might have an hour or two to say a few things that an audience will actually retain for more than a few minutes after they walk out the door. Everything we know and understand about memory retention is that it is optimized when there is some kind of active learning involved rather than just passive listening. So the challenge of a speaker in a large room is to figure out ways to get the audience involved in such a way that they can personalize and adapt the content to their own needs.

You've been in enough similar situations to know what you think works best. Presenters may ask the audience to close their eyes and do a visual imagery exercise, or ask them to share something meaningful in dyads or small groups. Some speakers (and standup comedians) pick out a few people in the audience to address indi-vidually as representatives of the group. Others enlist volunteers for demonstrations. One of my own favorite strategies is to end a program by asking participants (those brave enough to volunteer) to share out loud what they promise to do after the program ends—and how they will hold themselves accountable. But regardless of the chosen technique, the idea is that it is important to figure out ways to help participants to use immediately what they have just learned—or it will quickly be forgotten.

Sticking With a Clear Message

One common mistake is that presenters try to do too much. They rush through their notes and slides as if the goal is to get through everything that was planned rather than focusing on a few signifi-cant themes that are most likely to be valued and retained. They talk too fast, cover too much material, breeze through their slides, leaving people feeling lost, confused, and overwhelmed. You even see some speakers glowing in satisfaction because they managed to cover everything they planned within the limited time parameters—even though very little was understood and the most important messages were diluted by "fluff."

Good presentations begin by providing a key message in the form of a singular theme, metaphor, story, or an example that can be used throughout to hold all the pieces of the presentation together. This message is not really the subject of the presentation, which might be on stress, relationships, or whatever. The message would be something different that encapsulates a meaningful set of actions, such as "Empathy has little value until you can communicate it effectively" or "Stress can be as useful as much as it can be destructive, depending on how you harness the nervous energy." The most memorable speeches, song lyrics, theater productions, movies, and books often feature one strong message that becomes the chorus for anything else that is offered. Martin Luther King's "I Have a Dream," Abraham Lincoln's "Gettysburg Address," or Steve Jobs's iPod launch all followed this template.

Dr. King's speaking greatness was related, in part, to always presenting a simple but strong message that held a speech together. Each talk placed primary attention on one individual message throughout. Nonviolence, hope, strength of commitment, the unacceptability of bigotry, or equality for every human being would each get its turn in the spotlight for a given speech on a given day. Audiences could recognize all the concepts, but only one example and one message would be repeated throughout to pull everything together. The audience left knowing the one message so thoroughly that all the other pieces could eventually be learned through its context.

In deconstructing the greatest speeches of all time, Duarte (2010) found that they have a similar cadence and formula, not dissimilar from that of a well-orchestrated symphony. First there is a statement or story about "what is," the status quo. In Lincoln's case, "Four score and seven years ago our fathers brought forth . . ."

Next, there is an image presented of "what could be," a future so much better that what has already been accepted: "It is for us the living, rather, to be dedicated here to the unfinished work which they who fought here have thus far so nobly advanced." Or in Steve Jobs's case it was a matter of describing a new world in which it was possible "to carry one thousand songs in your pocket."

Finally, there is a "call to action," a new level of bliss or satisfaction that can result from effort to make things different. In Lincoln's seminal speech it was a matter of rallying the frayed nation to come together, "that we here highly resolve that these dead shall not have died in vain—that this nation, under God, shall have a new birth of freedom."

A Handful of Ancillary Points

Solid preparation will always leave you with more information to present than people can effectively remember at one time. It has been known for some time there are limits to how many things people can remember reliably, usually not more than a handful. Think of treating these ancillary points, which are part of your main message, as you would with any client. When a major insight occurs during therapy, you stop exploration and focus instead on stabilizing immediate gains. You highlight the insights, examine them in detail, review them, and send the client home to experience them in order to solidify the gains.

Giving time and emphasis to a few key client insights per session is the same principle as keeping key presentation points to a manageable number. Highlight them in the introduction, use vivid examples for emphasis, lay them out in an organized way in the body of the presentation, and summarize them during the conclusion. Give ample time to flesh out the logical and experiential connections between points. Answer questions in ways that show relationships between examples, the message, and key points. Make the relationships between points as memorable as the message itself. This will send the audience home with memories and definitive feelings about the importance of your points rather than a head spinning with details immediately to be forgotten.

As mentioned earlier, media experts who consult with CEOs and political figures consistently advise their clients to use as few slides as possible so the audience attention remains focused on *them*. Furthermore, the slides should not usually contain more than a dozen words (that's right, you heard me correctly), in high-contrast colors (Duarte, 2010). Better yet, use images instead of words, especially those that are emotionally moving and highlight the themes discussed.

What do you do with all the extra useful information that goes beyond the ancillary points? Put it in handouts that people can review later and inform them about additional resources. The best single purpose of handouts and related materials is to provide an audience with the means to expand on the concepts they hear in a presentation.

Uses and Misuses of Technology

Obviously, technological tools have become so much a part of daily life that we hardly notice anymore how rare it is that anyone delivers a talk or presentation just facing the audience, with no slides or visual aids. It is even more unusual that the presenter knows how to use the Powerpoint, Keynote, or Prizzi structure in such a way that it truly enhances and supports what is being presented rather than acting as a distraction or worse.

The biggest mistakes that presenters make include the following:

1. Using too many slides that rush the pace and overwhelm the audience with content.
2. Having too much content on the slides that invites the audience to focus on the screen instead of the presenter.
3. The slides are disjointed and fragmented, leading in many directions without telling a coherent story.
4. The slides are not visually interesting and simple enough to emphasize key points.
5. The images or content presented are not unique, unusual, or novel enough to be remembered.

6. The presenter turns his or her back to the audience to look at the slides (or even read them!), thereby losing contact with the audience.
7. The talk becomes bland, boring, and predictable because the presenter follows the script without making spontaneous or responsive adjustments.
8. Rather than helping the presenter to connect with the audience more intimately, the slides create more distance.

Probably the most radical strategy is not to use slides at all but concentrate instead on the conversation in the room. That's why I mentioned earlier that a number of corporations and organizations now forbid slide presentations, reasoning that they actually cut off discussion and inhibit spontaneous conversation and creative brainstorming. "Powerpoint makes us stupid," admits a former head of U.S. Central Command when he was planning a mission into Iraq (Yu, 2014). The audience goes into autopilot and listens with only half a mind.

Of course, there are also many advantages to using visual aids and other technology like "clickers" that invite audience responses and participation. The main problem is that most presenters don't know how to use these options to maximize their effectiveness and enhance their performances.

A Challenging Send-Off

It is daunting enough to consider that we meet with clients once a week or so for less than an hour, talk to them about what's on their mind, and expect that this is going to have much enduring impact. But what about the challenge of talking to people for a single meeting and expecting that this experience is somehow going to stick with them for more than an hour after they resume their lives outside the room? The prognosis is indeed pretty dismal.

It really isn't that hard to keep people entertained and engaged when they are in the room, at least for the first half hour or so. But the really challenging goal of any such program is to say or do something that is going to stick. An even more difficult task is to inspire participants to actually *do* something meaningfully different when they leave.

It helps to ask these questions directly:

1. How will you apply what you've just heard?
2. When and where are you going to do this?
3. How will you hold yourself accountable to make sure you follow through on what you say is important?

I've experimented with all kinds of ways of doing this, such as asking participants to write down their commitments or share them with someone else nearby, exchanging phone numbers to check up on one another. I've had people write letters to themselves, setting down their intentions and making promises to themselves, then collecting the envelopes and mailing them back a year later. I've asked them to sign contracts, complete with witness signatures. I've invited them to share out loud, in front of the whole group, what they are willing to do and when they will do it. All of these may sound like good ideas, but I'd still estimate the probability of people following through as pretty remote. It's just really, really hard to plan a single-session therapy with a big room and expect that it will matter very much. Sorry to be so pessimistic, but you have to admit that has been your experience as well: The vast majority of times you hear someone speak the effects are very temporary.

Therapeutic Strategies When Teaching

For those who have the opportunity to work with groups over a prolonged period of time, whether a semester or an 8-week program, there are additional opportunities to incorporate what we know and understand from our therapy practice into the classroom. Just as professors receive little, if any, instruction in how to teach, so, too, have therapists' training been neglected in this area.

And the bar isn't set very high because so many presenters and lecturers aren't necessarily very charismatic.

While it is true that doing therapy and teaching do involve somewhat different skills, they also have a lot in common. In both cases the value of the experience is based on addressing the most salient concerns and interests of the people in the room. Participants all want to learn something new that will be immediately helpful in some way. And the likelihood of that process occurring is directly related to the level of active engagement we can help create.

It is amazing how much you can learn about audience members just by watching them as you would with your clients. Their faces alone tell the stories of how much they know, what their mood is, whether they are with you or they have checked out. Anger, joy, frustration, confusion, satisfaction, disappointment, exhilaration, boredom, and enlightenment are all visible if you are watching carefully.

I have a friend who does workshops for a living, and I was following his visit with a workshop of my own. The organizer of the program was helping to set up the room when he remarked that my friend who had been there the previous week and taken off his shoes and walked around the space in his socks to get a feel for the room before the people arrived. I thought that was interesting, but it sparked for me a realization that I could care less about the room itself; it is the people present who make all the difference. I also realized that my willingness to take risks, to explore the unknown, to push my limits as a presenter is related to how comfortable I feel with those in attendance. If I feel a connection, if I feel that we have some rapport and trust developed, then I will try all kinds of things without fear of being written off. I get wild and crazy. I give myself permission to create a singular experience by experimenting with new and different methods, anecdotes, and ideas I might make up on the spot. If things are working well, then my excitement becomes contagious because we all realize that we are collaborating together to create something altogether fresh and unexpected.

So that's why I decided to stand outside the door (with my shoes on) and greet each participant individually, shaking a hand, touching a shoulder, introducing myself, making some kind of contact. By the time the program began I felt like I already "knew" the people in the room; we were no longer strangers. That was a breakthrough for me in my teaching, an insight that is an outgrowth of what I already do as a therapist. If we are going to have credibility, if the audience is going to trust us and be open to what we have to offer, it isn't just related to our perceived expertise but also our ability to connect with those in the room.

Fortunately, we do have all kinds of training that prepares us for this endeavor, even if many therapists fail to adapt their skills effectively to meet the unique demands of a classroom context. Whether speaking to people face to face, or via published works that we cover in the next chapter, the key is always going to come down to the relationships we create with our audience.

Chapter 11

WRITING AND PUBLISHING FOR PLEASURE, PURPOSE, OR PROFIT

What is a writer?

It is someone who writes.

Never before in history has it ever been easier to "publish" what you have created. Once upon a time it was next to impossible to disseminate a manuscript to a larger audience. Acceptance rates in scholarly journals are less than 5% of manuscripts submitted, and that is based on a sample of fairly high-level authors with lots of experience. To have a book proposal even considered, you often needed representation by an agent, which is no easy matter in the first place to find one willing to sell a project. Sadly still, more than 99% of book proposals are rejected by assistants and interns before they ever land on an actual editor's desk. And even for those books that are actually published, the average shelf life in a bookstore is less than a few weeks. No wonder aspiring writers are so easily discouraged.

There have been a lot of complaints about the evolution of the publishing world in recent years. Publishers are dying; those that survive (so far) are redefining themselves, merging, diversifying, struggling to find a solid footing. Nobody is quite sure yet how "books" will evolve in the future. Will they remain physical objects or perhaps electronic entities in the "cloud?" Will books eventually be replaced with some other vehicle for consuming information in much the same way that libraries are now becoming transformed into centers for electronic media?

Even the prospect of letter writing has become a lost art. Some of the greatest biographies of Thomas Jefferson, Winston Churchill, John Adams, Virginia Woof, Sigmund Freud, and others were constructed mostly from their correspondence. This had been a kind of private publishing with a limited audience of one. What legacy now remains of significant figures of the future? Their texts and tweets? Perhaps some e-mails or postings on Facebook?

Yet one of the consequences that has evolved in published writing is that there are now more outlets and opportunities for therapists to share their wisdom, knowledge, and experience in a variety of ways. Not only are there still traditional vehicles of writing articles and books, whether in physical or electronic form, but it is now possible for almost anyone to publish blogs, newsletters, or posts on social media.

One of the most exciting opportunities involves self-publishing opportunities on demand in which a therapist can create a manuscript, hire an editor, and distribute the work in limited and economical quantities for one's own clients or particular audience. Considering that the average number of books that are sold through a commercial publisher is a few hundred copies, it isn't much of a stretch to figure you could do just as well yourself.

Why Bother to Write With Everything Else on Your Plate?

You already work days, evenings, and when you can't get out of it, weekends as well. There is never enough time for it all: helping clients in distress, tending to emergencies, expanding your referral base, learning new therapeutic methods, consulting, perhaps supervising, teaching, and trying to earn a living. If you are lucky, you may even squeeze in a little leisure time. So why would any overloaded therapist consider taking on the additional work needed to write and publish original ideas? Therapists publish their ideas for a number of personal, professional, and economic reasons.

Recognition. There are few kicks in life more pleasurable than seeing your name in print. Likewise, there is tremendous satisfaction in showing your latest publication to your parents or children, your partner, spouse, colleagues, friends, and clients. It feels wonderful to be recognized for some small contribution you have made as a function of your unique way of describing and explaining things.

How often have you sat in session and articulated some concept or idea that went way over your client's head who was barely listening in the first place? Every therapist has discovered or invented some insight, or twist on an idea, that is worth sharing with others. We are all deep thinkers who spend our daily lives involved in the most interesting discussions with people about the most significant concerns of their lives. Each of us has something original to say about the state of the human condition.

Published works can lead to enhanced reputation for your expertise, increasing credibility. Given that many authors now take primary responsibility for marketing their own work, this also leads to increased networking and presence on social media, and it may provide other professional opportunities.

Immortality. One thing that is true for writers is that your words live long beyond your own physical occupancy of this planet. It is exciting to consider that in libraries, or even people's homes, there will rest on shelves (or in cyberspace) a copy of something you wrote long ago. Decades, even centuries from now, someone in the future can look back and read something that you once described.

Opening doors. There is no doubt that publishing leads to a number of options that would not be available otherwise. For those in academia, publishing is a necessary part of job survival. However, practitioners also find that publishing leads to opportunities for consulting and collaboration, speaking engagements, travel sojourns, media appearances, increased referrals, and visibility.

Fortune. Well, not exactly fortune; more like a few extra dollars for spending money. Despite myths to the contrary, very few writers ever make enough money to even compensate them for their time. The overwhelming majority of books that are published don't sell enough copies to break even, much less shower the author with wealth. Still, it is a motivation for some therapists to write with the hope that they will be paid a fair wage for their creative efforts. Certainly, it is a pleasant surprise to receive even a modest check in the mail for a magazine article or book that you have written. Although financial rewards for writing are rarely realized to the extent that the author hopes, this fantasy does act as an incentive for some to continue their efforts.

Personal satisfaction. This reason is the most crucial of all. Because the life of a writer is filled with rejection letters, critical reviewers, and endless drafts, it has got to be a labor of love, one you undertake because you enjoy the process of creation as well as the end result. It is important to write what you really love, and to love what you write, purely for the personal satisfaction from expressing creativity.

Procrastination and Inhibition

One of the aspects of writing that compromises enjoyment of the process is feeling blocked because you haven't discovered your authentic narrative voice. There is sometimes a disconnect between what therapists do regularly in their offices, that is, explain things and talk about ideas quite fluently, and then setting these or similar ideas down in print. Assuming that you choose to write about a subject you feel passionate and knowledgeable about, the process usually involves getting out of your own way and letting the ideas flow. This is a lot easier and fun if certain conditions are met.

1. *Write about a topic or content that stimulates a strong personal, as well as professional, interest.* Almost every project I undertake (including this one) involves exploring a subject that confounds, confuses, or disturbs me. I am writing as much for myself as I am to inform an audience.

2. *Figure out what is unique and singular about your message and the way you would communicate it.* I have always found this prospect most inhibiting of all, thinking that all the good books have already been written and most of the best ideas have already been explored. And yet what you, or anyone, has to offer is the personal way you make sense of things and the individual style with which you communicate these ideas.

3. *Recruit a coauthor.* Writing is a lonely business for sure. And it is a lot more fun to collaborate with someone else, if (a) you can find someone who complements what you do, (b) that person is totally reliable and delivers what was promised, and (c) you make the necessary time together to get things done. Most people talk a good game but rarely follow through on what they say they will do, and when they say they will do it.

4. *Say what you'll do and do what you say. Always. Without exception or excuses.* This might sound simple but most people can't—or won't—follow through. I've edited a lot of books and journal issues in my career, and I'd say that the majority of authors who are invited to contribute something do not deliver their manuscript on time. What makes a writer is someone who writes—every day.

5. *Create opportunities.* Like anything else in life, and anything we teach to our clients, you will wait a very long time if you are sitting around hoping for deliverance. You have to create opportunities for yourself by reaching out to publishing sources and not taking no for an answer (all the while making changes in light of feedback you receive). My first book idea was rejected by over 50 publishers. I used the form letters I received to paper the wall of my study as a reminder of the resilience and immunity to rejection it would take to finally be successful.

6. *Send stuff out into the world.* Always have something under review, something on your desk (or computer) that you are working on, something that a coauthor is making

edits or changes to, and some idea in your head that is still in a developing stage. Keep the queue moving along. When some manuscript is declined, send it somewhere else right away. Embrace the feedback you receive to make it better for the next round.

7. *Ask for help when you need it.* Be honest about your strengths and weaknesses as a writer. You get better not only through practice but also critical input from others you trust. Hire an editor if you need one.

The biggest obstacle that inhibits the ability to write is procrastination. People spend more time thinking about writing and talking about writing than they ever do actually sitting down and doing it. Certainly such reflection and engagement with others about ideas is useful, even necessary, in order to attain some degree of excellence in what you create. There is a difference, though, between systematic preparation, research, hypothesis testing, critical thinking, and actually getting those ideas down.

If you are going to write and attempt to publish your work, then criticism and rejection come with the territory. Whether your reasons for writing relate to profit or pleasure, you have the necessary abilities for success; most therapists do. What holds you back is an inability to engage the struggles needed for growth, to make the necessary time commitment, or to maintain an accurate perception of how the process works.

Publishing is a game with its own unique set of rules, some of which are accessible to most anyone who cares to investigate the arena and others that are rarely spoken about. Personal choice will dictate your commitment and willingness to engage in the process, while the information contained in this chapter and other sources can help you increase the likelihood of your success.

The Inside Rules of the Publishing Game

Writing is one thing; publishing is quite another. The insiders of the publishing world know what reviewers and editors are looking for, while the outsiders don't. Journals look for material that fits their audience just as book publishers seek manuscripts that can sell to specific markets. Most manuscripts are rejected out of hand after reading the first few paragraphs and discovering that what was submitted doesn't really match what the publishing outlet actually does. The first thing that journal editors (and their assistants) look for is whether the article actually fits the journal's content. Likewise, publishers screen out most proposals because the authors either miscalculated or overreached their market audience.

Each journal, publisher, or online outlet has a specific audience that they are ideally suited to reach. The editor of *The Counseling Psychologist* expects to see articles in a form and style that is different from *Psychotherapy Networker*. They may both be geared for practitioners in the field, but one has a far more academic slant while the other is written in a more accessible, journalistic style. Readers of the *Journal of Humanistic Psychology* expect thoughtful material on the human condition, not the latest behavioral approach. The *Journal of Experimental Psychology* or *Social Work Research* is looking for solid research, not thoughtful experiential pieces.

Even more precise are the target audiences of book publishers that have done extensive market surveys to determine exactly what will sell and what will not. For example, textbook publishers realize that although texts are written for students, it is really professors who decide whether to adopt them; such books are not actually sold to the consumers. Publishers know that the professional market is made up primarily of social workers and psychologists in their 30s and 40s who purchase books primarily through direct mail advertisements; they do not expect to sell therapists' material to the broader audience who frequent chain bookstores (the few that remain).

Each journal or book editor has a different set of readers to please. Although this point may seem rather obvious, you would be amazed by how often authors send their manuscripts to places that don't publish works remotely related to their own. The author did not investigate very carefully to see if what he or she created matched the style and scope of the particular publishing outlet.

There are several ways to gain inside knowledge about a particular publishing outlet. First of all, study previous publications. Make yourself a student of the content and style that have been used before. There is no sense in sending in an article or book idea if the journal or publisher already produced something similar a few years ago.

As mentioned earlier, you may also wish to consider working with a coauthor who already has a track record of successful publishing efforts. Book publishers, in particular, are not inclined to risk their money with someone who is, as yet, unproven. Even with article submissions that are reviewed blindly, readers can often tell whether the author(s) is a member of the inner club.

Whether you work alone or with a coauthor, it helps to talk with members of the editorial board, or even the editor, to find out about what they are looking for. Most editors are quite amenable to speaking with prospective authors about their ideas, letting them know if the plans fit their own agenda. This is not unlike the process we undertake when we work with families in therapy. We first study their patterns and rules before we try any direct intervention. Particularly with journal articles, when you are only allowed to submit an article to one place at a time and the turnaround time can take many months, you don't want to make the mistake of submitting a manuscript without being fairly certain that your piece fits what they are usually seeking.

What to Write About?

I am frequently asked how it's possible to be so prolific, to write three or four books each year for the past 30 years. I usually just shrug, mostly because I don't really understand the question. As therapists, we are paid to talk for a living, to explain complex ideas in language that is accessible. We use words to demonstrate our deep understanding of others' experiences, as well as to communicate the insights that seem most relevant. We are poets and sages. People pay for our wisdom.

I have never seen much difference between how I talk and how I write. Somehow I found my writing voice as simply an extension of the things I might speak aloud. So I have never experienced "writer's block" any more than you become tongue-tied during sessions. Once we are in the zone, the words just flow.

Pretty much every book I've ever written stems from some unresolved personal issue of mine or else some curiosity I feel about a subject that appears to have little already written. When I review my life as a writer, I see a catalogue that reflects my own struggles to make sense of things that in some way befuddled me. I'd do a literature review and find scant articles or search books and find them completely inadequate. And even when there was a body of literature on the topic, rather than following the usual "rules" of first doing a thorough review of what has been written previously, I'd first try to sort out what I know, what I might have to offer on the subject. I never could have written a single page otherwise, feeling that there's nothing new I could possibly say that hasn't been said before. I have felt that way for 40 years, and *still* feel that way—in case that might seem familiar to you.

I once had a traumatic experience while backpacking the wilds of New Zealand, coming close to dying from hypothermia. When I was brought back to life, I couldn't stop crying, knowing how close I came to leaving my family fatherless and husbandless. But what puzzled me most is that I hadn't cried in 10 years prior to this. Why had I stopped crying for so many years, and what now brought forth my endless tears? I began researching the subject and found very little was known and understood about the "language" of tears as a form of communication across cultures, contexts, gender, and meaning-making. This became a book called *The Language of Tears* (Kottler, 1996), followed afterward by another one about how such travel experiences can become so much more transformative than traditional therapy (Kottler, 1997). Whether I write about personal issues that interest me, or professional challenges I face, the projects are always driven by intense curiosity. If that is the case for me, or anyone, it is never a matter of "finding" time to write but rather making time to do other things that are far less interesting and fulfilling.

Every therapist muses about the most extraordinary and puz-zling aspects of human experience. In one sense I don't think it matters that much what you choose to write about as long as you discover a way to explore it that reflects your own style and view-point. I know that publishers and journal editors talk a lot about finding the "right" marketable topic, but it is also your take on it that can make the piece stand out. Personally, I don't even care what I write about as long as the process teaches me some things and allows me to explore new territory.

I've also heard it said to "write what you know," but I think I'd reframe that to write what you *live*. In other words, write about what is most sacred and precious to you and do it in a way that comes from both your head *and* your heart.

Forums for Publishing

As I've said before, publishing used to be a completely closed sys-tem for the elite members of the guild. The likelihood of breaking into the club as an unknown, without a mentor or sponsor, was pretty remote. In my first projects I had a very senior scholar as the first author even though I did most of the work. This seemed to be the only way that I could be admitted into the exclusive club.

It used to be so discouraging to learn that the acceptance rates for journals or publishers was so low, sometimes akin to winning the lottery. And when you don't have personal contacts or advocates within the industry, along with high stature in the field, the odds drop even further. For better or worse, it is now a brave new world for writers in which there are so many companies that now provide opportunities for self-publishing that were once considered a stigma. You may find it surprising that in today's climate authors who self-publish actually earn more money than those who go with the five largest publishing houses. Just as interesting, one third of all ebook sales now feature self-published works (Howey, 2014). The books *50 Shades of Grey* and *The Wool Trilogy* are two examples of such works that have been wildly successful and sold millions of copies.

The goal, realistically, is not to write a best seller but rather to be able to find an outlet to distribute your work to a wider audience, however this might be defined. One therapist had been practicing for more than 20 years and felt that she had accumulated enough wisdom that it seemed worthwhile to organize and formalize her ideas into a book she might share with her clients. "I had no big dream and maybe no interest in even having the book available in bookstores. It was just something I wanted to do for my own clients and I thought they might enjoy having an outline of the main ideas I like to cover with them in sessions."

The therapist settled on one company that didn't require any upfront costs and would produce the books on demand without her being stuck with boxes of books in her basement. It turned out to be the perfect outlet for the limited goals of her project.

An even more accessible vehicle, which doesn't require much (if any) external approval, is to publish via a blog or on a website. In one sense, posts on social media are also considered publications in that brief stories are told through photos or narrative updates. For those who yearn for a more traditional publishing source (and perhaps more widely distributed market), there are several opportunities.

Newsletters

Newsletters are the most overlooked and undervalued vehicle for publishing, especially by those who are just getting their writing careers going. As the workhorses of communication in professional organizations, newsletters are produced more frequently in order to provide the most timely and practical information to readers. The emphasis on timeliness brings about particularly strong requirements for brevity and practicality, where professionals can access content quickly and move on to the next article.

Newsletter articles are generally one of five types: (1) information on the business of the profession, (2) opinions about current issues, (3) reports of experiences in the field, (4) "how to" articles in which practical techniques are described, and (5) book reviews. You may also be surprised at how hungry editors are for submissions in any of these areas. As long as the author is willing to work on several drafts of the article to meet the editor's requirements, there is a high probability of eventually seeing it published to a fairly large audience.

Newsletter articles are usually designed to be brief, interesting, and most relevant to readers. They are written in a more journalistic rather than academic style, but what they may lack in professional credibility they make up for in accessibility.

Journals

Major professional organizations generally publish both a newsletter for currency, opinions, and greater flexibility of documentation, and a journal where evaluation of material is formalized and involves external reviewers. Two to four editors will generally review a manuscript submitted to a professional journal to assess its value, support for ideas, and the quality of writing. The process is slow and can take from 8 months to 2 years or more for an article to make it into print. Even getting an article into a specific journal is no sure task for the best of writers. Journal editors generally have many more manuscripts submitted than they can publish, so rejection is a regular occurrence for those who submit manuscripts. Some of the top-tier journals reject 90% of article submitted, whereas others may accept as many as half the manuscripts considered.

Details, careful reasoning, scrupulous methodology, and supporting documentation in scholarly journals replace the brevity and timeliness of newsletters. Extra professional credibility comes with the more scholarly approach to journal articles even if they are not read as widely as newsletter articles. Strong support of ideas and peer evaluation are demanded because journal articles represent the historical record of theory and practice of a profession. They also act as the "currency" of those who circulate in the academic world because their retention and promotion depend on the quality and quantity of these refereed articles, as well as how often they are cited by others.

Keep in mind that it is highly unusual to have an article accepted by the first journal you submit to. If your article is accepted, most often that will include some changes that are suggested (or required) by the reviewers and the editor. It's important to evaluate this feedback carefully, incorporating the best ideas into the next draft. Alternatively, you can make a decision to submit the piece to another publication. Although there are "rules" that you can only have an article under submission by one journal at a time, there are usually lots of options that can be considered. Before I submit an article I always make a list of three or four publications that might be suitable, starting with the one that is most desirable and then working my way down the list.

Rather than feeling discouraged by multiple rejections, there are also some "back doors" through which articles can also be accepted. Often special issues of journals invite particular authors to contribute articles. Although these manuscripts are also subjected to critical evaluation by reviewers, there is a high probability that they will make it into print once suggestions and edits are incorporated. Sometimes it is possible to collaborate with a more senior author who has been invited to be part of such a project. One other strategy is to contact the editor of a favorite journal and ask how you can most effectively contribute. Sometimes the publication is planning a special issue in the future or may even solicit a piece about a particular subject that may fit your interests or expertise.

It is at this point that I also want to talk about the realities of being a writer. There is a significant difference between writing and publishing. As difficult as producing an article or manuscript might be, it is even more challenging to get the piece into print and this is the part that most discourages aspiring authors. If you are serious about this enterprise, then you must immunize yourself against the frustrations of rejection, which are all too common. Until you develop your skills, learn the rules of the game, make contacts within the field, and develop a reputation, you are going to hear lots of bad news.

Magazines

One "cousin" of a journal is a commercial magazine, a profit-driven version of a monthly or quarterly publication that is designed for the general public rather than professionals. A few members of our profession have been successful in writing articles for magazines by talking about psychological issues in accessible terms, often related to their research areas.

One advantage of submitting to magazines is that you are allowed to contact several different ones at the same time because there is no prohibition against multiple submissions. Similar to book projects, there is often an advantage to notifying the editor that the piece is under consideration by others, which may expedite a response, as well as notify them that they have competition. On the other hand, it may be difficult to have an article considered by a reputable magazine unless you are represented by an agent or, at the very least, have established a track record.

Books

I will say again that if the main motive for writing a book is to make money, or even to expect reasonable compensation for your time, you'd best look elsewhere and concentrate on seeing more clients. Writing is mostly a labor of love.

There are different kinds of books—and thus publishers are positioned in different ways to reach these markets. First there are *trade books*, those for the general public that find themselves in retail establishments. Most aspiring authors imagine producing this sort of book, translating some area of expertise into a volume that is accessible to general readers. This is a common goal, not only because it is desirable to reach the largest possible audience but also because it is imagined that this is the most profitable path to fame and fortune. I'm sorry to disappoint you.

Many of the large trade publishers might receive thousands of book proposals each year from which they select a few dozen to offer contracts. Among this elite group, most of these authors would be established authors who have already worked with this or another publisher previously. In addition, most of these authors have an agent representing their interests. Before you run out and hire an agent of your own, you should know that the best ones are even more selective in choosing their clients than the publishers are in signing books.

Even if you should be so fortunate to obtain a book contract and publish with one of the big houses, that guarantees almost nothing. Trade publishers might release 20 books (or fewer) each season, but many allocate their marketing budget primarily to the two or three volumes that they think have the best chance of hitting the jackpot; the rest are left to flounder on their own. That's why books have such a brief half-life on the shelves and most of them never even complete their first printing. Once the author deducts production costs, indexing fees, and agent commissions, there is precious little left over as a prize.

Professional trade books are a second optional category. These are books like the one you are currently reading that are designed for professionals as resources. This is definitely a fertile area for therapist-writers to pursue in which specific topics related to the practice of therapy, or similar subjects, are explored. Publishers like W. W. Norton and others are always searching for novel ideas, or seminal volumes that might be of interest to their professional market. One of the best places to explore this possible partnership is at a professional conference in which you can arrange face-to-face meetings with the acquisition editors in attendance. Alternatively, you can always send a proposal directly to the editor at one of your target publishers.

Textbooks are a third type of book and, surprisingly, perhaps the most profitable. One reason for this is that once a textbook becomes minimally successful and receives enough adoptions, it stays in print for a long time through subsequent new editions. Furthermore, if a university or professor decides to adopt a text, this means a large number of sales that are potentially renewed each year. But before you hurry and grind out a textbook in some area that you think is needed, you should understand that the publishing industry in general is in such a state of flux with diminishing sales, reduced profits, mergers, government regulation, and uncertainty because of new technologies, that many publishers are not signing very many new texts any longer and instead trying to just stabilize sales with their current offerings.

I don't mean to be discouraging, just realistic about what you can reasonably expect. And I'd like to return to one of the earliest points I made—that the overriding goal and purpose of writing should be to express yourself in a meaningful way for the pure pleasure and satisfaction of doing so. Whether this takes place through journaling, blogging, social media, writing essays for limited distribution, or aiming for conventional publication, it is about the process rather than the outcome.

Writing a Proposal

If you do decide to pursue a book idea, the first place to start is a conversation with an editor who works for one of your target publishers. You'll first want to do your homework to make sure that this publisher markets and distributes books in the particular subject area and doesn't already have a similar title. I can't tell you how many proposals are rejected out of hand for these two reasons.

One thing you do *not* want to do is to complete your manuscript and then look for a publisher. First of all, editors don't have time to read a whole manuscript before issuing a contract. Secondly, it is likely that you wasted a lot of time because the editor will have some suggestions and input that might change the whole trajectory of the project. "That's a great idea," an editor might tell you. "And we like what you've done a lot." Pause. Long silence. Wait for it . . . "But what we really need is a book about . . ." In other words, they like one part of your idea but want you to reshape it in a different direction altogether. And by then it's really too late because you are overcommitted to what you've already done. That's why the relationship between an author and a good editor is a true partnership in which the collaboration leads to a product that may end up very different from what was started.

One case in point is this book you hold in your hands, a collaboration with my editor, Ben Yarling. I would estimate that only about one third of these pages were part of the original plan, and the balance was the result of an ongoing organic discussion and series of compromises. I love that part of the process, but it also means you have to be open to other possibilities you may not have previously considered.

Although most publishers have their own preferred formats for submitting a proposal, there are some standard sections that you will want to include. The whole document is usually not more than 30 pages or so, including a sample chapter. This includes a brief introduction and overview of the project, a detailed chapter outline, and sections that describe how your book is unique, competing books in this area, and how you are the one qualified to complete this book. It is also a good idea to have your sample chapter reviewed and edited before you subnit it so you can present the best possible first impression of your writing skills.

There are sources you can consult like *The Writers Digest* and a book by Bill O'Hanlon (2013), *Becoming a Published Therapist*, which discusses some of the ins and outs of converting an idea into a salable project. In addition, conference programs often have panels of editors or published authors who speak about the practical realities of getting into print. While this inside information is certainly instructive and helpful, I wonder about its role in promoting false and unrealistic hope for future prospects. The reality is that it is really, really hard to get something published in traditional outlets, which is why I'm so excited about alternative avenues that have opened up in recent years, making it possible for therapists to share their ideas in a variety of other forums.

Writing for Yourself

Writing for publication ultimately involves being at the mercy of others' judgments. Editors decide whether they believe your contribution has merit, whether it is good enough. This is a most unpleasant, helpless position to be in, and it hasn't gotten that much better over time.

One way to get around the situation of faceless editors being the gatekeepers who determine whether a wider audience will read your stuff is to write primarily for yourself. Write because it gives you pleasure, because it helps you clarify your ideas, because it stretches your thinking, because it forces you to be more disciplined. Write because you wish to do so for yourself.

Should you be fortunate enough to have your product published, that is an added bonus, not a necessity. You may be thinking, "That's easy for *you* to say; after all, your words do get in print." I worked diligently and compulsively for a long time, sometimes writing every day, before a first article was finally accepted for publication—in a small, state journal that only a few people ever read.

It is truly lovely when something you write is published. It feels wonderful to know that many others will be reading your words, perhaps years from now when you are no longer around. But this is a luxury rather than a necessity. If this book had never seen the light of day, I would still have learned so much trying to make sense of the differences between how we were trained and what goes on in the real world of practice. I would still have enjoyed the pleasure of expressing myself.

Write because it makes you happy. Write because it makes you a better therapist and a better thinker and a better communicator. Share what you've written with those whom you most respect and like. Circulate your manuscripts among your friends and colleagues. Create position papers for your clients. Most of all, to be a writer means that you have to write. Every day. Whether what you create becomes published is not totally within your control. First and foremost, you must write for yourself.

Chapter 12

NAVIGATING ORGANIZATIONAL POLITICS

As challenging as some difficult clients may be, such as those who present intractable mental disorders, chronic addictions, or florid personality disorders, sometimes the greatest source of stress in our jobs may be our own colleagues. Every human organization presents certain challenges as staff compete for resources or power, but sometimes mental health organizations can create some dysfunctional systems that are quite difficult to manage.

You would think that as human relations experts we would be more than a little sensitive and skilled at dealing with interpersonal conflict. You would think we would be more tolerant and flexible than most folks, more willing to compromise and support one another. You would also expect that we would be especially able to recognize power struggles as they are occurring and intervene constructively, just as we do in our clients' family systems. Although I'm talking about some of the more unsavory aspects of our profession, I do want to emphasize a strong belief that it doesn't have to be this way and that we are capable of doing so much better.

Necessary Casualties?

Some of us do not recall our days in graduate school as especially pleasant. It was a competitive environment, one with its fair share of stress in many ways. Certainly it was frightening to be continuously evaluated and wonder if you're really good enough. There was all the work involved, the uncertainty about the future, the mixed messages you might have received from faculty. You learned that certain instructors didn't much care for one another, and you figured out how to be very cautious in navigating the treacherous interpersonal waters.

During sincere attempts to make sense of discrepant feedback from different faculty, students are often caught in the middle. Each instructor and each supervisor had strong beliefs regarding the best way to function as a therapist—and these visions were not necessarily compatible. One mentor might tell you to do one thing, while another would tell you just the opposite. In some cases, it wouldn't take much awareness to observe and understand that some of those in power didn't much like one another at all, and it was wise to try and stay out of the line of fire, that is, unless you were coopted as a surrogate pawn.

When students are exposed to the kinds of power games, one-upmanship, coalitional battles, and backstabbing that are sometimes so much a part of academic life, they come to accept this behavior in their mentors as almost normal. They hear their heroes bad-mouthing one another. They observe the intricate patterns of engagement that take place between warring camps. They join in the battles themselves, playing active roles as scouts, messengers, sometimes even firing off a few salvos of their own against the designated targets of the other side. Worst of all, most of us still have the scars to prove our courage, wounded in battle for what we imagined was an honorable cause.

What, then, did we learn in graduate school about the inevitability of factionalism, with its accompanying political games? We internalized far more than what our mentors said; we sometimes imitated the ways they act. If they presented themselves to us as noble crusaders fighting against the infidels, we learned to view hurtful actions as necessary casualties in a holy war.

If I seem unduly cynical about this state of affairs, it's because I was caught in the crossfire more often than I'd prefer to remember—and it was all my own damn fault. If only I could have learned to keep my head down and my mouth shut. If only I hadn't felt so insecure about my own position that I felt the need to fight battles I could never win. If only I hadn't aligned myself with players in the drama who thrived on power and would do anything to keep it.

Lessons Learned Well

Before we ever began our first jobs as therapists, and entered an environment that might already have been highly toxic, we had been shaped and molded as warriors, ready to add fuel to the flames of discontent. In the case of surviving organizational politics, we also learned a set of lessons that were certainly not part of the organized curricula.

Students are rewarded for individual success rather than working well together as team members. They live in continual fear that they will be weeded out, that their professors will discover their deepest, darkest secret—that they are really quite ordinary and have been faking competence all their lives. They see some of their comrades giving in to the pressure and vow that they will rise above the fray, attain the highest honors, and therefore the choicest jobs.

These are bright people. They are folks who have been successful most of their lives playing academic games. They have learned their lesson well: You make yourself look better when others look worse.

Graduate school also taught us not to trust ourselves but rather to put our faith in what authority figures tell us about how we are doing. You could write the best paper of your life, convinced you have integrated the research on the subject and articulated your ideas with such clarity you feel dizzy with pride, and yet if some professor gives you a B+, your self-assessment will be diminished. You could make the most brilliant comment in class that you have ever formulated, much less said aloud, and yet if the teacher doesn't like what you said, you assume it was some shortcoming on your part. You could make an absolutely flawless execution of an intervention, yet while viewing the video with your supervisor, you are easily convinced that your efforts were misguided. In other words, you learned over and over again that it is others' opinions of your performance that matter most. By "others" I am not referring to who really matters (clients), but to authority figures like teachers and supervisors who are continuously judging whether you are worthy of remaining part of this exclusive club.

Each of these lessons, while compromising our personal confidence and initiative, did its job well in preparing us to work in an environment where being competitive, political, manipulative, dominant, and achievement oriented would be valued over values that lead to cooperation and mutual support. These, however, are only a few of the ingredients that help account for why the political squabbles in our work can be so vicious.

An Explosive Recipe

Imagine what would come out of the oven if you mixed together the following ingredients and stirred vigorously. First, you have a half dozen or more individuals who make a living convincing others to do things they don't really want to do and are used to getting their way and not taking no for an answer. They have been trained, molded, and drilled to be exquisitely sensitive to other people's weaknesses and vulnerabilities, also attracted to relationships in which they can be in control and in charge of the proceedings. They tend to be more than a little narcissistic and self-centered, with an inflated sense of self-importance. They make a living pretending to know more than they really do.

Add to this mix that these individuals are used to being in the middle of heated conflicts in which people are fighting ferocious, vicious, intractable battles that have been going on for years. Thanks to their strong personalities, charismatic interpersonal styles, and unbridled confidence, they actually get paid to tell people what to do, to impart wisdom, and to enjoy special status as a sage.

Put a bunch of these people together in an organization with different professional specialties in which they can't agree on which discipline is best qualified to do this work, which approach to helping is most effective, and what setting is best designed for this work. Stir in to the pot a cultural climate in the larger community that shows increasing skepticism and disrespect for what therapists do and how they do it, puts more and more pressure on practitioners to defend their activities, prove their effectiveness, and justify their existence, and then enforces fiscal cutbacks that create more competition and less cooperation among clinicians.

Next, throw in an organizational structure in which there is usually hierarchical power that may value efficiency rather than quality work and prefers product over process. This system also invites disagreement even if it doesn't actually tolerate defiance. Then remember that the participants in this system are those who usually love to analyze every nuance and underlying meaning to everyone else's behavior. They have a marked oversensitivity to perceived slights and often feel hurt or misunderstood. Then consider that within this group there is likely to be one or more individuals with surprisingly poor interpersonal skills, if not gross psychopathology.

Taken together, this indeed is a recipe for disaster, or at least a lot of drama. It is no wonder that so much uncooperative, if not toxic, behavior is spawned.

Monsters Among Us

It is our dirtiest secret. We speak about it in whispers with our closest friends. We ruminate about it constantly. It invades our sleep in the form of restlessness, nightmares, even insomnia. It dominates our most private discussions with staff members.

I am speaking about those among us whose behavior is not only disruptive but also borders on being pathological. If this field attracts the Joan of Arcs, the Florence Nightingales, the Martin

Luther Kings who want to be healers and saviors, to set things right and make the world a better place, then we have also attracted the forces of darkness. What a great place to hide, even blossom, for those who thrive on manipulating and controlling others.

Indeed, look around you. The odds are pretty good that if you work in an organization with more than a dozen people, there is a toxic colleague among you, one masquerading as a healer who really goes around hurting people—not only clients but also colleagues. I'm not saying that therapists have more than their fair share of sociopathy within their ranks, just that we do have some dangerous colleagues and they are far better equipped and positioned to do damage than others might be. These dysfunctional professionals are predators in the sense that they hunger for chaos around them. They like being around other people in pain; even better, they seem to enjoy causing it. It gives them a sense of power and potency. It helps them to feel in control.

It is too bad we were not provided with a diagnostic guide to identify such dysfunctional colleagues in graduate school. Not to sound too conspiratorial, but one reason this critical information was withheld, of course, is that such disturbing (and disturbed) individuals lurk in the hallways of academia in disproportionate numbers. And why not? If you get off on dominating and humiliating people, what better place to do that than with students?

People who have been trained as therapists are far more skilled at disguising their disabilities. We all realize this; it is another of our secrets—that we entered this field in the first place as a way to hold ourselves together and hide our own imperfections. Some people are far better at this than others. Nevertheless, if you look carefully around you, you will easily recognize the same symptoms you see in your clients in a few of your colleagues. (Of course, you are exempt because you are reading this book.)

The Spoils of War

At least with overt hostility you know what is happening even if you don't like it. In the case of those who are manipulative behind the scenes, sometimes you never know what hit you until it's too late. These are the sneaky ones, the colleagues who will be so cordial and considerate to your face but look for every opportunity to stab you in the back if it meets their needs. In the jargon of our profession, we would call these people passive-aggressive, or perhaps practitioners of a different sort of sociopathy than direct intimidation. Then again, they may be just extraordinarily well-schooled at playing the political games that are part of human organizations. If that involves deceit, exploitation, and manipulation, so be it. If other people get hurt along the way, that is their problem. It is survival of the fittest.

Some of the strongest bonds of friendship are often predicated on a common enemy. In his book on the political strategies of chimpanzees, de Waal (1982) provided a fascinating glimpse into the coalitional affiliations that take place as individuals wish to attain power and status and enjoy the fruits of those conquests in terms of greater resources. In the world of chimps, or a group of therapists, nobody can rule without the consent of those who are governed. A member who is skilled at using any means available, especially deception and manipulation, is likely to be rewarded in terms of the spoils of war.

What is it that therapists are maneuvering for, such that they would be willing to invest energy and effort in political pursuits? What's really at stake that makes it worthwhile to spend time trying to win friends and influence people?

Savage political struggles are part of the therapist's existence because the rewards are perceived as worth the emotional risks. For one thing, those who are best connected get the choicest referrals and are more likely to be promoted. Like the chimpanzees that are part of the dominant male's social circle, there is status by association. We may not be after the best bananas or selection of mates, but we are very interested in having access to "insider" information that makes it easier for us to do our jobs. Obviously, those who have managed to maneuver themselves into the "in" group also have a greater likelihood of enjoying the rewards that this brings.

These external rewards are certainly reason enough to get involved in political action, but there are internal motives as well.

The unfortunate reality is that some people like to become embroiled in political struggles because they love the action. They wish to distract themselves from the emptiness of their lives. They feel powerless in other areas and so thrive on the exhilaration that comes from knowing they played a role in stirring things up. Like gambling addicts, they get high on the thrill of the action, spinning the roulette wheel while their hearts pound in anticipation. Finally, they like the way it feels to be in the thick of things, action stirring every which way. They no longer get as much of a kick from their therapy sessions. Like an addict who graduates to increasingly more powerful drugs, they need a bigger rush, the kind that comes from not only manipulating a helpless client or two but also a whole room full of therapists.

Brands of Toxicity

So far, I've been talking about political squabbles as if they emanate from a single source, as if one or even two individuals are responsible for the work climate that we function in. I've listened to enough stories of placing blame on a scapegoat to realize that most conflicts are far more complex than we prefer to recognize and most often are embedded in complex systemic patterns.

In the taxonomy of toxicity, there are a number of different systemic dysfunctions that you may recognize among groups of therapists.

Hierarchical Oppression

This organization is run like a single parent with a bunch of delinquent children. The administrator rules with an authoritarian style, which in turn sparks the rebelliousness of therapists who, by and large, resent any intrusion into their lives and work. After all, they became therapists to escape parent figures telling them what to do.

Although the staff may complain incessantly about being treated like children, about not being given respect or responsibility, on another level many of the staff members enjoy their conspiratorial ploys to undermine the administrator and assert their independence. The more they act out, of course, the more the administrator feels justified in cracking down further, exerting more control, and thereby eliciting more dramatic acting out.

Surface Cordiality

You would think that this organization is the antithesis of the previous one, and in some ways you would be correct. Staff members are very respectful to one another, almost painfully polite in their dealings.

During a staff meeting you would be struck not so much by what they talk about as what they *don't* talk about. Things pretty much stick to safe areas of business and avoid anything resembling emotional risk taking. This might surface most dramatically when one therapist is discussing a case and everyone jumps in with helpful suggestions but carefully avoids dealing with some of the negative feelings the therapist may exhibit toward the client.

Although this group functions quite well on the surface of things, especially in completing appropriate forms and generating client contact hours, the morale of the staff members may be quite low. Digging beneath the surface, you find much hidden discontent. There are "family secrets" in this agency, long buried by mutual consent. They conspire to pretend their problems don't exist, satisfying themselves with a minimal level of collegiality that includes little intimacy or trust.

Gross Ineptitude

A government-funded department within a larger organization consists of four members, three of whom have worked there for more than 20 years. Whereas once upon a time they may have been quite good at what they do, the newer team member muses about what that must have been like: He finds it difficult to imagine that any of them were ever very competent.

Prior to his arrival on the scene, this group functioned together in an uneasy truce of live and let live. Their level of job performance was marginal by anyone's standards, but with so much seniority there was no way that any of them could be fired or transferred against their will. Adding the fourth therapist only aggravated an already difficult situation.

Although his clinical work was flawless, the younger therapist inadvertently sparked a lot of conflict with his colleagues by undermining their authority. When people from other departments began to come to him for answers instead of his more senior staff members, they all banded together for the first time in years to protect themselves from a perceived assault to their integrity. In less than six months, the younger therapist moved on to another job, the third time this had happened at this agency in as many years.

Denial and Enabling

The only thing worse than ruminating constantly and complaining incessantly about the incompetent practitioners among us (without doing anything constructive to help them or their clients) is to pretend that they are not really impaired. Collective denial, or even enabling the dysfunctional behavior, is a common coping strategy among alcoholic or addicted families. The same holds true for groups of therapists.

In an institution that specializes in the training and supervision of therapists, two members of the staff demonstrate clear signs of major depression. Both are taking antidepressant medication (without accompanying psychotherapy!) and seem to take turns spinning out of control. They were hired in the first place by the benevolent and accepting administrator who believes in supporting his staff no matter what they are going through. Even though days sometimes go by in which each of them might not speak to anyone, make eye contact, or do anything but shuffle from their offices to the coffee pot or to fetch the next supervisee, the other staff members cover for them as best they can. People often wonder how these two impaired colleagues manage to get any of the therapists to return for supervision and conclude that they must feel sorry for them, just as the staff does.

Most of the staff members in the institute feel embarrassed by the degree of dysfunction in their two colleagues and never confront the idea that they, along with the administrator, are part of the problem. The only way such impaired professionals could continue to practice is with the collusion of everyone else who is protecting and covering for them, including their own clients.

Islands in the Stream

In a group private practice, each therapist is quite adamant about issues of autonomy and freedom. They share rent for their office space but otherwise contract for their own phone, secretarial, and support services. This, by itself, is hardly an indictment of dysfunction as much as it may be a preferred business model. However, most of the practitioners hardly speak to one another besides a mumbled hello, much less ever talk in a meaningful way.

Most of the practitioners do not exactly enjoy the isolation they feel; in fact, the majority of them are exploring other practice arrangements as soon as their lease expires (only 21 more months!). For reasons that are guessed at but never discussed, mistrust is rampant between them. It is impossible to know who is in or out on any given day because their doors are inevitably kept closed, regardless of their occupancy.

Acting Out Behind Closed Doors

In another clinic, composed of a dozen or so practitioners of various disciplines, an ethos of camaraderie prevails. The administrators work hard to create a spirit of family among them. Biweekly case conferences offer not only guest supervisors but also gourmet catered lunches. Regular retreats are scheduled. All policies and decisions are made democratically, by group consensus. New staff members are not brought on board until everyone, including the administrative and clerical staff, has provided input. In many ways, it seems like a utopian setting in which to practice therapy, one in which both morale and productivity are high.

But if you look closer, you'd discover the shenanigans going on behind the scenes. One therapist was convicted of fraud for double-billing an insurance company. Another therapist was found to be having sex with his clients; another was actually doing so in the office while charging for his services! As things unfolded, what appeared to be a model office of decorum and professional conduct was actually a hidden jungle of deceit and immoral behavior. We therapists kid ourselves about our powers to ferret out truth, and yet it is frightening how often we have no idea what is really going on. And I assure you that everything just described actually occurred because I worked in this place for a number of years until I fled to a solo practice with a few other colleagues.

Chaos Abounds

This final example of toxicity in action occurs in those organizations without any leadership at all. A group of therapists can't agree on who should lead them, whether someone should emerge from within or whether they should find someone outside the setting. So they settle on a compromise position of trying to function without any leadership at all, doing everything by committee.

They find that no matter how much time they spend talking about issues they never get around to settling anything, much less taking any constructive action. In frustration, they disperse to conduct their own agendas, oblivious to the ways they are contradicting and undermining one another; or, if they are aware of their mutual interference, they don't seem to care.

It is a miracle that anything is ever accomplished in this atmosphere of ever-present chaos. Decisions are never deliberately made; policy is established through simple neglect. Nobody is quite aware of what is going on or where things are headed. In this spirit of inertia, the place seems to run itself on stored energy that is slowly running down. Like each of the toxic environments mentioned as examples, this one permits therapists to function at minimal levels of competence even if morale is severely compromised.

The Nature of Human Organizations

An office takes on both the best and the worst characteristics of the people who work there. Organizations are not theoretical concepts we can manipulate in the ways most logical, reasonable, and beneficial for all. Instead, they reflect every one of the strengths, weaknesses, fantasies, fears, and appropriate or inappropriate behaviors that are a part of any group of humans. Organizations that include therapists are not exempt from these human frailties just because of the noble nature of the work.

Therapists require support more than most other professionals because of the nature of the stressful and emotionally laden work that we do, matched by the uncertainty and mystery that accompanies so much of the journey. In addition, we may often feel caught between paradoxical and often conflicting needs. On the one hand, we need to feel safe, secure, and unthreatened in order to maximize productivity and creative work, yet on the other hand, we want to be challenged and stimulated. We feel a need to demonstrate what we know and understand, yet we have to acknowledge that some of the time we have no idea what is happening or why. And like most others, we want approval and validation, yet we also want to assert our independence and control.

The same client-focused approach that we employ in therapy is closely related to the goals and practices of effective human resource management in which the focus is on understanding and meeting the physiological, social, and psychological needs of staff. Effective organizations bring people together on a regular basis to provide formal support and to make difficult but consensual decisions. Sometimes these processes are given formal recognition with terms and procedures like participative management, self-managing work teams, or organizational democracy. Other times they exist as a part of the informal structure of an organization.

Groups that wind up gathering on a regular basis for lunch, drinks after work, coffee breaks, or Friday afternoon debriefing sessions often do so to provide the personal attention and support that their formal office structure may not offer.

Strategies for Survival, If Not Flourishing

Clearly, therapists are ideally prepared and suited to convert our systemic knowledge and interpersonal skills to the workplace in order to create and maintain an optimally healthy environment. Why we aren't able to do that more often is a bit of a mystery but one that can at least be addressed if there was a more open discussion of the issues among colleagues—and a willingness to take responsibility for one's own role in the mutual dissatisfaction.

Examine Your Role in the Conflict

It is so easy to blame others for difficulties, to point the finger at others who are making life so difficult. Far more interesting, and also in line with what we tell our clients, is what role *you* play in the struggles.

There is a marked tendency, not only on the part of our clients, who are always pointing fingers at someone else, but also for us to blame others for our troubles. We know, from both research literature and our own experience in sessions, that assigning blame to others may temporarily provide some relief but that ultimately it creates a different set of problems. We know, for example, that when people see themselves as victims of circumstances outside their control, they are less likely to adapt and recover successfully.

Denying responsibility for problems at work creates a number of negative side effects. First, such a condition creates more animosity and alienation through a paranoid outlook that others find unappealing. Second, this mentality contributes to a sense of helplessness in that you have little control over what happens (and it does often feel that way). Third, being in an excuse-making mode tends to create more stress, worry, and a more sour mood. Fourth, blaming others limits the range of options you have to adapt to changing circumstances. Finally, making excuses and blaming others leads to other distortions and denial of reality, producing challenges to self-esteem.

Diversify Your Life

One of my closest friends and colleagues was literally on his death-bed. Although a relatively young man, his body was riddled with cancerous tumors. He knew that his life was limited to a matter of weeks and so wished to record his last thoughts and reflections, not only for his profession but also for his family and friends.

"There are some things I want to tell you," he said in a hoarse whisper as I sat by his bedside. We had been friends throughout graduate school, then later taught at the same university and eventually ended up in private practice together. I had come by to say a final goodbye, and I could barely keep myself together. He looked at me fiercely, virtually ordering me to pay close attention to what would be his last words to me.

"I wish that I had spent less time concerned with the things I thought were so important at work, and more time doing the things that really matter." As he said this, he smiled, knowing me all too well and our shared tendency toward workaholism.

Bob was looking back on his life with regret—and it was making me really uncomfortable with some of my own priorities. He was sorry that he had allowed himself to get so caught up in the petty politics at work and that he had devoted so much time and energy to being productive. This took me by surprise because he'd always been so proud of what he'd accomplished during his distinguished career.

"I wish I had spent more time skiing," he whispered. I had to lean closer because I hadn't been sure I'd heard him right. He was thinking about skiing more as he lay dying?

"And I wish I had spent more time flying my plane," he said as he pointed to a photo that his wife had pinned on the wall by his bed-side. He spent a lot of time staring at the image, perhaps imagining himself still in flight instead of in agonizing pain. As if to emphasize that point, he pushed the button that controlled his morphine drip.

"Most of all, I wish I had spent more time with my wife, my children, and my friends." He looked at me meaningfully. It was indeed a source of frustration that I could never pin him down even to take the time to have lunch occasionally, even though our offices were next to one another. He scheduled his clients continuously throughout the day, usually without a break.

"I was so good at being productive, accomplishing things, succeeding in my teaching and my practice, that I let myself become seduced by my own competence. I forgot, though, that there were other things that were really more important."

In a strange, perverse way, Bob almost felt grateful for his cancer in directing his attention to areas of his life he had been neglecting. In the few weeks he had remaining, he found to his delight that he was able to build a level of intimacy with his friends and family that he had never thought possible. It took impending death to get his attention.

I have obviously never forgotten every moment of our last time together and that conversation has haunted me throughout my life. I picture Bob looking over my shoulder, whispering to me, asking me if what I'm really doing, and how I'm spending my time, is what really matters most.

When we keep things in perspective, the political squabbles at work mean so little in the grand scheme of things. We exist to help people; everything else is secondary. I sometimes wonder what is missing in others' lives when they seem to have so much discretionary time to stir up trouble and obsess about petty things that don't matter much to anyone. The truth is that if our family lives are rich and satisfying, if we are surrounded by friends who support us, if we have interests outside our roles as therapists, then any conflict at work becomes a minor annoyance rather than a major upheaval.

Confront Injustices

I'm about to contradict myself, or at least muddle the waters a bit. As much as we might like to stay out of the fray and mind our own business, there are times when we can't allow ourselves to stand by and watch others being neglected or abused. Becoming indignant, or even furious, at injustices committed is partially what mobilizes our energy to confront wrongdoings and try to change a system that marginalizes or hurts others. Yes, that may result in increased stress and loss of sleep, but sometimes that's the price paid for fighting the good fight and standing up for what we believe.

Of course, success, not to mention peace of mind, depends very much on how you go about challenging some injustice or unscrupulous practice. It is difficult indeed to do so in such a way that you don't end up making things worse by ratcheting up the level of conflict, threatening others to the point they look for retribution, and increase your own stress to unmanageable levels.

Trust and Be Trustworthy

I've had some really lousy supervisors in my life, a few of whom were downright abusive. I've also experienced examples of visionary leadership in which people within the team were respected and honored and provided with ample opportunities to have a voice in the direction that things go.

I've seen so much backbiting and undermining within organizations. Staff members would gossip about one another and complain to others about their dissatisfactions. They would go to the supervisor and lodge complaints about someone but almost never say anything to the person directly. There was very little trust that anyone felt toward others, except for a few confidantes who were part of one coalition or another.

I vowed that if I ever attained a position of leadership in an organization (something I tried to avoid as much as possible), I would focus on trust issues among the staff most of all. When I finally found myself in such a position (not by choice), I implemented a policy that I would not permit complaints or criticisms about others until such time they were first communicated directly. I made sure that every person had the opportunity to speak in every meeting. I eliminated voting on issues because that resulted in winners and losers and instead initiated every decision by consensus. I organized retreats that were not focused on business but rather on building trust, collaboration, and intimacy among participants.

I have to say that things worked out marvelously well for a while. But even with all this intentional effort and policies in place, there were still perceived breeches of trust among one or two people. I think this is inevitable, but I also think that the key principle is to address these issues as openly as possible rather than letting them fester behind closed doors.

I also recognize that within some organizations such trust among staff is not really possible, given the members involved, or past experiences in which there have been serious wounds inflicted. But I still believe that it is worthwhile for each person to take responsibility for at least recruiting and nurturing a group of like-minded colleagues who can provide ongoing support. If that isn't feasible, then it's time to ask yourself what you are doing there.

Go Somewhere Else

When all else fails and you are unable to live with the daily political battles or conflict within a work setting, it is time to pursue other options. Of course, this is a lot easier said than done. There are many legitimate reasons why this may not seem feasible, many of which mirror the things our clients tell us why they can't (or won't) make needed changes. There are no other jobs available. You can't afford a pay cut. Your clients depend on you. You aren't qualified for other positions. You don't want to abandon your friends. As I said, these are all perfectly good reasons to stay where you are—but only if the complaining stops and you accept the limitations that are in place.

Perhaps it is time to recruit a new mentor, someone who can help to process things more constructively, whether in the workplace itself or in challenging sessions with clients.

Chapter 13

✦

ON SUPERVISION, MENTORING, MASTERY, AND CREATIVITY

Students often can't wait to escape school and get on with their lives. Yet one of the frequent complaints after graduation is that there are precious few opportunities to work with extraordinary professionals who can mentor and guide us throughout our careers. Certainly there are options and requirements for supervision, but it takes proactive effort to seek out the kinds of individuals who can truly teach you what you most want to learn. The counterpoint to this is related to how little preparation we've received in learning how to mentor others in meaningful ways, especially if the goal is not just to promote mere competence but true mastery and the kind of creative output that leads to excellence.

Hierarchical Relationships and Traditional Supervision

Most of us were never really taught how to get what we needed most from supervision and training as much as how to be compliant and cooperative with the agenda that was to be followed. If the supervisor preferred to examine unresolved attachment issues, defense mechanisms, countertransference reactions, schematic incongruences, systemic processes, or diagnostic anomalies, then that's how we spent our time. We would often be asked questions or invited to talk about issues that were thought to be most significant—to the supervisor.

Rarely did we entertain the idea, much less mobilize the courage, to say, "Excuse me, but this is what *I* want and how I learn best."

Once we left graduate school and got a real job, we were ecstatic about the possibility that now, finally, we could get the kind of supervision that would take us to the next level of competence. No longer would we have to worry so much about figuring out what our supervisors wanted to hear and then give it to them in the exact language they mandated. We could talk about the issues that bothered us most, ask the questions that most befuddled us, and structure our consultation sessions with the same freedom and self-responsibility we bestow on our own clients. What a surprise it was to discover that in some ways little had changed.

Imagine, for instance, a staff meeting that is being managed (and I do mean "managed") by the clinic administrator and clinical director. Sprinkled around the table are a dozen other mental health professionals—psychologists, social workers, counselors, a psychiatric nurse, a medical resident, and a few interns. They are working through cases under review, and there are some very strong opinions in the room about how to best proceed with them, especially by the more senior staff. There is a clear hierarchy of power evident by how often and how stridently that individuals control the meeting.

Traditionally speaking, supervision has been conceived as a kind of "super-vision" in which those in positions of authority are able to recognize and see things that may be invisible to mere mortal beings. There are a number of conflicting, sometimes paradoxical, motives at work that may have little to do with the growth and development of clinicians and far more to do with protecting against liability and minimizing risk.

Consider that, on the one hand, a supervisor expects full disclosure of your doubts, fears, failures, and mistakes, yet he or she is also in a position to evaluate your performance based on what you say and do. Depending on the judgment formed, you may or may not be recommended for licensure, promotion, expanded responsibilities, or a future position. The mixed message you hear is, "Tell me everything about what you are doing. Be honest. Leave out nothing. I will not only offer you support and guidance, but I will evaluate what you have said and done afterward."

Adding to the mixed messages, although the consultations with a supervisor are supposed to be "mostly" confidential, what you reveal about your clients, how you handled the cases, and how you respond to suggestions will likely be shared with others. Sometimes this includes critical judgments about your performance. Needless to say, these may not be the most ideal circumstances to further your growth and development.

What You Always Wanted—and Deserve—From Supervision

I don't mean to imply that the kind of tutorial supervision that is commonplace in many agencies is not helpful, because it very well can be the most appropriate model. However, its usefulness depends to a great extent on the clarity of boundaries that have been established, the degree of flexibility in the supervisor's role, the amount of safety the therapist feels, the means by which confusion is handled, the manner in which disagreements are worked through, and the clear and open ways that evaluation takes place.

If you are fortunate, then perhaps at some point in your career you have been privileged to work with a supervisor in which it was perfectly safe—and even encouraged—to discuss your greatest fears and uncertainties. You were supported and rewarded for being completely honest about what you didn't know and understand and felt grateful for the opportunities to explore areas that interested or disturbed you the most. But this is the exception, not the rule, at least based on what many therapists report occurred during the training and internship experiences.

Imagine yourself disclosing any of the following honest confessions to a past or current supervisor who played a significant oversight role:

- "I'm scared that deep down inside I don't have what it takes to be a good therapist. I'm just faking it most of the time. I don't really know what I'm doing. I feel stupid and incompetent. Furthermore, I don't think I'll ever know enough to be good at this stuff."
- "I sure blew that one! I really misjudged things, and as a result of my error, I don't think the client will ever come back. I didn't write that in the progress notes, but that is really what happened. I just totally miscalculated things and think I seriously screwed things up."
- "No, I know nothing about that theory/technique/strategy you are mentioning that you say is so widely used and that I should be quite familiar with its application. Actually, I've never heard of it before. I don't know if I missed that class, I was sleeping, or they just left that one out of my education."
- "Frankly, I don't have any idea what to do with this case. I don't even know where to begin. I'm not sure what you are really asking me, whether you are testing me to see if I know what to do, or whether you are just stalling because you don't have any idea either. I wish you would just say what you really want instead of playing games with me."
- "I can't believe how attracted I feel to some of my clients. They are talking to me, and I'm sitting there pretending to listen. All the while, though, I am thinking about how attractive they are. Do you ever do that, or am I some sort of pervert or something?"
- "You're wrong! You are so certain that you know all the answers, but this time you've missed it by a mile. You don't understand what I'm saying because you are listening to yourself rather than hearing what I am saying. With all your experience, you still don't know everything all the time. You act like you are so flexible, and sometimes you even pretend to

give in, but we both know that you believe that you are really seeing things clearly and that I'm not. I wish you'd listen to me instead of give lectures all the time."

These examples highlight that sometimes the things that we most need to talk about in supervision are pushed underground because it doesn't feel safe enough to bring them up. Instead, we follow the lead offered by the supervisor, reasonably satisfied that although we are not getting everything we want, at least we are getting other stuff that may be useful. This attitude is probably a healthy adaptation to a difficult situation, reminding ourselves to focus on the positives about what we can be learning rather than what is being omitted.

What if you were going to take charge of your own learning and growth in such a way that you wished to move beyond mere competence to reach a level of mastery that you had always hoped was within reach? Our field talks a lot about attaining a degree of competence in various domains, but what about those who wish to attain a higher standard of mastery and excellence?

Master Therapists: Who Are They . . . and How Do I Become One?

Before you can hope to become extraordinary in your clinical performance, it first helps to have some idea of what matters most in achieving excellence and what doesn't seem to matter much at all. There have been a number of studies investigating what it takes to become a master therapist, producing some surprising results (Betan & Binder, 2010; Chi, 2006; Duncan, 2010; Kottler & Carlson, in press; Miller & Hubble, 2011; Norcross, 2011; Orlinsky & Ronnestad, 2005; Skovholt, 2012).

It would seem the first and most important characteristic is the deep and overriding motivation and commitment to be really, really good and invest all the hard work that it takes on a daily basis to make that happen. This occurs not just when we are in session, but just as important, the amount of time and effort we devote toward reflective practice between sessions.

There are many variables that don't appear to matter very much at all, even though our profession seems to devote so much attention to these things. For example, there's been so much discussion and debate regarding the most suitable theoretical orientation, the preferred interventions to be employed, the optimal degree or license, yet those factors don't seem to have much to do with predicting excellence as a clinician. Likewise, even years of experience, number of continuing education credits, and amount of supervision aren't necessarily key variables.

First of all, there are certain personal qualities that have been found to be important, such as the ability and willingness to be fully present, an aura of composure as well as wisdom, compassion and caring, extraordinary interpersonal skills, and a degree of honesty and willingness to accept and process feedback. It is this flexibility, more than anything else, that distinguishes master therapists from their brethren because they are able to continually make adjustments according to what clients really need most at any moment in time. They also realize that far more important than any particular technique or intervention or theoretical approach is the quality of the relationship they develop with clients, optimized for the particular client needs and stage of treatment.

If you aspire to attain mastery, to be far more than competent in your clinical practice, to take your skills to the next level, there are several questions you might wish to consider:

1. How can you find your own "voice" when your head and heart are so dominated by other influences?
2. How do you limit your options by the ways you define yourself as a therapist and person, including your theoretical orientation, specialties, and style?
3. What are some of your most cherished beliefs you hold dear but have been unwilling to challenge critically in light of new opportunities and experiences?
4. What are some things your clients (and others) find annoy-

ing or off-putting about you, yet you remain oblivious or in denial?

5. What are some examples of how you tend to blame your clients or other external factors outside of your control when sessions don't proceed the way you prefer?

6. What are some aspects of the profession that have always bothered you but you've never chosen to challenge?

7. In what ways do you feel confused and uncertain about aspects of your work but don't feel safe or comfortable admitting this to yourself and others you trust?

8. How do you live with your doubts, imperfections, mistakes, and failures, treating these experiences as valuable "gifts" and learning opportunities?

9. Which clients most consistently get underneath your skin and trigger the most negative personal reactions?

10. What are some ways you use your work to hide from unresolved issues in your life or compromise your personal relationships?

11. If you are really, *really* honest with yourself, what are some of your biases, prejudices, and entrenched beliefs that lead you to judge others critically, inaccurately, or unfairly? These could be based on race, economic status, religion, ethnicity, age, sexual orientation, gender, or even involve personal appearance, profession, and other characteristics that consistently trigger negative reactions.

12. How do you limit your creativity by following in the footsteps of others rather than investing the time and energy to personalize your own unique style of practice that is better suited to your personality, background, values, skill set, and needs of your clients?

13. What are some ways you could broaden or diversity your life through new experiences, exposure to different stimulation, immersion in novel cultures or environments, and exploration of new subject areas?

14. How are you a hypocrite, unable or unwilling to practice what you preach and teach to others?

You may have found some of these questions intriguing, some threatening or disturbing, and others just not that relevant to what you do and how you think about your work and life. Surely, some of the queries sparked some reflective thought, if not stymied you a little (or a lot). Here's the bottom line: What are you willing to do to commit yourself to some action in order to invigorate your practice and instill greater passion into your life? What proactive steps are you willing to take to recruit new mentors who might inspire or support you to move to the next level of personal and professional mastery?

Reading a book like this is a solitary, private experience. Any promises you make become silent commitments that you may, or may not, follow through with. In fact, there is a lot of research on the poor prognosis of private declarations, which is why the same New Year's resolutions are made each year. So, one of the most important and useful things you could do is to recruit some friends and trusted colleagues to talk to about these questions, especially those you find most challenging.

Obstacles to Creative Breakthroughs

Sticking with the theme of achieving excellence rather than minimal standards of competence, one additional area worth exploring is what occurs during creative breakthroughs in therapy. I'm talking about those extraordinary experiences in session that are almost transcendent, when something wholly new was coinvented, perhaps something that never occurred previously—by anyone. This sort of innovation does not occur every day, nor perhaps not even every week, but the bliss and joy that accompanies such creative effort can sustain us for a long time afterward.

In another project, we interviewed what we considered to be the most creative practitioners in our field, at least those who are most well known for their originality and resourcefulness. Jon Carlson and I (Kottler & Carlson, 2003, 2009) invited dozens of these individuals to describe their most creative breakthrough, perhaps in some cases the particular session that led to them abandoning their previous ideas and developing the approach that now bears their name. We talked to the likes of Jeff Zeig, Judy Jordan, Bill O'Hanlon, William Glasser, Albert Ellis, Laura Brown, Cloe Madanes, Jay Haley, Susan Johnson, Jim Bugental, Donald Meichenbaum, Peggy Papp, Arnold Lazarus, and others to tell us about those cases that were instrumental in shaping their views and clinical style. What we learned from these conversations was that most of these groundbreaking discoveries occurred as a result of them overcoming many of the obstacles that get in the way of us becoming more imaginative. In some cases this wasn't necessarily the result of some heroic brilliant new insight as much as it was a collaboration with a client to create something special.

One of the most persistent barriers to creativity—in therapy or any field—is the overallegiance to a particular theory or model that prevents one's ability to see whatever is happening with fresh eyes. In that sense, beginners have an advantage over veterans because to them almost *everything* looks new and different and they are not yet overreliant on automatic responses. It is certainty that can compromise choices and limit opportunities. And as long as you stick with what is tried and true, then there are no chances to experiment with other alternatives that might be more suitable and effective. The same thing can be said with respect to the kind of diagnostic assessments that put clients into boxes rather than viewing them as unique individuals with their own personal set of traits, issues, and behavior, not to mention the novel interactive effects that take place in sessions.

I know that it took me the longest time to find my own stride as a therapist, to clarify my own beliefs and ideas, to develop my own unique style, because I was busy imitating others whom I admired and worshipped. Of course, I didn't fully trust myself and was terrified of making a mistake; I figured as long as I followed in the footsteps of others before me, I would mostly stay out of trouble. And that is probably true to a certain extent, even if it set a lower limit on what I could achieve, or rather what my clients and I could achieve together.

Evidence-based practice relies on different kinds of "evidence," including empirically supported research, data-driven studies, and accumulative wisdom in the literature, but also one's own intuition and felt sense that have been honed through years of systematic experience. Even beginners start to get a feeling for what may work best in a given situation.

Creativity is Facilitated Through Relational Connection

"When I first started seeing clients," Candace explained, "some very unusual things started happening during the sessions. When in a relaxed, open and present state, I experienced a feeling like a gateway of energy opens and connects me to my clients on a deep emotional level." She admits with a laugh that there was no thunder and lightning but sometimes it felt that way.

"I remember the density of the energy field that was opened up like a gateway to a human soul—to my client's soul. The best way I can describe it is that it felt like invisible feathers surrounding me, soft and dense at the same time, creating a passage of energy from my client to me."

Once in this transcendent state, Candace felt the kind of effortless concentration and focus that almost allowed her to read a client's mind, as well as feel the raw emotions. She noticed that the more she relaxed and opened this connection with her clients, the more creative she felt and the more quickly things moved along. She felt embarrassed and uneasy about this experience, not prepared to talk about this to her supervisor, who might judge her critically or label her a flake. But it really did feel like there was an almost telepathic connection with clients when both she and they would let go. She later learned this was the kind of deep, empathic listening that had been described so much earlier by the likes of Carl Rogers and Rollo May. Indeed, she had come upon one of the seminal discoveries that led to creative breakthroughs in therapy—the power of relational connection to permit taking risks that would otherwise not be possible.

Candace was nevertheless uncomfortable acknowledging, much less talking about, what almost felt like a supernatural power. She recalled a teenaged client with whom she had a similar feeling of a creative breakthrough. The boy felt complete despair and hopelessness that she, or anyone else, could help him. Again she felt the energy field that allowed her to connect to him. "I felt his innermost thoughts and his desperate feelings. I actually *knew* what was going on inside him and I communicated this to him, hearing his plea for help."

The boy just started to cry and Candace let him go for more than 20 minutes before he started talking about his fears and opening up. When during the next session, the boy's mother accompanied him, there was a different kind of breakthrough that led them each to support one another after years of conflict between them. Candace wonders where this gift of deep understanding and relational connection comes from. Is it empathic listening? Mirroring? Telepathy? A gift from God? She's really not sure.

What she does know is that when she was seeing 50 clients each week, plus all the accompanying paperwork, she lost her ability to connect deeply with her clients. It was if she was squandering too much energy. "I felt depleted. I still applied the techniques I learned in graduate school. I still did the best I could to be a good enough therapist, but the results were never the same. In three months three of my clients asked to be transferred to another therapist, which never happened in six years. Other clients did not seem to improve much. I made a decision to quit this job—the job of working for a non-profit agency—even though I did not have another job lined up for me. I needed time for myself. Time to attend to my own needs. Time to synchronize myself. Time to get in touch with my spirituality."

Candace needed to slow down the pace of her life, make some changes, in order to access her creative energy. I'd add to that the idea that in order to be most innovative and experiment with possibly new breakthrough strategies, it requires a degree of trust on the part of *all* the participants in the process. There's all this talk about earning the client's trust but, likewise, they have to earn *our* trust. When we feel safe with a particular client, when there has been a solid alliance established, we feel freedom to experiment, to make mistakes, to take risks, and know we will be forgiven and cut some slack.

Admitting You Are Lost

As long as you are convinced you know what's going on, where you're heading, and which path to take, you are going to take a route that is tried and true. It is at the point that you realize that you really *don't* understand what is going on, nor know what to do next, that you are most inclined to experiment. Creative breakthroughs often result from desperation.

The creative process is not usually an orderly experience but one borne of chaos and uncertainty. We are usually not willing to take risks or try something new until after we have already exhausted everything in our existing repertoire. Creative efforts are thus fueled, in part, by the curiosity related to what might happen next once you abandon what you are already doing that isn't quite turning out as you hoped.

There are certain assumptions that we hold so dear that even when they prove to be inappropriate in a given situation we are reluctant to surrender them. Most of the examples of creative breakthroughs occur in circumstances in which several conditions are met:

1. *Challenging conventional wisdom.* Almost by definition creative acts involve breaking rules or thinking outside the box. When you think about some of the most innovative practitioners such as Milton Erickson, Fritz Perls, Virginia Satir, and Carl Whitaker, what immediately comes to mind is how differently they thought about their work and how far outside the bounds of conventional practice that they were willing to operate in order to help their clients.

2. *Risk taking and courage.* Let's face it: trying something you've never done before is frightening precisely because you can't predict the likely outcome. You are taking a leap into the unknown, even when due diligence guides your behavior as safely and cautiously as possible.

Most creative interventions are improvisational. They depend as much on intuition as any kind of logical reasoning. An idea strikes you, from where you are neither certain nor very much interested. All you know is that this strategy *might* be helpful, certainly more so than what has already failed multiple times.

At other times you and your client simply grin at one another sheepishly. Something remarkable just happened, something you can't quite describe and certainly can't make much sense of. But the result is still the same—a new insight or different perspective that seems to make all the difference.

3. *A different therapy for every client.* Even during an era when treatments are becoming more and more standardized, homogenized, and manualized, there is still plenty of room to customize and individualize what we do and how we do it. Most creative breakthroughs are not necessarily dramatic and groundbreaking innovations but rather derivative in nature, adapting or building on what was conceived previously.

One of the reasons why many therapists don't think of themselves as particularly creative is that they feel intimidated and self-conscious by that label. And yet you do all kinds of creative things every day, almost every session, figuring out ways to reach your clients, given their unique backgrounds and issues, or at least the ways they are experienced.

Creative innovations (or adaptations) take place when you individualize strategies, catering to the personalized language, preferences, interests, and needs of each client and context. Rather than telling the same old story the same old way, you change many of the details to better resonate with the client's way of being.

4. *A collaborative partnership.* One thing I learned from interviewing prominent therapists about their most creative innovations is that they have very different ways of viewing the process. Whereas many see the breakthroughs as courageous, singular, heroic actions on their part that reflected their own brilliance and wisdom, several others (mostly female) preferred to conceptualize any progress or outcomes as the result of their mutual collaboration. The theorists didn't even view themselves as all that creative but rather just claimed to have creative clients. While I appreciate this modesty, I think it is a clear understatement because they also discovered their own innovative ways of accessing this inventive energy in sessions.

Being creative in any endeavor is mostly about giving yourself permission to think differently about what you do and how you do it. You enter a zone or flow state in which it really feels like you've entered an alternate state of consciousness, one in which you surprise yourself with novel ways of solving problems or at least conceptualizing them.

The reality is that most of the time creative efforts don't work out very well, at least the first time you try them. How could they when they are almost always awkward, tentative actions that require a bit of fine-tuning before they are completed?

Getting the Most From Supervision and Mentoring

Creativity, and for that matter, any kind of professional effectiveness, depends on the support you get from others. If you work in a threatening and unsafe environment, under the supervision of someone who does not appear to have your best interests in mind, then you are not going to feel very comfortable stretching yourself in beneficial ways. On the other hand, if work under the care of someone you trust, with like-minded colleagues, there are all kinds of exciting possibilities that open up to you. But in the same way that we teach our clients to get the most from therapy, so too must we take responsibility for our own growth and development. This means teaching mentors and supervisors what we need most and how to help us obtain that knowledge or wisdom in optimal ways.

Just as we understand that positive outcomes in therapy are more likely when there is mutual agreement on the methods and goals targeted to the client's needs, so too do mentoring relationships work best when the process is mutually negotiated. This is sometimes less than ideal with the supervisor, manager, or mentor who holds evaluative power, but still absolutely essential for the experience to be productive, much less satisfying.

This is all predicated on the assumption that we were prepared to get the most from supervision, which is by no means the case. During training we were often forced to go along with whatever structure or program was mandated, often without much input. Because we've left what can be viewed as a fairly rigid, if not oppressive, environment, we now have far more choice in who we seek out for consultations and how we want the process to unfold.

Express Curiosity Rather Than Doubt

Regardless of the setting and established norms for any supervisory relationship, there are some guidelines that are usually helpful, beginning with the ways that disagreements are handled. Questioning a supervisor's ideas, advice, suggestions, directives, or evaluations is a normal part of the learning process when you want to understand the rationale for these choices, as well as to grasp the underlying thinking. When you can bring these questions into the relationship through a self-focused inquisitive approach, you stand a greater chance of having them resolved productively rather than making the supervisor feel challenged or confronted. This more diplomatic approach allows for assertive behavior without the drawbacks of more traditional argumentative options.

Traditional models of supervision acknowledge the power inequities between the participants, yet that doesn't mean that this reality is always recognized. That's why it is generally more effective to own the problem (e.g., "I'm not making myself clear" or "I don't understand what you mean") rather than launching what could be perceived as an attack (e.g., "You're contradicting what you told me before" or "You're not making a lot of sense"). This might seem quite obvious, especially in a relationship with someone who is an authority figure, but I'm sometimes shocked at how insensitive and inappropriate interns can become when they are anxious and confused. In all fairness, I'm just as surprised at how often supervisors, instructors, or mentors can be brutally critical and threatening in the way they offer feedback that causes the therapist or student to shut down rather than hear what was offered.

Convey Humble Knowledge

Power imbalances in supervision models do not account for the reality that the relationship can be egalitarian and reciprocal. There are, in fact, times when you are convinced that a supervisor is misguided or wrong. There are instances when you actually know far more about an issue or topic or your client than your supervisor does. And there are other times when your supervisor may be out of line.

If the choices come down to ignoring the situation, or confronting it directly (e.g., "I think you're wrong about that"), either result may lead to an undesirable outcome. It therefore helps if your different opinion or informed knowledge is offered in a spirit of humility rather than arrogance. Again this may seem obvious, but so many of the difficulties encountered in mentoring relationships occur because one, or usually both, parties feel threatened rather than supported by the other.

Ask for Examples

Many times when something is explained to me, I don't really (or fully) understand what is meant—including what I just said. So here's an example. My supervisor asked me to justify why I made a particular decision related to an intern who I believed (and documented) was not performing to minimal standards.

"I'm not sure what you mean," I pressed her, "could you give me an example?"

She then went on to cite a specific instance in which I didn't provide the intern with the extra time she needed to complete a case report. When I asked for further clarification about why this intern would receive special consideration, it was pointed out to me that she had a learning disability and was, therefore, allowed to make other arrangements. Was I not aware of this?

Oops.

I mention this example of asking for examples because it was a case in which it was clearly the result of my neglect. But what you may not catch from this description is that the emotional temperature in the room was quite cool during the conversation, meaning that we were both calm and neither of us felt criticized or challenged. I was genuinely grateful for the input, which only hit home after I could relate to specific behavior.

We were taught in graduate school that feedback is most valuable to clients (or anyone) when (1) it is specific, personalized, and detailed; (2) it is offered in a spirit of caring and support rather than as criticism; and (3) it is supported with an example.

Request Demonstrations

When a descriptive example does not make things clear enough, the next best option is a demonstration. "Can you *show* me?" is always more interesting and engaging than "Can you *tell* me?"

A supervisor tells a therapist that what might make a difference in his relationship with a resistant client might be to employ more immediacy interventions rather than interpretations to keep things focused on the present rather than only the past.

"I'm not sure what you mean." (This therapist obviously read the previous section.)

"Well, for instance, I notice right now when I said that, you seemed to startle for a moment, as if you were caught by surprise and somehow felt attacked."

"No, no, that's not how I . . ."

"Even still, as you protest, you've covered up your chest and your hands are clenched. It could be my imagination, but I'd guess you are feeling uncomfortable right now. And as I'm pressing this further, you seem to be withdrawing. I wonder if you would be willing to talk about what's going on right now between us?"

Some of the most powerful interpersonal interactions occur when, instead of merely talking about something, we are living it in the moment. Any opportunity to role-play or act out a scenario or demonstrate a skill or idea is going to be more useful than just describing it.

Peer Consultation as an Alternative

Traditional supervision, as described earlier, is hierarchical in the sense that the supervisor is seen as an expert or at least a person in a position of authority. We've discussed how there is an inherent inequality in the relationship, based on experience, position, authority, or perceived knowledge. Whereas most therapists have someone in their life who acts as a mentor or supervisor, most of the consultations we have about cases take place with trusted colleagues and peers who are far more accessible and available.

Clearly there is a trade-off when seeking professional guidance in a context that no longer includes a sanctioned expert, especially one who is specifically compensated to provide this service. It could even be said that during peer consultations it is often a matter of the blind leading the blind. It is for this reason that collegial connections act as adjuncts rather than as the sole form of supervision. On the other hand, feedback and suggestions from a peer are often based on more than self-reports because he or she has had the opportunity to observe behavior in a variety of contexts and over a long period of time.

One example of the best in peer supervision models is that which takes place between co-therapists in family or group therapy. One of the reasons this practice is so desirable and interesting, even if it is less cost-effective, is because of the opportunities for debriefing that take place afterward. I can honestly say that most of what I've learned as a therapist that has been most helpful occurred as a result of working with a trusted co-leader who has experienced the same therapeutic situation, observed me in action, partnered with me in our joint work, and had access to his own reactions and feelings as the group has unfolded. I've found our meetings afterward to be invaluable, especially because my co-leader and I have developed such a high level of trust and honesty. He can tell me what he didn't like, what he thinks gets in my way, but just as important, we can both compare notes on what we observed and thereby hone the accuracy of our assessment skills. It's even better than having someone review a video because there are opportunities to actually change the direction that things are going as they are happening.

We might occasionally take "time-outs" in the middle of a session to check in with one another, calibrate our thinking, or even provide feedback to one another right in front of the group. It might look something like this.

JEFFREY: "So, Camille, although you say you don't want to go much further with this, I sense that some part of you would like to work on this issue if . . ."

MATT: "Excuse me, Jeffrey?"

JEFFREY: "Ah, sure."

MATT: "I'd just like us to take a break for a minute. I know you want Camille to talk more about the abuse, but I have a different take on this and sense that she is continuing mostly to comply with your request. After all, she's talked before about how much she defers to authority figures and I think that's what's happening now."

JEFFREY: "So, you'd like us to check this out with her before we go further?"

MATT: "Exactly."

I must admit that when this sort of intervention takes place, especially in front of the group, I do feel a certain amount of shame feeling censured. But after a minute or two of reflection, what comes next is an incredible feeling of gratitude, not only because my client was rescued from me being too pushy but also because I learned something really helpful that I can use during future interactions.

Whether working as co-leaders, or consulting a peer to review a case, the quality of the input is directly related to how knowledgeable, skilled, and sensitive the colleague might be. Obviously, everyone has an opinion about almost everything. So if you ask a workmate, anyone in the office, what you should do about a situation, you are going to hear a variety of responses, many of them less than helpful.

One additional problem that can develop is that although you'd like the most honest feedback possible, this can also lead to hurt feelings with a peer. Far more likely is that people become so polite and cautious in order not to hurt anyone's feelings that they avoid telling one another those things that most need to be brought out into the open.

There are other challenges that arise when professionals get together to try and help one another. For one thing, a lot of complaining and whining takes place in which therapists compete with one another over who is most unappreciated and worst treated by their clients.

"I've been seeing this one guy," a therapist begins the conversation in the staff lounge. "He comes into my office each time, proceeds to tell me how much worse he's feeling, and then spends the rest of his time telling me what a lousy therapist I am. When I tell him that there is only so much that I can do, that the rest is up to him, he . . ."

"Oh yeah?" the other therapist interrupts. "You think *you've* got it bad?

"There's this woman I've been seeing for over four months. Just like clockwork she shows up for her appointments. We've been making incredible progress. Then, this week, no show, no phone call, no nothing. I call her to find out what happened, and her phone has been disconnected. No forwarding address. Just gone. Not even a good-bye, much less a thank-you."

This type of complaining often continues when therapists get together during a break. Ostensibly, we are trying to help one another, but what really happens is that we often end up feeling worse by only stating our woes. As in many self-contained groups, nobody is likely to confront anyone else that they may be adopting a victim mentality where we blame everyone else for our problems.

Advice is liberally dispensed in peer supervision, but it often comes too late to do much good. Weaker groups have a tendency to focus on past occurrences rather than future actions. Members can end up feeling stupid, believing they should have thought of the advice being given beforehand. Now that the information is brought to their attention, they realize the situation will have changed dramatically by the next session, rendering most of the suggestions obsolete.

Teaching People to Help You When You're Stuck

One alternative peer supervision format involves working with a single partner during times when you feel stuck with a case. It is designed to avoid the power- and expertise-based issues of traditional supervision. This model provides a framework for creating a professionally supportive session at almost a moment's notice and dealing with each of the stages in a single session of less than an hour.

This strategy can prove useful in a variety of circumstances. It works equally well with *any* conflicted relationship found to be at an impasse. Although a particular client will most often be the focus of a session, the strategy is also productive for dealing with conflicts related to a supervisor, colleague, or friend. No matter what the specifics of the problem situation, there are several basic steps that should make the system work for you.

1. *Find a partner you can trust.* The choice of the partner may be the single most important decision that deter-

mines the effectiveness of this method. Make a mistake and you risk betrayal. Choose someone you work with too closely, and you can jeopardize a friendship during those times when you must be painfully frank. Find someone who will always choose answers to make you feel good and growth will be stunted. A good compromise is to pick someone you trust to be flexible in following your direction and honest enough to make you aware of your cognitive and emotional blind spots.

2. *Describe your most difficult case right now.* The starting place is to briefly provide necessary background of the one case that is giving you the most trouble. Don't dwell on the details. Focus on *one relationship* rather than a complex web of influences associated with numerous relationships. Limit your presentation to just a few minutes. Resist the temptation to whine, complain, and seek sympathy. The focus will be on you, so your description of the problem individual(s) should take up as little time as possible.

> *I am having trouble with a couple who, while polite and respectful during sessions, refuse to talk about anything or do any work once they walk out the door. I have been seeing them for a few months, but they don't seem to be improving. After fifteen years of being together, they are on the verge of splitting up. These sessions are their last resort. I've tried everything I know how to do. They act like these ideas are absolutely brilliant and surely will make the difference, but nothing changes. They come in every session feeling hopeless. Now I'm feeling that way as well.*

3. *What things does the client do that you find frustrating?* This is the time to be specific; generalities will only confuse the issues and delay the process. Describe a few examples of the type of behavior you find most irritating, the situations in which this is most likely to occur, and the consequences to you and the relationship.

Well, there are several things they do that drive me nuts. For one, they don't listen to one another, nor to me. It is as if each of them has already rehearsed what they want to say, and it is the telling of this story that is their first priority. When I reflect what is going on, they both smile, thank me for my brilliant observation, and then proceed to continue doing the same thing. Then they keep bringing up stuff from the past, even though we've already agreed that isn't helpful. They take turns, like a wrestling tag team—one of them accuses the other of some misconduct, while the other acts like a victim of some minor misunderstanding. I watch them go at it, always painfully polite. I feel like I'm at a tennis match where my head keeps following the ball back and forth across the net.

4. *What feelings are being elicited in you?* Stop talking about the client and speak about yourself. Tell your partner about all the feelings that come up as a direct and indirect result of your interactions with the client. As much as you feel willing and safe to go, dig deep inside yourself for what is being triggered by these interactions. You are searching for those most human parts of your being that operate beyond your regular conscious control rather than the formal professional parts that are more consciously accessed.

These people make me feel hopeless and foolish. Left unsaid is the accusation that I don't really know what I'm doing, which in this case, is mostly true. I don't know what to do with this couple. I have exhausted all my favorite techniques. I feel sad as well. I really like these people and so badly want to help them. Yet I feel inadequate because I am up against the limits of what is possible. I tell myself over and over again that there is only so much I can do, that the rest is up to them, but I guess I don't believe that. There should be something else I can do.

5. *Conduct an assessment of what has been going on, along with a corresponding list of your personal reactions.* Your partner may have been reflecting your ideas and seeking some understanding up to this point. Now it is time to directly request significant involvement from your partner. Ask for reactions, but mostly address specific questions that focus on how you've been stuck and what *you* have been doing to stay that way.

6. *List what you have tried that hasn't worked.* Similar to any strategic or problem-solving method, you now need to figure out what you are doing that is consistently ineffective. The very nature of being at an "impasse" in a relationship should confirm that ineffective actions need to be identified and discarded. Write down what you've been doing and the relative impact. Make a promise not to do those things anymore so you can try something else.

7. *Brainstorm a list of other options.* This is when having a partner, or even multiple partners, comes in really handy for generating ideas that you hadn't yet considered. It doesn't really matter what you come up with as long as it breaks you loose from the dysfunctional patterns that are already keeping you at an impasse. A flexible and creative partner is invaluable at this stage. You were stuck and that is the worst possible framework in which to creatively develop new ideas on your own. An effective partner will help you generate a long list of possibilities from a wide assortment of frameworks.

The intention at this point is *not* to come up with a correct solution to the problem, but rather to spur thinking along more innovative lines. A relationship impasse by definition is when two or more people are stuck in a frustrating, dysfunctional pattern characterized by each of them blaming the other. Once you let go of who is at fault, abandon strategies that are not producing desirable outcomes, and begin a creative exploration of new strategies, then it is only a matter of time until you discover one combination of ingredients that breaks things loose.

On Being Mentored

We next move from the specific focus on case supervision to the more general subject of recruiting mentors to guide your personal and professional growth. Graduate school may have disappointed us in many sectors, but not in the area of providing support. For many of us, being a student was a time of camaraderie in which we came together to aid one another. We studied together. We worked on group projects. We sat together over coffee or beer, complaining about how unfair our professors were. During times of difficulty or special challenges, we supported and helped one another.

Then, there were the other sources of support available to us: financial aid, graduate assistantships, computer laboratories, study skills centers, tech support, social events, counseling services, student organizations, and faculty advising—both through an assigned mentor and also through informal relationships. Despite how badly we wanted to graduate and get back into the real world, we didn't realize at the time how much we would miss the spirit of camaraderie. We didn't realize how much of the time we would feel so alone.

One of the most frequent complaints voiced by practitioners everywhere is how little support we receive from the organizations we work in and the colleagues we work with. In the way that time heals all wounds, we even feel wistful about our days in graduate schools, longing for those special times when we felt supported. Furthermore, we absolutely need this support in order to survive, if not flourish.

There are three things involved in transforming ourselves in such a way that we can meet the challenges of a rapidly evolving profession: a clear vision of where we are headed, retooled skills for adapting to these changes, and a support system for carrying through with our intentions. Among those sources of support that are available to us from family and friends, colleagues and peers, is the able assistance of a mentor who is concerned for our welfare and in a position to do us some good.

If you already have someone in your life who acts as a benevolent figure and wise guide, then you are well aware of how critical that is to sustain your passion, metabolize confusion and stress, and act as an advocate on your behalf. Ideally that is someone with senior status who has the power and position to speak out on your behalf or help you network within the professional community. In addition, this person is a confidante to whom you can go to when you are overwhelmed or confused. As discussed earlier, a mentor or supervisor can provide you with useful feedback about your behavior, not only within sessions but also within the organization. He or she acts as a tutor, filling in gaps in your knowledge. Most critically, a mentor helps guide your career path, especially as it relates to important decisions regarding future opportunities and choices. Finally, a mentor acts as a role model, someone who you wish to emulate in a lot of ways.

If all this sounds pretty wonderful, the challenge is to find someone (or several people) who fits these requirements. We recruit our mentors from among a wide variety of sources. The authors of our favorite books provide us guidance and direction within the context of somewhat limited one-way relationships. We may talk back to them, ask questions, plead for elaboration, but then we must construct the answers ourselves from whatever we can deduce from their dialogue.

Senior colleagues and supervisors at work are other obvious candidates for mentors. Unfortunately, it takes a certain degree of luck to be placed in a work group in which there is someone qualified, interested, and available.

Hiring our own therapist is another obvious choice, although one that is all too often avoided by those of us who should know better. Certainly, we make lousy clients, by and large. We play games, second-guess our therapists, critique their performances, intellectualize, and hide behind our experience watching others do the same. Still, if we are honest and talk about our resistances, if we hire someone with experience working with other therapists, the protective facade will eventually come down.

We don't look for mentors often enough outside our own field. If we are searching for people who are wise and experienced, who can teach us things we never learned in graduate school, then they are most likely those who are operating in a different arena altogether. In fact, most of us need more of such diversity in our lives. We spend altogether too much time thinking about therapy, talking about therapy, reading about therapy, and doing therapy that we leave little opportunity to expand our worlds from outside influences.

Ultimately, one of the things that compromised my growth the most in graduate school was the belief that the best way to become a better therapist was to read, study, practice, and learn more about therapy. This is true only to a certain extent. As we well know and understand with our clients, sometimes the best way to promote dramatic and lasting changes is to push people to move beyond the safe boundaries of what they already know, to delve into areas that are unknown, even a little frightening.

In graduate school, we learned to avoid risks, to play it safe, to do what is expected, to meet the approval of others. We learned to read accurately what others wanted from us, whether that was the correct choice on an exam, the perfect formula for a term paper, or the ideal comment to make in class. Once we secured our first jobs, we continued this pattern of pleasing others. Because we were already well-trained as approval seekers, it didn't take much for us to do whatever we could to fit in, to get others to like us. Indeed, being likable and delivering what others want and expect is critical to getting clients to return.

Somewhere along this path, however, what has been lost is our own ability and willingness to mentor ourselves. Yes, it certainly helps to have mentors like professors, supervisors, therapists, and wise and experienced friends, who can show us the way, just as we do for our own clients.

When You Supervise Yourself

The best kind of supervision and mentoring, whether it takes place with someone in a position of authority, a peer, or during inner dialogue, is designed to meet your particular needs during a period of maximum readiness. In that sense, almost all such instruction is actually a form of *self*-supervision in which you are the one who translates input into a form that is meaningful and relevant. You hopefully reach a point where you have internalized the voices of the best mentors in your life: You hear them speaking to you during the most opportune moments.

Ultimately, experienced therapists may continue to have a need for mentors and supervisors, but in the real world most of the time we have to rely on ourselves to make decisions on the fly and take responsibility for our own growth and development. To the extent that we have attained some level of self-awareness, clarity, and honest self-scrutiny, self-monitoring behavior can be either extremely useful or contribute to increased denial and self-deception.

It certainly helps to pay close attention to what our clients need most, what they say, what they do, what they tell us is most important to them. And it is just as important to listen to ourselves, to watch ourselves, to review sessions critically. In addition, it's absolutely imperative that we admit when we feel lost, when we've made mistakes, when we've failed our clients—or ourselves. Unless we are willing to recognize and acknowledge our limitations and weaknesses, there isn't much chance to improve them. This is a lot easier said than done as the difficulties are occurring in the moment. It helps if we've been prepared and trained by previous mentors and supervisors to watch for the kind of internal "noise" that leads us astray.

We also have an obligation, an ethical responsibility, to challenge our biases and prejudices. These may not necessarily be related to ethnicity, religion, age, socioeconomic background, gender, or sexual orientation, but perhaps to other assumptions we make about people based on prior experiences. I know that for experienced therapists one of the hardest things to do is to not jump to conclusions too quickly when we first meet new clients. It is far too easy to categorize people, to relegate them to diagnostic entities or classifications that reduce them to their labels.

Self-supervision is strongest when you avoid settling for what you already do well but strive for new knowledge, more advanced skills, and increased therapeutic options. Expertise in therapy is not necessarily developed from what you know, or what you think you understand, but rather from the kind of "deliberate practice" that goes beyond mere repetition to include adjustments and improvements in light of immediate feedback (Ericsson, Charness, Feltovich, & Hoffman, 2006). This all sounds good, but the reality is that very few experienced therapists actually collect systematic feedback, much less change their patterns as a result of what they hear (Tracey et al., 2014). More concerning is that therapists, like most everyone else, aren't very accurate judges of their own performance and usually fail to recognize their own incompetence (Dunning et al., 2003; Walfish, McAlister, O'Donnell, & Lambert, 2012). To complicate matters further, even if we rely solely on what clients tell us about their relative satisfaction with their treatment, those reports are often distorted, biased, and less than accurate (Kottler & Carlson, 2011), usually favoring far more positive assessments than might be deserved and so-named the "Barnum effect" (Meehl, 1956).

As mentioned earlier, this journey is not only related to staying current on advances in our profession but also venturing far afield to learn about ideas across a variety of disciplines. This means reading widely, traveling to other cultures and communities, and diversifying the kinds of people you hang out with. In a sense, it is about modeling for our clients the kind of growth and learning that are possible with sufficient commitment and motivation. We help them not only by what we say and do in sessions but also how we live our lives.

Practicing What You Preach

One final issue that is often neglected in graduate school is the importance, not to mention the opportunity, to walk our talk, to become the kinds of individuals that we would wish for our own clients. This means that we are able to infuse all of their relationships with the consideration and caring that we demonstrate when serving others. It also means that we can apply our expertise to develop a deeper understanding of many things that affect our lives.

One of the most remarkable aspects of our profession is that we have opportunities to use what we know and understand to work on our own unresolved issues. Few of us are as healthy as we appear to others, or even as we would like to be. There is a dark side to each of us, a part we keep hidden from view. Late at night when we are unable to sleep, or at other times when we are daydreaming, we are haunted by unresolved issues of our past, by things we have done for which we feel regret or shame, by our secrets long buried, by our weaknesses, our failures, and our imperfections.

Yet despite our flaws and limitations, most of us function reasonably well on a daily basis. We go about the business of helping people, doing the best we can. Through self-monitoring, workshops, growth experiences, peer consultations, professional training, supervision, and personal therapy, we confront our demons and can usually hold our most unsavory or self-defeating impulses in check. Sometimes, however, our efforts do not work that well and some among us may hurt their clients, or themselves.

Each one of us knows another professional who is, or has been at some time, seriously impaired. There are also times when each of us offered our clients far less than they deserved. This could have involved instances when we were suffering from boredom, burnout, clinical depression, incapacitating anxiety, or any number of other diagnoses that we readily bestow upon clients.

We know therapists who drink too much or lead self-destructive lifestyles, those who are undergoing major life transitions, suffering financial strain, relationship breakups, child custody battles, legal disputes, and a host of other problems that can substantially reduce personal and professional effectiveness. We also know therapists with full-fledged personality disorders—those who are emotionally abusive, who thrive on having others dependent on them, who are overcontrolling and manipulative, or who demonstrate extreme levels of narcissism or sociopathy.

The professional work of every therapist undergoing a life transition or experiencing personal problems is not necessarily impaired.

Diminished? Certainly. After all, how could any of us be expected to operate at optimal levels of performance when we are unduly distracted or distressed? It is certainly possible for us to be helpful to others even when we are struggling with our own difficult issues. Yet we can all identify individuals in our midst who we know, beyond any doubt, are hurting people more than they are helping them because of their impairments. How can these observable problems continue to go unattended? After all, we learned in graduate school that ethical problems are relatively straightforward: You simply do what the codes of our profession instruct you to do.

Indeed, there is a whole collection of such codes—by social workers, psychiatrists, psychologists, counselors, family therapists, and other groups—and they all say basically the same thing: We have an obligation to intervene when either ourselves or other professionals may be harming clients. This action may take the form of self-monitoring, confronting an impaired individual directly, or reporting suspected problems to state licensing boards. However, only a small fraction of the problems are actually dealt with in such an organized manner.

Taking This Personally

Before pointing elsewhere, each one of us needs to consider how well we are functioning in various aspects of our lives. There isn't a day that goes by that I don't feel less than ideal in some way, hopefully not to the point that I hurt others, but at least to the point that my levels of competence are diminished. I am a voyeur, a perfectionist, an approval seeker, an obsessive-compulsive achiever, a do-gooder, a meddler, a reckless risk-taker, and each of these urges has compromised me in some way.

Yet these qualities have also been among my greatest strengths as a therapist and teacher. They have helped me to understand other people's pain through my own struggles. I have been committed to learning from my clients, as well as my therapists and supervisors, so that I have brought my impairments under sufficient control that I can function quite well. Along the way, there have been a number of colleagues who have been instrumental in offering the caring, support, and honest confrontation that it takes to make me face my own demons.

I mention these vulnerabilities not because I enjoy admitting my weaknesses, but because I wish to emphasize the very personal nature of this subject. It is easy to shake my head in disgust when a colleague commits some ethical transgression or otherwise acts inappropriately.

Any one of us can lose control, become depressed, abuse drugs or alcohol, or suffer a tragedy from which we cannot recover. None of us is immune from the potential to lose our way, slowly, so slowly we don't even realize what is happening. We all have the ability to so distort our view of a personal disability that we fail to recognize the damage we are doing. Any of us can hurt so badly that we can become threatened by others' attempts to be helpful. I am not just speaking about "them"; I am talking about *us*.

We have an opportunity to be among the most high-functioning human beings on the planet, given what we do for a living. We have endless possibilities for applying concepts to ourselves that we teach to others. We have plenty of reflective time to consider the most important issues in life that provide meaning and satisfaction. We are constantly honing our interpersonal skills and increasing the breadth of our knowledge. We are sojourners on a path to our own enlightenment just as we act as guides for others. We challenge people all day long to consider ways they could be more effective in their lives, all the while we experience a parallel process. In all these ways, and so many others, we have an incredible impetus, if not mandate, to become as fully functioning as possible, not only to empower our therapeutic actions but also to engage more actively in whatever matters most to us.

Congruence Versus Hypocrisy

You likely have witnessed your fair share of hypocrisy in graduate school, dealing with faculty or supervisors who would tell you one thing but do quite another. You heard a lot about how important it was to develop your capacity for empathy, compassion, and caring toward others, but all the while you may have experienced something quite different from your instructors or peers. You may have also encountered more than a few members of the profession, perhaps even seasoned veterans, who barely seem to function in their own lives yet purport to act as models for their clients.

It is interesting that although training to be a therapist includes all kinds of attention devoted to learning diagnostic assessment, intervention strategies, reflective skills, clinical specialties, research methodology, and writing papers with suitable documentation, there is sometimes very little focus on those personal qualities that are most associated with being persuasive and influential. If we agree that being kind, respectful, and sensitive are such important ingredients in therapeutic relationships, how come we don't more directly develop those characteristics? If we believe that it is important to be authentic and genuine, charismatic and passionate, why don't we spend as much time strengthening these traits as we do anything else we learn?

We may all agree that characteristics of the therapist, as well as those of the client, are among the best predictors of successful outcomes, but on some level, we must not really believe that or we'd spend a whole lot more time and energy targeting our own personal development. Although there would also be a consensus among us that therapists who are more fully functioning in their own lives, more able to apply to themselves what they teach to others, have distinct advantages over others who aren't nearly as personally effective, we don't spend nearly as much time on that facet of our development as we do attending continuing education workshops.

Reading books like this one is certainly helpful at times, but they certainly have their limits if the content, or dialogue with the author, doesn't lead to deep reflection, altered beliefs and attitudes, and new, more inspired and personally effective action. Once we graduated from school, we thought we'd finally moved beyond the boundaries of needing—or wanting—to be pushed and cajoled into working more diligently on our own growth, learning, and development. But that is truly the greatest gift of our profession—

that we have this incredible opportunity to walk our talk, to practice what we preach, to be who we wish our clients to become.

None of us have ever really left graduate school behind once we
entered the real world. And we never will. We hold within us the
passionate commitment to learn as much as we can, and become
the best we can at what we do, not only with our clients but in our
daily lives.

REFERENCES

Adler, J. M., Wagner, J. W., & McAdams, D. P. (2007). Personality and the coherence of psychotherapy narratives. *Journal of Research in Personality, 41,* 1179–1198.

Appel, M. (2008). Fictional narratives cultivate just-world beliefs. *Journal of Communication, 58,* 62–83.

Appel, M., & Richter, T. (2007). Persuasive effects of fictional narratives increase over time. *Media Psychology, 10,* 113–134.

Baldwin, S. A., & Imel, Z. E. (2013). Therapist effects: Findings and methods. In M. J. Lambert (Ed.), *Bergin and Garfield's handbook of psychotherapy and behavior change* (pp. 258–297). New York: Wiley.

Bavonese, J. (2013). What's in a brand? *Psychotherapy Networker, Sept/Oct,* 33–37.

Bergner, R. M. (2007). Therapeutic storytelling revisited. *American Journal of Psychotherapy, 61*(2), 149–162.

Betan, E. J., & Binder, J. L. (2010). Clinical expertise in psychotherapy: How expert therapists use theory in generating case conceptualizations and interventions. *Journal of Contemporary Psychotherapy, 40,* 141–152.

Bettelheim, B. (1976). *The uses of enchantment: The meaning and importance of fairy tales.* New York: Knopf.

Birch, C. D., Kelln, B., & Aquino, E. (2006). A review and case report of pseudologia fantastica. *Journal of Forensic Psychiatry and Psychology, 17,* 299–320.

Boston Process Change Study Group. (2010). *Change in psychotherapy: A unifying paradigm.* New York: Norton.

Bowen, E., Brown, S., & Howat, D. (2014). Client engagement in psychotherapeutic treatment and associations with client characteristics, therapist characteristics, and treatment factors. *Clinical Psychology Review, 34*(5), 428–450.

Breggin, P. R., & Breggin, G. R. (2014). *Talking back to Prozac.* New York: Open Road.

Brehony, K. A. (1999). *Ordinary grace.* New York: Riverhead.

Brennan, C. (2013). Ensuring ethical practice: Guidelines for mental health counselors in private practice. *Journal of Mental Health Counseling, 35*(3), 245–261.

Bruner, J. S. (1990). *Acts of meaning.* Cambridge, MA: Harvard University Press.

Burns, G. W. (2001). *101 healing stories: Using metaphors in therapy.* New York: Wiley.

Burns, G. W. (2005). *101 healing stories for kids and teens: Using metaphors in therapy.* New York: Wiley.

Burns, G. W. (Ed.). (2007). *Healing with stories: Your casebook for using therapeutic metaphors.* New York: Wiley.

Burns, J. P., Goodman, D. M., & Orman, A. J. (2013). Psychotherapy as moral encounter: A crisis of modern conscience. *Pastoral Psychology, 62,* 1–12.

Burns, S. T. (2008). Utilizing fictional stories when counseling adults. *Journal of Creativity in Mental Health, 3,* 441–454.

Bussolari, C. J., & Goodell, J. A. (2009). Chaos theory as a model for life transitions in counseling: Nonlinear dynamics and life's changes. *Journal of Counseling and Development, 87,* 98–107.

Castonguay, L. G., & Beutler, L. E. (Eds.). (2006). *Principles of therapeutic change at work.* New York: Oxford University Press.

Castonguay, L. G., & Hill, C. E. (Eds.). (2012). *Transformation in psychotherapy: Corrective experiences across cognitive, behavioral, humanistic, and psychodynamic approaches.* Washington, DC: American Psychological Association.

Chi, M. T. H. (2006). Two approaches to the study of experts' characteristics. In K. A. Ericsson, N. Charness, P. J. Feltovich, & R. R. Hoffman (Eds.), *The Cambridge handbook of expertise and expert performance* (pp. xx–xx). New York: Cambridge University Press.

Clement, P. (2013). Practice-based evidence: 45 years of psychotherapy's effectiveness in a private practice. *American Journal of Psychotherapy, 67*(1), 23–46.

Corey, M. S., & Corey, G. (2015). *Becoming a helper* (7th ed.). Belmont, CA: Cengage.

Cronin, C. (2001). Storytelling: The future of nursing. *Nursing Forum, 36*(3), 4.

Cummings, J. (2011). Sharing a traumatic event: The experience of the listener and the storyteller. *Nursing Research, 60*(6), 386–392.

Cummings, N. A. (2014). The first decade of managed behavioral care: What went right and what went wrong. In R. D. Weitz (Ed.), *Psycho-economics: Managed care in mental health in the new millennium* (pp. 19–35). New York: Routledge.

Cummings, N. A., & Cummings, J. L. (2013). *Refocused psychotherapy as the first line intervention of behavioral health.* New York: Routledge.

Dawes, R. M. (1994). *House of cards: Psychology and psychotherapy built on myth.* New York: The Free Press.

Devlin, A. S., & Nasar, J. L. (2012). Impressions of psychotherapists' offices: Do therapists and clients agree? *Professional Psychology: Research and Practice, 43*(2), 118–122.

de Waal, F. (1982). *Chimpanzee politics.* Baltimore, MD: Johns Hopkins.

Djikic, M., Oatley, K., Zoeterman, S., & Peterson, J. B. (2009). On being moved by art: How reading fiction transforms the self. *Creativity Research Journal, 21*(1), 24–29.

Doherty, W. J. (1995). *Soul searching.* New York: Basic.

Donovan, J. (2012). *How to deliver a TED talk: Secrets of the world's most inspiring presentations.* San Bernardino, CA; Jeremy Donovan

Downs, R. B. (1983). *Books that changed the world.* New York: Signet.

Duarte, N. (2010). *Resonate: Present visual stories that transform audiences*. New York: Wiley.

Duncan, B. L. (2010). *On becoming a better therapist*. Washington, DC: American Psychological Association.

Duncan, B. L., Miller, S. D., Wampold, B. E., & Hubble, M. A. (2010). *The heart and soul of change: Delivering what works in psychotherapy* (2nd ed). Washington, DC: American Psychological Association.

Dunning, D., Johnson, K., Ehrlinger, J., & Kruger, J. (2003). Why people fail to recognize their own incompetence. *Current Directions in Psychological Science, 12*(3), 83–87.

Ekman, P. (2009). *Telling lies: Clues to deceit in the marketplace, politics, and marriage*. New York: Norton.

Elder, D., & Holyan, R. (2010). *Life lessons through storytelling*. Bloomington: Indiana University Press.

Ericsson, K. A., Charness, N., Feltovich, P. J., & Hoffman, R. R. (Eds.). *The Cambridge handbook of expertise and expert performance*. New York: Cambridge University Press.

Evans, I. (2013). *How and why people change: Foundations of psychological therapy*. New York: Oxford University Press.

Falkenstrom, F., Granstrom, F., & Holmqvist, R. (2013). Working alliance predicts psychotherapy outcomes even while controlling for prior symptom improvement. *Psychotherapy Research, 24*(2), 146–154.

Fanelli, D. (2009). How many scientists fabricate and falsify research? A systematic review of meta-analysis of survey data. *PLoS One, 4*(5), 1–11.

Fawcett, J. (2013). What is the future of psychotherapy in psychiatry? *Psychiatric Annals, 43*(11), 1.

Fluckiger, C., Del Re, A. C., Wampold, B. E., & Symonds, D. (2012). How central is the alliance? A multilevel longitudinal meta-analysis. *Journal of Counseling Psychology, 59*(1), 10–17.

Frank, J. D. (1973). *Persuasion and healing*. Baltimore, MD: Johns Hopkins.

Frankel, Z., & Levitt, H. M. (2009). Clients' experiences of disengaged moments in psychotherapy: A grounded theory analysis. *Journal of Contemporary Psychotherapy, 39*, 171–186.

Fredrickson, B. L. (2003). The value of positive emotions: The emerging science of positive psychology is coming to understand why it's good to feel good. *American Scientist, 91*, 330–335.

Gallo, C. (2014). *Talk like TED: The 9 public-speaking secrets of the world's top minds.* New York: St. Martin's Press.

Gaudiano, B. A. (2013, September 29). Psychotherapy's image problem. *The New York Times.* Retrieved December 2014, from http://www.nytimes.com/2013/09/30/opinion/psychotherapys-image-problem.html?hp&_r=2&&pagewanted=print

Gergen, K. (1991). *The saturated self: Dilemmas of identity in contemporary life.* New York: Basic Books.

Gladwell, M. (1996, June 3). The tipping point. *The New Yorker,* pp. 32–38.

Goldfried, M. R. (2010). The future of psychotherapy integration: Closing the gap between research and practice. *Journal of Psychotherapy Integration, 20*(4), 386–396.

Gordon, D. (1978). *Therapeutic metaphors.* Cupertino, CA: Meta.

Gottschall, J. (2012). *The storytelling animal: How stories make us human.* New York: Houghton Mifflin.

Greenberg, M. A. (2008). Emotional storytelling after stressful experiences. In S. J. Lopez (Ed.), *Positive psychology: Exploring the best in people* (Vol. 3, pp. 145–169). Wesport, CT: Praeger.

Haber, R., Carlson, R. G., & Braga, C. (2014). Use of an anecdotal client feedback note in family therapy. *Family Process, 53*(2), 307–317.

Hamilton, R. (2013). The frustrations of virtue: The myth of moral neutrality in psychotherapy. *Journal of Evaluation in Clinical Practice, 19*, 485–492.

Hansen, J. T. (2007). Counseling without truth: Toward a neopragmatic foundation for counseling practice. *Journal of Counseling and Development, 85*, 423–430.

Healy, D. (2004). *Let them eat Prozac.* New York: New York University Press.

Heinonen, E., & Orlinsky, D. E. (2013). Psychotherapists' personal identities, theoretical orientations, and professional relationships: Elective affinity and role adjustment as modes of congruence. *Psychotherapy Research, 23*(6), 718–731.

Herbert, W. (2014, July 18). Why psychotherapy appears to work (even when it doesn't). *Association for Psychological Science.* Retrieved December 2014, from http://www.psychologicalscience.org/index.php/news/were-only-human/why-psychotherapy-appears-to-work-even-when-it-doesnt.html

Herman, D. (2013). *Storytelling and the sciences of mind.* Cambridge, MA: MIT Press.

Hesley, J. W., & Hesley, J. G. (2001). *Rent two films and let's talk in the morning: Using popular movies in psychotherapy* (2nd ed.). New York: Wiley.

Hess, M. (2012). Mirror neurons, the development of empathy and digital storytelling. *Religious Education, 107*(4), 401–414.

Higginson, S., & Mansell, W. (2008). What is the mechanism of psychological change? *Psychology and Psychotherapy: Theory, Research, and Practice, 81*, 309–328.

Hodgetts, A., & Wright, J. (2007). Researching clients' experiences: A review of qualitative studies. *Clinical Psychology and Psychotherapy, 14*, 157–163.

Hodson, P. (2012). *The business of therapy: How to run a successful private practice.* New York: Open University Press.

Holmes, J., & Lindley, R. (1989). *The values of psychotherapy.* New York: Oxford University Press.

Howey, H. (2014, February 19). The 50k report. *AuthorEarnings. com.* Retrieved December 2014, from http://authorearnings.com/report/the-50k-report/

Hoyt, M. F. (Ed.). (2013). *Therapist stories of inspiration, passion, and renewal.* New York: Routledge.

Hoyt, T., & Yeater, E. A. (2011). The effects of negative emotion and expressive writing on posttraumatic stress symptoms. *Journal of Social and Clinical Psychology, 30*(6), 549–569.

Hsu, J. (2008). The secrets of storytelling: Our love for telling tales reveals the workings of the mind. *Scientific American Mind,* *19*(4), 46–51.

Iacoboni, M. (2008). *Mirroring people: The new science of how we connect with others.* New York: Farrar, Straus & Giroux.

Ingemark, C. A. (Ed.). (2013). *Therapeutic uses of storytelling.* Lund, Sweden: Nordic Academic Press.

Johnson, S. B. (2012). Psychology's paradigm shift: From a mental health to a health profession. *Monitor on Psychology, 43*(6), 5.

Joseph, S. (2011). *What doesn't kill us: The new psychology of posttraumatic growth.* New York: Basic Books.

Kahana, E., Bhatta, T., Lovegreen, L. D., Kahana, B., & Midlarsky, E. (2013). Altruism, helping and volunteering: Pathways to well-being in later life. *Journal of Aging and Health, 25*(1), 159–187.

Karia, A. (2012). *How to deliver a great TED talk.* Seattle, WA: Amazon Digital Services.

Kazdin, A. E. (2009). Understanding how and why psychotherapy leads to change. *Psychotherapy Research, 19*(4–5), 418–428.

Keeney, B. (2007). *Shaking medicine: The healing power of ecstatic movement.* Rochester, VT: Destiny Movement.

Keeney, B. (2009). *The creative therapist: The Art of awakening a session.* New York: Routledge.

Keeney, H., & Keeney, B. (2012). *Circular therapeutics: Giving therapy a healing heart.* Phoenix, AZ: Zeig, Tucker, Theisen.

Kirsch, I. (2011). *The emperor's new drugs: Exploding the antidepressant myth.* New York: Basic Books.

Kottler, J. A. (1987). *On being a therapist.* San Francisco, CA: Jossey-Bass.

Kottler, J. A. (1990). *Private moments, secret selves: Enriching our time alone.* New York: Ballantine.

Kottler, J. A. (1991). *The compleat therapist,* San Francisco, CA: Jossey-Bass.

Kottler, J. A. (1992). *Compassionate therapy: Working with difficult clients.* San Francisco, CA: Jossey-Bass.

Kottler, J. A. (1994). *Beyond blame: A new way of resolving conflict in relationships.* San Francisco, CA: Jossey-Bass.

Kottler, J. A. (1996). *The language of tears*. San Francisco, CA: Jossey-Bass.

Kottler, J. A. (1997). *Travel that can change your life*. San Francisco, CA: Jossey-Bass.

Kottler, J. A. (2000). *Doing good: Passion and commitment for helping others*. New York: Routledge.

Kottler, J. A. (2006). *Divine madness: Ten stories of creative struggle*. San Francisco, CA: Jossey-Bass.

Kottler, J. A. (2010a). *On being a therapist* (4th ed.). San Francisco, CA: Jossey-Bass.

Kottler, J. A. (2010b). *The assassin and the therapist: An exploration of truth in psychotherapy and in life*. New York: Routledge.

Kottler, J. A. (2011). *Lust for blood: Why we are fascinated by death, horror, and violence*. Amherst, NY: Prometheus Press.

Kottler, J. A. (2012). *The therapist's workbook: Self-assessment, self-care, and self-improvement exercises for mental health professionals* (2nd ed.). New York: Wiley.

Kottler, J. A. (2013). The power of transcendent empathy: Empowering lower caste girls in Nepal. In J. Kottler, M. Englar-Carlson, & J. Carlson (Eds.), *Helping beyond the fifty minute hour: Therapists involved in meaningful social action*. New York: Routledge.

Kottler, J. A. (2014). *Change: What leads to personal transformation* New York: Oxford University Press.

Kottler, J. A. (2015). *Stories we've heard, stories we've told: Life-changing narratives in therapy and everyday life*. New York: Oxford University Press.

Kottler, J. A., & Blau, D. S. (1989). *The imperfect therapist: Learning from failure in psychotherapy*. San Francisco, CA: Jossey-Bass.

Kottler, J. A., & Carlson, J. (2002). *Bad therapy: Master therapists share their worst failures*. New York: Brunner/Routledge.

Kottler, J. A., & Carlson, J. (2003). *The mummy at the dining room table: Eminent therapists reveal their most unusual cases and what they teach us about human behavior.* San Francisco, CA: Jossey-Bass.

Kottler, J. A., & Carlson, J. (2006). *The client who changed me: Stories of therapist personal transformation.* New York: Brunner/Routledge.

Kottler, J. A., & Carlson, J. (2007). *Moved by the spirit: Discovery and transformation in the lives of leaders.* Atascadero, CA: Impact.

Kottler, J. A., & Carlson, J. (2008). *Their finest hour: Master therapists share their greatest success stories* (2nd ed.). Bethel, CT: Crown Publishing.

Kottler, J. A., & Carlson, J. (2009). *Creative breakthroughs in therapy: Tales of transformation and astonishment.* New York: Wiley.

Kottler, J. A., & Carlson, J. (2011). *Duped: Lies and deception in psychotherapy.* New York: Routledge.

Kottler, J. A., & Carlson, J. (in press). *On being a master therapist: Practicing what we preach.* New York: Wiley.

Kottler, J. A., Carlson, J., & Keeney, B. (2004). *An American shaman: An odyssey of ancient healing traditions.* New York: Brunner/Routledge.

Kottler, J., & Englar-Carlson, M. (in press). *Learning group leadership: An experiential approach.* Thousand Oaks, CA: Sage.

Kottler, J. A., & Hazler, R. (1997). *What you never learned in graduate school.* New York: Norton.

Kottler, J. A., Englar-Carlson, M., & Carlson, J. (Eds.). (2013). *Helping beyond the 50 minute hour: Therapists involved in meaningful social action.* New York: Routledge.

Kottler, J. A., & Marriner, M. (2009). *Changing people's lives while transforming your own: Paths to social justice and global human rights.* New York: Wiley.

Kottler, J. A., Sexton, T. L., & Whiston, S. C. (1994). *Heart of healing: Relationships in therapy.* San Francisco, CA: Jossey-Bass.

Krippner, S. (1994). Humanistic psychology and chaos theory: The third revolution and the third force. *Journal of Humanistic Psychology, 34,* 48–61.

Kuhn, T. S. (2012). *The structure of scientific revolutions.* Chicago, IL: University of Chicago Press. (originally published 1970)

Lakoff, G., & Johnson, M. (2003). *Metaphors we live by.* Chicago, IL: University of Chicago Press.

Lambert, M. (2010). *Prevention of treatment failures: The use of measuring, monitoring, and feedback in clinical practice.* Washington, DC: American Psychological Association.

Lambert, M. J. (Ed.). (2013). *Bergin and Garfield's handbook of psychotherapy and behavior change.* New York: Wiley.

Lambert, M. J., & Shimokawa, K. (2011). Collecting client feedback. *Psychotherapy, 48*(1), 72–79.

Lampropoulos, G. K., & Spengler, P. M. (2005). Helping and change without traditional therapy: Commonalities and opportunities. *Counselling Psychology Quarterly, 18*(1), 47–59.

Lankton, C. H., & Lankton, S. R. (1989). *Tales of enchantment: Goal-oriented metaphors for adults and children in therapy.* New York: Routledge.

Larsen, D. J., & Stege, R. (2012). Client accounts of hope in early counseling sessions: A qualitative study. *Journal of Counseling and Development, 90,* 45–54.

Laska, K. M., Gurman, A. S., & Wampold, B. E. (2013). Expanding the lens of evidence-based practice in psychotherapy: A common factors perspective. *Psychotherapy, 51*(4), 467–481.

Lee, J., Lim, N., Yang, E., & Lee, S. M. (2011). Antecedents and consequences of three dimensions of burnout in psychotherapists: A meta-analysis. *Professional Psychology: Research and Practice, 42*(3), 252–258.

Levine, M. (2004, June 1). Tell your doctor all your problems, but keep it less than a minute. *The New York Times.* Retrieved December 2014, from http://www.nytimes.com/2004/06/01/health/tell-the-doctor-all-your-problems-but-keep-it-to-less-than-a-minute.html?pagewanted=all&src=pm

Levitt, H. M., Rattanasampan, W., Chaidaroon, S. S., Stanley, C., &

Robinson, T. (2009). The process of personal change through reading fictional narratives: Implications for psychotherapy practice and theory. *The Humanistic Psychologist, 37,* 326–352.

Lilienfeld, S. O., Lynn, S. J., Ruscio, J., & Beyerstein, B. I. (2010). *50 great myths of popular psychology: Shattering widespread misconceptions about human behavior.* Chichester, UK: Wiley-Blackwell.

Lilienfeld, S. O., Ritschel, L. A., Lynn, S. J., Cautin, R. L., & Latzman, R. D. (2013). Why many clinical psychologists are resistant to evidence-based practice: Root causes and constructive remedies. *Clinical Psychology Review, 33*(7), 883–900.

London, P. (1986). *Modes and morals of psychotherapy* (2nd ed.). Washington, DC: Hemisphere.

Lorenz, E. (1963). Deterministic nonperiodic flow. *Journal of Atmospheric Sciences, 20,* 130–140.

Macdonald, J., & Mellor-Clark, J. (2014). Correcting psychotherapists' blindsidedness: Formal feedback as a means of overcoming the natural limitations of therapists. *Clinical Psychology and Psychotherapy.* Epub ahead of print. Retrieved December 2014, from http://onlinelibrary.wiley.com/doi/10.1002/cpp.1887/abstract;jsessionid=E383E1BE3CA8FC12BEACCFDC233DB33C.f01t02

Mahoney, M. (1991). *Human change processes: The scientific foundations of psychotherapy.* New York: Basic Books.

Mahrer, A. R. (1989). *The integration of psychotherapies.* New York: Human Sciences.

Malhotra, H. (2014). *Metaphors of healing: Playful language in psychotherapy and everyday life.* Lanham, MD: Hamilton Books.

Malinowski, A. J. (2013). Characteristics of job burnout and humor among psychotherapists. *Humor, 26*(1), 117–133.

Manthei, R. J. (2007). Clients talk about their experience of the process of counselling. *Counselling Psychology Quarterly, 20*(1), 1–26.

Mar, R. A., & Oatley, K. (2008). The function of fiction is the abstraction and simulation of social experience. *Perspectives on Psychological Science, 3*(3), 173–192.

Mar, R. A., Oatley, K., Djikic, M., & Mullin, J. (2011). Emotion and narrative fiction: Interactive influences before, during, and after reading. *Cognition and Emotion, 25*(5), 818–833.

Marshall, J. (2014). Mirror neurons. *Proceedings of the National Academy of Sciences USA, 111*(18), 6531.

McAdams, D. P. (1993). *The stories we live by: Personal myths and the making of the self.* New York: Morrow.

McAdams, D. P. (2006). The problem of narrative coherence. *Journal of Constructivist Psychology, 19,* 109–125.

McGregor, I., & Holmes, J. (1999). How storytelling shapes memory and impressions of relationship events over time. *Journal of Personality and Social Psychology, 76,* 403–419.

Meehl, P. E. (1956). Wanted—a good cookbook. *American Psychologist, 11,* 263–272.

Mehl-Madrona, L. (2010). *Healing the mind through the power of story.* Rochester, VT: Bear and Company.

Miller, S., & Hubble, M. (2011). The road to mastery. *Psychotherapy Networker, March/April,* 22–31.

Miller, S., Hubble, M., & Duncan, B. (2007). Supershrinks: What's the secret of their success? *Psychotherapy Networker, Nov/Dec,* 27–35

Miller, S. D., Duncan, B. L, Brown, J., Sorrell, R., & Chalk, B. (2006). Using feedback to inform and improve outcomes. *Journal of Brief Therapy, 5,* 5–22.

Miller, S. D., Hubble, M. A., Chow, D. L., & Seidel, J. A. (2014). The outcome of psychotherapy: Yesterday, today, and tomorrow. *Psychotherapy in Australia, 20*(3), 64–75.

Miller, W. R., & Rollnick, S. (2002). *Motivational interviewing: Preparing people for change* (2nd ed.). New York: Guilford Press.

Mukherjee, S. (2012, April 19). Post-Prozac nation. *The New York Times.* Retrieved December 2014, from http://www.nytimes.

com/2012/04/22/magazine/the-science-and-history-of-treating-depression.html?pagewanted=all

Neimeyer, R. A. (Ed.). (2012). *Techniques of grief therapy: Creative practices for counseling the bereaved.* New York: Routledge.

Newman, C. F., & Strauss, J. L. (2003). When clients are untruthful: Implications for the therapeutic alliance, case conceptualization, and intervention. *Journal of Cognitive Therapy, 17,* 241–252.

Nigam, S. K. (2012). The storytelling brain. *Science and Engineering Ethics, 18,* 567–571.

Norcross, J. C. (2006). Integrating self-help into psychotherapy: 16 practical suggestions. *Professional Psychology: Research and Practice, 37*(6), 683–693.

Norcross, J. C. (Ed.). (2011). *Psychotherapy relationships that work.* New York: Oxford University Press.

Norcross, J. C., & Glencavage, L. M. (1989). Eclecticism and integration in counseling and psychotherapy: Major themes and obstacles. *British Journal of Guidance and Counselling, 17,* 227–247.

Norcross, J. C., & Guy, J. D. (2007). *Leaving it at the office: A guide to psychotherapist self-care.* New York: Guilford Press.

Norcross, J. C., & Rogan, J. D. (2013). Psychologists conducting psychotherapy in 2012: Current practices and historical trends among Division 29 members. *Psychotherapy, 50*(4), 490–495.

Norcross, J. C., Pfund, R. A., & Prochaska, J. O. (2013). Psychotherapy in 2022: A Delphi poll on its future. *Professional Psychology: Research and Practice, 44*(5), 363–370.

O'Hanlon, B. (2013). *Becoming a published therapist: A step-by-step guide to writing your book.* New York: Norton.

Omer, H. (1987). Therapeutic impact: A nonspecific major factor in directive psychotherapies. *Psychotherapy, 24,* 52–57.

Orlinsky, D. E., & Ronnestad, M. H. (2005). (Eds.). *How psychotherapists develop: A study of therapeutic work and professional growth.* Washington, DC: American Psychological Association.

Paul, A. M. (2012, March 17). Your brain on fiction. *The New York Times*. Retrieved march 2013, from http://www.nytimes.com/2012/03/18/opinion/sunday/the-neuroscience-of-your-brain-on-fiction.html?pagewanted=all&_r=0

Paulson, B. L., Turscott, D., & Stuart, J. (1999). Clients' perceptions of helpful experiences in counseling. *Journal of Counseling Psychology, 46*(3), 317–324.

Polkinghorne, D. E. (2013). Narrative identity and psychotherapy. In C. A. Ingemark (Ed.), *Therapeutic uses of storytelling* (pp. 21– 41). Lund, Sweden: Nordic Academic Press.

Post, S. G. (Ed.). (2007). *Altruism and health: Perspectives from empirical research*. New York: Oxford University Press.

Post, S. G. (2011). *The hidden gifts of helping: How the power of giving, compassion, and hope can get us through hard times*. San Francisco, CA: Jossey-Bass.

Prochaska, J. O., & DiClemente, C. C. (1984). Transtheoretical therapy: Toward an integrative model of change. *Psychotherapy, 19*, 276–288.

Prochaska, J. O., & Norcross, J. C. (2014). *Systems of psychotherapy: A transtheoretical approach* (8th ed.). Belmont, CA: Wadsworth.

Puig, A., Yoon, E., Callueng, C., An, S., & Lee, M. (2014). Burnout syndrome in psychotherapists: A comparative analysis of five nations. *Psychological Services, 11*(1), 87–96.

Reese, R. J., Toland, M. D., & Slone, N. C. (2010). Effect of client feedback on couple psychotherapy outcomes. *Psychotherapy: Theory, Research, Practice, and Training, 47*(4), 616–630.

Reynolds, D. J., Stiles, W. B., Bailer, A. J., & Hughes, M. R. (2013). Impact of exchanges and client-therapist alliance in online-text psychotherapy. *Cyberpsychology, Behavior, and Networking, 16*(5), 370–378.

Reynolds, G. (2012). *Presentation Zen: Simple ideas on presentation design and delivery*. Berkeley, CA: New Riders.

Rhodes, P. (2012). Why clinical psychology needs process research: An examination of four methodologies. *Clinical and Child Psychology and Psychiatry, 17*(4), 495–504.

Rieff, P. (1961). *Freud: The mind of the moralist*. Garden City, NY: Anchor.

Rizzolatti, G., & Craighero, L. (2004). The mirror-neuron system. *Annual Review of Neuroscience, 27*, 169–192.

Roberts, G., & Holmes, J. (Eds.). (1999). *Healing stories: Narrative in psychiatry and psychotherapy*. New York: Oxford University Press.

Roberts, P. (1995, January 1). Prozacville, USA. *Psychology Today*. Retrieved December 2014, from http://www.psychologytoday.com/articles/199501/prozacville-usa

Ronnestad, M. H., & Skovholt, T. M. (2013). *The developing practitioner: Growth and stagnation of therapists and counselors*. New York: Routledge.

Rosen, S. (Ed.). (1982). *My voice will go with you: The teaching tales of Milton H. Erickson*. New York: Norton.

Rosenzweig, S. (1936). Some implicit common factors in diverse methods in psychotherapy. *American Journal of Orthopsychiatry, 6*, 412–415.

Sapyta, J., Reimer, M., & Bickman, L. (2005). Feedback to clinicians: Theory, research, and practice. *Journal of Clinical Psychology, 61(2), 145–153.*

Schulenberg, S. E. (2003). Psychotherapy and movies: On using films in clinical practice. *Journal of Contemporary Psychotherapy, 1*, 36–48.

Schwartz, B., & Flowers, J. V. (2006). *How to fail as a therapist*. Atascadero, CA: Impact

Shaw, S. L., & Murray, K. W. (2014). Monitoring alliance and outcome with client feedback measures. *Journal of Mental Health Counseling, 36*(1), 43–57.

Silverman, W. H. (2013). The future of psychotherapy: One editor's perspective. *Psychotherapy, 50*(4), 484–489.

Skovholt, T. M. (2012). *Becoming a therapist: On the path to mastery*. New York: Wiley.

Skovholt, T. M., & Trotter-Mathison, M. (2011). *The resilient practitioner*. New York: Routledge.

Smith, P. L., & Moss, S. B. (2009). Psychologist impairment: What is it, how can it be prevented, and what can be done to address it? *Clinical Psychology: Science and Practice, 16*, 1–15.

Solomon, G. (2001). *Reel therapy: How movies inspire you to overcome life's problems.* New York: Lebhar-Friedman Books.

Spaulding, A. E. (2011). *The art of storytelling: Telling truths through telling stories.* Lanham, MA: Scarecrow Press.

Spence, D. P. (1984). *Narrative and historical truth.* New York: Norton.

Stanton, A. (2012). The clues to a great story. *TED.* Retrieved March 2013, from http://www.ted.com/talks/andrew_stanton_the_clues_to_a_great_story.html

Stewart, G. (2013). Psychotherapy and relationship-based change: It's about leadership. *Journal of Psychotherapy Integration, 23*(4), 345–358.

Strupp, H. (1973). On the basic ingredients of psychotherapy. *Journal of Consulting and Clinical Psychology, 41*(1), 1–8.

Sussman, M. B. (1992). *A curious calling: Unconscious for motivations for practicing psychotherapy.* Northvale, NJ: Jason Aronson.

Tracey, T. J. G., Wampold, B. E., Lichtenberg, J. W., & Goodyear, R. K. (2014). Expertise in psychotherapy: An elusive goal? *American Psychologist, 69*(3), 218–229.

Truax, C. B., & Carkhuff, R. R. (1967). *Toward effective counseling and psychotherapy.* Chicago, IL: Aldine.

Tschacher, W., Martin, U., Pfammatter, J., & Pfammatter, M. (2014). Towards a taxonomy of common factors in psychotherapy—Results of a survey. *Clinical Psychology and Psychotherapy, 21*(1), 82–96.

Walfish, S., McAlister, B., O'Donnell, P., & Lambert, M. J. (2012). An investigation of self-assessment bias in mental health providers. *Psychological Reports, 110*, 639–644.

Wallach, M. A., & Wallach, L. (1983). *Psychology's sanction for selfishness.* San Francisco, CA: W. H. Freeman.

Walsh, R. (2011). Lifestyle and mental health. *American Psychologist, 66*(7), 579–592.

Wampold, B. E., & Imel, Z. (in press). *The great psychotherapy debate: The evidence for what makes psychotherapy work* (2nd ed.). New York: Routledge.

Warneken, F., & Tomasello, M. (2009). The roots of human altruism. *British Journal of Psychology, 100,* 455–471.

Wedding, D., & Niemiec, R. M. (2003). The clinical use of films in psychotherapy. *Journal of Clinical Psychology, 59*(2), 207–215.

Wooder, B. (2008). *Movie therapy: How it changes lives.* UK: Rideau Lakes Publishing.

Wylie, M. S. (1995). The new visionaries. *Family Therapy Networker, September/October,* 21–32.

Yu, A. (2014, March 16). Physicists, generals, and CEOs agree: Ditch the Powerpoint. *NPR.* Retrieved December 2014, from http://www.npr.org/blogs/alltechconsidered/2014/03/16/288796805/physicists-generals-and-ceos-agree-ditch-the-powerpoint

Zipes, J. (2006). *Why fairy tales stick.* New York: Routledge.

INDEX

academic performance
  formal testing and evaluation,
    23–24
  personal qualities of therapist
    versus, 24–25
accountability, 43, 116–17
aging, population, 118
alcohol dependence, 130
altruism, 199–200
antidepressant medications,
    44–46
assessment
  of client's perception of ther-
    apy, 132–34
  scientist-practitioner model
    for, 26–28
attention span, 206

Bavonese, J., 89
Becoming a Published Thera-
    pist (O'Hanlon), 237
behavioral psychology, 147
Bettelheim, B., 180
bias and prejudice, therapist's,
    284
bibliotherapy, 177–79
blogs, 222, 231
branding, 88–89
brief interventions, 46–48, 147
  chaos theory and, 90–91

current practice environ-
    ment, 39–40, 117
  insight and, 176–77
  out-of-session work and, 114
Brown, L., 142, 265
Bugental, J., 265
burnout
  manifestations of, 64–65
  prevention in private prac-
    tice, 195–96
  risk of, 115–16
business education, 189–90,
    191–92
Bussolari, C., 91

Carlson, J., 53
Carson, Rachel, 168
case studies, 95
change process
  benefits of witnessing, 138–
    39
  client resistance to, 95–96
  clinicians' limited under-
    standing of, 49–50, 53,
    77–80, 127, 131
  content-driven approach to
    training versus understand-
    ing of, 23
  current practice environment
    and expectations for, 39–40

change process (*continued*)
  eliciting client's story in, 82, 113–14
  emotional processing in, 82–83
  experimenting with new behaviors as part of, 83
  hope as important element of, 82
  lessons from chaos theory, 90–94
  misperception of client's progress, 131–32
  non-therapeutic factors in, 127–28
  role of insight in, 83
  role of storytelling in, 162–63
  role of therapist in, 109–13
  scientist-practitioner model for study of, 26–28
  significance of therapeutic relationship in, 81, 148–49
  significant variables in, 80–84
  storytelling in, 171–73
  talking as part of, 82
  task facilitation in, 83–84, 114–15
  therapeutic relationship as mediator of nonspecific factors in, 149–52
  therapist's optimistic belief in, 128–29
  therapist's self-perceived role in, 127–28
  third-party review and, 48–50
chaos theory, 89–94
Civil Disobedience, On (Thoreau), 168
cognitive therapies, 162, 168, 176
collaboration, 32–34
Common Sense (Paine), 168
competition within profession, 42–43, 117
  psychopharmacotherapy and, 45
confirmation bias, 129–30
conflicting opinions on treatment policies and techniques, 15–17
constructivist therapies, 162, 170, 173
control, 128–29
cost-effective service delivery, 41, 42, 117
countertransference, 135–36
couples therapy, after individual therapy, 15–17
creative breakthroughs in therapy
  conditions for, 268–70
  obstacles to, 264–66
  relational context of, 266–68, 270
cultural sensitivity, 117–18

deception, in client's story, 168–71
developmental needs of professionals, 18–20
developmental theory, 91
de Waal, F., 245
diagnostic skills, 22–23, 69–71

Doherty, W., 50
dream interpretation, 130
Duarte, N., 213
duration of treatment, 39–40, 46–48, 192–93

effective therapy
    academic qualifications versus personal characteristics, 24–25
    common factors of, 106–7
    cost-effectiveness concerns, 41, 42
    current paradigm shifts within psychotherapy, 84–87
    difficulty in delivering, 69–71
    importance of attending to client in, 123–25
    peer consultation for stuck case, 277–81
    placebo effects, 126–27
    psychotropic medications, 45–46
    resources for, 71–73, 125
    scientist-practitioner model for evaluating, 26–28
    soliciting client's perception of, 132–34
    therapist's confirmation bias in assessing, 129–30
    therapist's perception of cause and effect in, 130–31
    therapist's self-perceived role in, 125–26, 127–28
    trends toward integrative conceptualizations of, 52–53, 84

    see also change process; creative breakthroughs in therapy
elderly clients, 118
Ellis, A., 140, 142, 265
emotional arousal and processing, 82–83
emotionally-focused therapy, 95
Erickson, M., 180, 184
Ericksonian therapy, 162, 173, 184
ethical practice
    graduate school preparation for, 73–74
    impaired practitioners, 286–87
    moral responsibility, 50–52
ethnography, 95
evidence-based treatment, 26–28, 48, 116–17, 149, 266
evolutionary theory, 199–200
existential therapy, 168
expectations of beginning therapists
    confidence in training and abilities, vii, 55–59, 62–63
    private practice versus public service, 185–86
    reality versus, 37–38, 61
    for supervision, 258
expectations of clients
    novelty effects, 126–27
    for quick results, 46, 108
expertise, development of, 19–20
expert practice
    development of, 284–85

feminist therapy, 95, 162
fictional stories, 177–79
Freud, S., 95, 135–36, 147

Gandhi, M., 168, 202
Gladwell, M., 90
Glasser, W., 53, 142, 265
Goodell, J., 91
graduate training
    benefits of, 25–35, 281
    changes in clinical theory and
        practice after, vii–viii, 21–22
    content-driven approach of,
        23–24
    coverage of personal and
        interpersonal issues in,
        viii–ix
    creation of common profes-
        sional heritage in, 28–29
    emphasis on objectivity and
        detachment in, 51
    evolving requirements for, 21,
        22
    exposure to faculty conflicts
        in, 240–41
    fragmented nature of, 22–23
    goals of, 18, 20–21
    neglected areas in, 59–61
    preparation for private prac-
        tice, 189–90, 191–92
    preparation for team collabo-
        rations, 32–34, 241
    in professional ethics, 73–74
    recognized limitations of,
        18–19, 21
    seeking approval and profes-
        sional recognition in, 30–32,
        241–42

    skills for maintaining confi-
        dence and discipline pro-
        moted in, 34–35
    in storytelling, 162–64
    student's motivation for, 67–68
    support for clinician's profes-
        sional development in,
        29–30
    therapists' confidence in ade-
        quacy of, 55–59
    therapists' satisfaction with,
        vii, 119
    trends in professional special-
        ization and, 87–89
group functioning, 155–58
group therapy, 93–94
    advantages of, 176
    practice trends, 118
    therapist experience and
        leadership of, 19–20

Haley, J., 83, 91, 265
homework, 83–84, 114–15
hope, 82
hopelessness, 150
hospice care, 98–99
humor, 116

impaired practitioners, 248–49,
    286–87
insight, 83, 150
insurance
    evolution of industry atti-
        tudes toward mental health
        issues, 87
    fraudulent practice, 43
    trends affecting service deliv-
        ery, 41, 46

integrative theories and therapies, 52–53, 84, 118
interpersonal relationships
challenges for therapists in
maintaining, 107–8, 140–41,
152–55
cooperative and collective
orientation in, 155–57
coverage in graduate school,
viii–ix
leadership and, 157–58
storytelling and, 158
stresses for therapists, 60,
64–67, 115–16
therapists' preparation for
team collaborations, 32–34,
241
see also organizational politics

Jobs, Steve, 213
Jordan, J., 265
journals, professional, 232–33
Jungle, The (Sinclair), 168

Keeney, B., 115
Keynote, 215
King, Martin Luther, Jr., 213
Kohlberg, L., 91
Krumboltz, J., 142
Kuhn, T., 84

Language of Tears, The (Kottler), 229
Lankton, S., 184
law school, 18
Lazarus, A., 265
leadership, 157–58
organizational, 250–51

licensing
graduate training requirements for, 22
trends affecting practice, 52
Lincoln, Abraham, 213
Listening to Prozac, 44
Lorenz, E., 90–91

Machiavelli, N., 168
Madanes, C., 50, 265
magazine articles, 233–34
malpractice claims, 52
managed care, vii, 41, 96
marketing of therapy services,
88–89, 102–3
May, R., 266
Mead, M., 95
meditation, 117
Meichenbaum, D., 265
memory, 163
trauma effects, 173
mentors, 281–83
metaphors, 173–74
mindfulness movement, 117
mirror neurons, 163
moral responsibility, 50–52

narrative analysis, 95
narrative therapy, 21–22, 95,
162, 168, 170, 173, 176. *see
also* storytelling
Nepal, 196–98, 200–201
neurolinguistic programming,
101–2
new clinical techniques and
concepts
celebrity advocates for, 102–3
chaos theory and, 89–94

new clinical techniques and
concepts (*continued*)
client's influence in discovering or adopting, 142–43
current paradigm shifts
within psychotherapy,
84–87
future prospects, 116–19
graduate school preparation
and, 21–22
incessant flow of, 101–2
openness to, 96–99, 103–6
paradigm shifts, 84–87, 96
postmodernism and, 94–95
trends toward integration,
52–53, 84, 118
see also creative breakthroughs in therapy
newsletters, 231–32

O'Hanlon, B., 237, 265
organizational problems
in authoritarian organizations, 246–47
buried secrets, 247
confronting injustice arising
from, 254–55
graduate school preparation
for, 240–41
human needs and, 251–52
impaired practitioners, 248–49
incompetent practitioners,
247–48
lack of leadership, 250–51
maintaining healthy perspective on, 253–54
personality types leading to,
242–46
preventing, 255–56
self-assessment for contributions to, 252–53
as source of stress for therapists, 239
structural and institutional
factors leading to, 246–51
unresolvable, 256

Paine, Thomas, 168
Papp, P., 265
paradigm shifts within psychotherapy, 84–87, 96
past-life regression, 130
pattern recognition, 93
peer consultation
as alternative to supervision,
274–77
for stuck case, 277–81
personal life, therapist's, 61–62
person-centered therapy, 168
phenomenology, 95
physical health, 117
Piaget, J., 91
placebo effects, 126–27
postmodernism, 94–95, 96, 170
PowerPoint, 206, 215, 216
power relations, 95
practice design and operations
evolution of profession, 38–40
future challenges and opportunities, 116–19
graduate school preparation
for, 18–19, 189–90, 191–92
market pressures affecting,
38–44, 46
soliciting client's perception
of, 132

stresses of, 60, 64–67
theoretical framework for, 103
therapist's personal life and, 61–62
see also private practice
presentations, professional
ancillary points in, 214–15
awareness of audience in, 209, 210
challenges in making an impression with, 216–17
in extended workshops, 217–19
goals of, 211
good qualities in, 206, 208–15
graduate school preparation for, 205
human attention span and, 206
key message, 213
pace and scope of, 212–13
presumptions about therapists' capacity for, 206–7
rewards of delivering, 207–8
storytelling in, 210
strategies for audience involvement in, 211–12
structure, 213–14
use of slides, 215–16
use of technology, 216
Prince, The (Machiavelli), 168
private practice
burnout prevention, 195–96
business management, 189–90, 191–92
compensation, 187–88
expenses, 187
freedom of, 188–89

instability of, 189
perceptions of, versus public service, 185–86
practitioner characteristics and, 189
preparation for, in graduate school, 189–90, 191–92
sales and marketing activity in, 190–91
social and professional isolation in, 193–95
social justice and pro bono work in, 196–202
therapy termination decisions in, 192–93
vacations, 187
working hours, 186–87
see also organizational problems
Prizzi, 215
professional development
approval and recognition from colleagues, 30–32
attaining mastery, 261–64
from beginner to expert practitioner, 18–20
client's influence on, 134–35, 139–40, 142–45
exposure to new ideas and environments for, 285
getting the most from mentoring relationships, 270–74
graduate school preparation for, 29–30, 60
ongoing nature of, 119
personal change in, 152–55
personal development and, 285–86, 288–90

professional development
(*continued*)
  recruiting mentors for, 281–
    83
  risk-taking and, 283
  self-supervision for, 283–85
  writing for publication and,
    223
  see also creative break-
    throughs in therapy
projective identification, 135–36
Prozac, 44–46
Prozac Nation, 44
psychiatry, as profession, 118
psychodynamic therapy, 117,
    135–36, 162
psychopharmacology, 44–46,
    118
public service employment
  challenges and obstacles in,
    196, 200–201
  commitment over time,
    201–2
  motivation for, 196–99
  perceptions of, versus private
    practice, 185–86

quality of care, market trends
    and, 38–44
queer studies, 95

rational-emotive therapy, 176
recovered memories, 130
reflecting, 144
reframing, 176–77
relapse prevention, 118
relational-cultural therapy, 95
research

misrepresentation of results
    in, 104
  postmodern innovations,
    94–95
resistance to change, 95–96
resource-oriented therapies, 118
resources for therapists
  to build storytelling skills,
    180
  mentors for personal and pro-
    fessional growth, 281–83
  on publishing, 237
  for treatment planning, 71–73
Rhodes, P., 27
Rogers, C., 147, 266
Rosen, S., 180
rural practice, 62

Scharf, D., 142
scientist-practitioner model,
    26–28
secondary traumatization, 136–
    38
self-disclosure, 164–65, 174–75
self-help groups, 118
self-supervision, 283–84
shamanic healing, 115, 136
Silent Spring (Carson), 168
Sinclair, Upton, 168
social justice work, 196–202
social media, 222, 231
social support
  for client, 118
  for therapist, 115–16
solution-focused therapy, 95,
    162
specialization, 87–89
spirituality, 98–99

transcendent experience in therapeutic relationship, 151–52

spiritually-based therapies, 168

spontaneous remission, 128

storytelling
in bibliotherapy, 177–79
clinical applications of, 82, 113–14, 159–62, 164–65
in groups, 176
in human experience, 158
manipulation of truth in, 168–71
neural processing, 163
in professional presentations, 210
reinterpretation of client's story, 176–77
skill building, 179–80
techniques, 180–84
theoretical orientation and, 168
therapeutic functions of, 165–68, 171–73
therapist self-disclosure in, 164–65, 174–75
therapy as, 113, 151, 162–63
trauma effects on, 173
use of metaphor in, 173–74
using stories similar to client's, 175–76

Stowe, Harriet Beecher, 168

strategic therapy, 91, 114, 147, 176–77

strengths orientation, 118

stresses for therapists, 60, 64–67, 115–16

Structure of Scientific Revolutions (Kuhn), 84

supervision
conflicting feedback in, 15–17
conflicting motives of supervisors in, 258–59
expectations for, after graduate school, 257, 258
getting the most from, 270–71
handling disagreements or misunderstandings in, 271–72
peer consultation as alternative to, 274–81
power relationships in, 271–72
preparation for making good use of, 257–58
requesting examples or demonstrations to clarify issues in, 272–74
self-supervision and, 283–85
shortcomings in, 259–60

swimming after eating, 104–6

symptom substitution, 130

task facilitation, 83–84, 114–15

teaching, 217–19

technological advances
clinicians' adaptation to, 95–96
future prospects, 117

TED Talks, 206, 210

termination of treatment, 192–93

testing and evaluation
academic performance versus personal qualities of therapists, 24–25
graduate school emphasis on, 23–24

textbook publishing, 227, 235

therapeutic relationship

authenticity and presence in, 74–75, 108–9, 152–53

change factors mediated by, 149–52

client characteristics and, 148

clinical conceptualizations of, 147–48

clinical significance of, 81, 109–10, 148–49

communicating understanding in, 108–9

creative breakthroughs in therapy and, 266–68, 270

development of therapist's interpersonal skills in, 143–45

exchange of stories in, 171–73

manifestations of chaos theory in, 93–94

peer consultation for impasse in, 277–81

secondary traumatization risk, 136–38

spiritual transcendence in, 151–52

therapist's development influenced by, 134–35, 139–40

therapist's perception of, 125–26

transference and projective identification in, 135–36

transitioning to couples therapy after individual therapy, 15–17

validation of client in, 151

therapist qualities

academic qualifications versus personal characteristics, 24–25

awareness of one's strengths and limitations, 57–59, 60, 75, 284–85, 287–88

characteristics of master therapists, 261–62

confidence and discipline, 34–35

false confidence, 63–64

interpersonal skills, 143–45

leading to conflict with colleagues, 242–46

suitability for private practice, 189

Thoreau, H. D., 168

trade publishing, 234–35

transference, 135–36

trauma

as disordered story, 173

fragmented memory in, 114

significance of therapeutic alliance in intervention with, 151

traumatic stress debriefing, 130

treatment planning, resources for, 71–73

Uncle Tom's Cabin (Stowe), 168

underserved populations, 42–43, 117–18

utilization review, 48, 49

virtual reality, 117

websites, 231
White, M., 173
Writers Digest, The, 237
writing and publishing
  book proposals, 236–37
  choosing a topic, 224, 228–30
  with coauthor, 225
  current market for, 221–22
  on demand, 222
  finding publishers and media outlets, 226–28, 230–31
  magazine articles, 233–34
  newsletters, 231–32
  professional books, 235
  professional journal articles, 232–33
  reasons for, 222–24, 235–36
  resources, 237
  risk of rejection, 233
  self-publishing, 222, 230
  self-satisfaction in writing, 237–38
  textbooks, 227, 235
  trade books, 234–35
  writing process, 224–26

Yarling, Ben, 236
yoga, 117

Zeig, J., 265

ABOUT THE AUTHOR

Jeffrey A. Kottler is one of the most prolific authors in the fields of psychology and education, having written over 80 books about a wide range of subjects, many of them featuring his lifelong interest in therapists' inner experience and path to excellence. Jeffrey has authored more than a dozen texts for counselors and therapists that are used in universities around the world and a dozen books each for practicing therapists and educators, many of which represent stories of seminal change. His books have been translated into more than two dozen languages. Some of Jeffrey's most popular books include *On Being a Therapist, Learning Group Leadership, Change: What Leads to Personal Transformation, Divine Madness, The Therapist's Workbook,* and *On Being a Master Therapist: Practicing What We Preach.*

Jeffrey has served as a Fulbright Scholar and senior lecturer in Peru (1980) and Iceland (2000), as well as worked as a visiting professor in New Zealand, Australia, Hong Kong, Singapore, and Nepal. He has taught counseling and therapy in universities and workshops throughout the world. Jeffrey is professor of counseling at California State University, Fullerton and the University of St. Thomas (Houston), and the founder of Empower Nepali Girls, an organization that provides educational scholarships for at-risk children in Nepal.